And They Planted Trees

Memoirs and Lessons

A work of creative non-fiction

David Newton Sneed

Copyright © 2019 David Newton Sneed

All rights reserved.

Published by

L Cross Ranch - Bootjack Press.
PO Box 22142
Cheyenne WY 82003
dsneed@lcrossranch.com

Cover Design by Hannah Fields.

Printed in the United States of America.

No part of this book may be reproduced, stored in a retrieval system, or transmitted, in any form or by any means, electronic, mechanical, photocopying, recording, or otherwise without prior written approval of the author.

This is a work of creative non-fiction. The events are portrayed to the best of my memory and notes. While the stories are true, some names and identifying details have been left out or changed to protect the privacy of the people involved. In some cases I have written permission. Many stories of me and and great folks I have known have been omitted for space reasons.

ISBN: 978-0-692-07970-6

DEDICATION

To Cheri, my wife of over 51 years, who has always extended acceptance, support, encouragement, and love to me for all the worthy things I have attempted to do. She has sacrificed much for me and for our children.

To all of our children and grandchildren. I love you no matter what you choose to do or how you want to think. You should be yourself.

CONTENTS

Acknowledgments
Preface   1
Introduction   7
1   The Relevance of Mobility   10
2   Very Early Days   29
3   I Lived In Many Places   31
4   Education After High School   62
5   Formal Career Start   85
6   McKesson Laboratories   116
7   How I Diversified   133
8   Dictaphone   149
9   I Go Out On My Own   157
10   North Carolina   208
11   New England   272
12   Berkshires   281
13   "Go West Young Man"   310
14   Reinvention   336
15   Quotes and Notes   367
16   I Learn The Meaning of Faith   370
17   Is Healing For Today?   376
18   Does God Heal Through Doctors?   380
19   Not Yet The End For Me   383

ACKNOWLEDGMENTS

Thanks to the many people who influenced my ideas.

Heartfelt thanks to those that motivated me to write this book.

A special thanks goes out to Hannah Fields. She designed the cover, and did the legwork to the book into print. I could not have done it myself.

PREFACE

On one trip I had a most memorable experience with one our sons.

I don't recall his age at the time. He was old enough to talk but was not much older.

We drove across the Albemarle Sound in North Carolina, the largest freshwater estuary on the Atlantic coast. Work was just starting for the building of a new bridge for the four mile crossing. I told him what was going on. He took it all in. As we crossed he certainly that only open water can be seen.

Later that day we crossed the Chowan River west of the western end of the Albemarle Sound. At the point that we crossed there are many trees that grow in the water, trees such as cypress and water tupelo. There are some other really bushy trees, oak and others. That bridge was fairly new.

"It looks like they finished the new bridge," I said.

He looked around. "And they planted trees," he replied.

A child can easily believe that all things are possible. I decided to give this book the name *And They Planted Trees*. I have included stories of faith, my faith, and faith of others.

There are many definitions of the word "faith." Growing up as a preacher's kid, I had heard them all. The definition I prefer is from the Bible in Hebrews 11:1:

"Now faith is the substance of things hoped for, the evidence of things not seen."

It is a substance and it is evidence.

For years I had thought about writing my story yet felt it both impossible and unnecessary. I don't like doing something unless it has, at least what I believe, value to someone else.

From the days of clipping and mailing in years past, I have often sent newspaper and magazine articles to selected others. Now I send emails and links. I do appreciate the ones that I get. This long term activity is today a part of what is called content curation.

Near the end of March 2017, I was prompted to think about writing a book. I had reasons that I thought were valid to not write one.

- Everything that I could say had already been written.
- The book contents would become obsolete, to me if no one else.
- I would likely have a change of thought after the book was written.
- I could pass along someone else's book that would be better than I could write.

One of our daughters asked me the same thing about writing a book yet with some specific content possibilities and needs.

I threw out all of my reasons for not writing a book. I began this book right after getting off the phone with her and did about ten pages that day.

I had several ideas in mind.

1. Originally the book was to be for family and as a memoir would be of family stories involving me.
2. I did want for my grandchildren, and for that matter some of my younger children, to know about me before they came along.
3. The book would be a way to preserve and convey specialized knowledge and cultural history.
4. It would be a book of memoirs and lessons learned, not necessarily in chronological order.
5. I wanted to make an attempt to convey tacit knowledge, using explicit examples in a context of one life in a given time. Each anecdote has a lesson learned.
6. It would be stories of spiritual power that are available to all believers.

Family history is good to know. I regret that I did not get to know my maternal grandfather, Simeon Newton Dorris. He died five months before I was born. I know nothing about him, what he did, or for that matter, anything he did. Of what he died is not clear. Cancer is one theory though not much was known of cancer when he died. I did know my maternal grandmother, Lillian Reese Dorris, and both paternal grandparents, Henry and Belle Sneed, as they all lived well into my adult life.

Granny Sneed's favorite saying was: "That suits me and I'm hard to please."

G. C. Bevington.
I got an idea from the itinerant Methodist evangelist G. C. Bevington.

Bevington was a man of great faith and prevailing prayer, who in his lifetime saw extraordinary things that were accomplished through the power of God. To quote directly:

"I got a large book, and when I would come in for a little rest, I would write down the important incidents as a stimulus to my faith. Many a time, after coming in from a very hard pull, without money, and but little to show by way of visible results, and feeling none the best, I dived into that book, and invariably was greatly encouraged. Several times when I was getting pretty low in faith, the records in that book lifted the clouds and gave me great victory knowing that what God had done once He could do again if conditions were kept. I generally kept a close watch on the conditions, to see that they were up to the standard."

I have not kept a book like Bevington did but I have kept index cards, notebooks, and scraps of paper. I have kept much in memory and have been able to recall victories when needed. I have kept note of many scriptures and have memorized them. I wanted to make an organized book for me and to whoever else can benefit. I have come in like Bevington, after a "very hard hard pull," and "needed encouragement."

Bevington wrote in the Foreword of his published book: "I hope that these incidents will be as great a blessing to you and to others as they have been to me. If they are, pass the book on, keep it traveling, and hence spreading the deeper truths of the hidden nuggets contained in God's great goldmine, the Bible. Read, pray, lay hold, take in, and give out. Eat, and get fat."

Bevington's first manuscript and his notes were lost in a fire. He was encouraged to rewrite it.

Bevington wrote: "So I related to him all that I have said here relative to my first book, and told him that I had no record of names, dates, or places. He said that they are of little importance in such a work as this. So after praying over it I concluded to rewrite the incidents. Read as impartially as you can for all that follows is true."

Lincoln Steffens.

The Autobiography of Lincoln Steffens was required reading when I was in college and was in high schools. For dates, the book only has 1866 when Steffens was born and 1895 when he started college. It is however chronological by design. It is a good story and is written like a novel. It is quite lengthy.

There is one excerpt of his book that is worth knowing. At the beginning of part two, chapter 1, *"I Become a Reporter,"* we see that at one time that Steffens got off the ship in New York his father's agent brought him a letter:

"My dear son: When you finished school you wanted to go to college. I sent you to Berkeley. When you got through there, you did not care to go into my business; so I sold out. You preferred to continue your studies in Berlin. I let you. After Berlin it was Heidelberg; after that Leipzig. And after the German universities you wanted to study at the French universities in Paris. I consented and after a year with the French, you had to have half a year of the British Museum in London. All right. You had that too. By now you must know about all there is to know of the theory of life, but there's a practical side as well. It's worth knowing. I suggest that you learn it, and the way to study it, I think, is to stay in New York and hustle. Enclosed please find $100, which should keep you till you can find a job and support yourself."

In my story, like Steffens, I have also elected to remove dates, though from 1967 onward. I had some dates and did not have others. The greater issue might be that presenting my life chronologically after my career start has overlap problems. I would have had to stop in the middle of one story, insert another, and then resume. My jobs, travels, and other activities overlapped in time. Some covered short times; others longer. One of them covered 36 1/2 years. To fit chronology, dates would have had to be month, day, and year. There would be start and stop dates. Start dates would be tough. End dates just about impossible.

I'm reminded of Luke 8:41-56 in the Bible of one day when Jesus had overlapping events.

- Jairus approached Jesus to ask help for his 12 year old daughter who was dying at home (41-42.)

- A woman with an issue of blood for 12 years touched Jesus. He was aware and stopped what he was doing to deal with her (43-48.)

- "While he yet spake," a man arrived from Jairus' house to announce that the 12 year old daughter had died. Jesus then went to the house to deal with resurrecting the daughter (49-56.)

I'm also reminded of the time in the Bible when Jesus' friend Lazarus was sick. The story is in John 11.

- Lazarus, a good friend of Jesus, was sick in Bethany, 15 furlongs, almost two miles, from Jerusalem.

- Word was sent to Jesus. Someone had to have walked to tell him.

- Jesus stayed put for two days.

- Jesus suggested making a trip to Judea.

- Jesus and disciples went to Bethany to see Lazarus. When they arrived Lazarus was already four days in the grave.

Where I have needed some semblance of a resume, I have usually just put down my employment in my corporation, a common practice of employees of consulting firms. Often those employees have non-disclosure agreements prohibiting naming client assignments.

I think of job applications. Last job start and stop. Then previous job start and stop. Explain all time gaps. I can't do that.

In some years I may have done work for many client companies. In some years I have had gaps doing selling or idea development while doing some work with long term projects.

For me and fir others today, the best resume is to tell what you have done, so that you can tell what you will do if the employer involved hires you.

Even if I knew the start and stop dates, the need to link one event at one time to others in other times, or one event in one location to others at the same or similar location, would turn this book into a lot of dates. Times before 1967 were somewhat easier.

Putting the birth of children, certainly an important part of anyone's life, into the chronological context of this story, was not going to work.

Over the years the lady who did the billing at first and longest term client, kept a list in the back of her desktop calendar and reminded me of my children's birthdays. When she and her boat skipper husband retired, I was out of luck, not being able to remember the dates.

My wife, Cheri, of course kept me up to date. She did not have to keep a list.

We were blessed with 14 children of our own. I have left out the names for privacy reasons.

At this writing, we have 26 grandchildren and one great grandchild. I have left out the names for privacy reasons.

To quote from the Bible: "Lo, children are an heritage of the Lord: and the fruit of the womb is his reward. As arrows are in the hand of a mighty man; so are children of the youth. Happy is the man that hath his quiver full of them: they shall not be ashamed, but they shall speak with the enemies in the gate." Psalms 127:3-5.

INTRODUCTION

"It is difficult to get a man to understand something if his salary is dependent upon his not understanding it." - Upton Sinclair.

I am 72 years old at completion of this writing. Is that old? It doesn't have to be old.

At my last birthday, I decided that I would reverse the numbers of 72 and my age became 27.

My life story includes things that are no longer so. At that time they were. I am presenting what was reality then.

Some have said that I have no right to claim credit to what I did with race and gender. I beg to differ. I dealt with individuals. At that time I was the catalyst of change for those individuals.

As a disciple of Jesus and as a scientist, science being organized knowledge, I have developed some positions on race and gender, all subject to change.

I like simplicity.

"Jesus loves the little children, all the children of the world. Red and yellow, black and white, they are precious in His sight, Jesus loves the little children of the world." A great song. I love it. I agree with it.

Science tells us that all people are of the same species, Homo Sapiens.

You like science? Race has no scientific basis. Race is a social construct. Race is "bad" because it means that each race, a species difference if you will, has specific characteristics.

Now how "woke" is that?

In Genesis 11:1 we read that "And the whole earth was of one language and one speech."

What happened is quite simple. See Genesis 11:4:

"And they said, Go to, let us build us a city and tower, whose top may reach unto heaven; and let us make us a name, lest we be scattered abroad upon the face of the whole earth."

In short, God, jealous of his position, confronted arrogance by confounding their language and scattering them.

Homo sapiens, with different environments and with natural selection, split and became what today we call races.

As a white American, my exposure is mostly to white people, black people, and what we know as Indians. To a smaller extent I am exposed to various other immigrants.

Our children and grandchildren are exposed to a variety of viewpoints, mostly of political origin.

Problems occur, within families, then within society.

Within each segment of scattered mankind there are good and bad, intelligent and stupid.

I am sad about disabilities of any humans. I wish there was something I could do.

Plain and simple, pass all the laws you want, you cannot make full equality.

This book is a memoir and a textbook.
A major subject is faith. chapter 16, followed by chapters 17 and 18, is a primer on that subject. You can either go there now, pick it up at the end, or you can skip it altogether.

From a story standpoint, my life is not the typical one of beginnings in the mid-20th century.

It is more typical of beginnings in the 21st century.

Into my early adulthood there were remnants of at least believing in spending a whole career at one company, often in the same job. Clearly you will see in this book that I did not do that.

For me as a seeker of new ideas, new technologies, and better ways, there are quotes that have been particularly related to the development of my philosophy and actions in my career life.

"It must be considered that there is nothing more difficult to carry out nor more doubtful of success nor more dangerous to handle than to initiate a new order of things; for the reformer has enemies in all those who profit by the old order, and only lukewarm defenders in all those who would profit by the new order; this lukewarmness arising partly from the incredulity of mankind who does not truly believe in anything new until they actually have experience of it." - Niccolo Machiavelli.

"With all thy getting get understanding." - Proverbs 4:7

"Never run out of money." - Anonymous.

"Freedom is the ability to comprehend your own bondage. - Anonymous.

"….if he owns ships and sails them, he attends to shipping, and he ceases to insure his own ships just as soon as he has surplus capital and can withstand the loss of one without imperiling solvency…." - Andrew Carnegie.

"A leg of a successful, sustainable business involves its bank."

I have a long and good relationship with my bank. The same should be said about any bank of any business. The bank is the agent to process financial transactions.It is a key to a community reputation. It is important for a bank customer to maximize average daily deposits in deposit accounts as this is the inventory of the bank to carry out its business. Don't complain about fees. There are ways to avoid fees and all the methods relate to increasing the bank's inventory of money available to lend. The process of receiving deposits and then lending is what creates money in a capitalistic society. Respect your bank. Respect its advice." - David Newton Sneed.

Why I count things.
I count everything. Lord Kelvin nicely summarized the subject:

"When you can measure what you are speaking about, and express it in numbers, you know something about it, when you cannot express it in numbers, your knowledge is of a meager and unsatisfactory kind; it may be the beginning of knowledge, but you have scarcely, in your thoughts, advanced to the stage of science."

CHAPTER 1: THE RELEVANCE OF MOBILITY

Birds have wings; they're free; they can fly where they want when they want. They have the kind of mobility many people envy." - Roger Tory Peterson.

"It is not our feet that move us along. It is our minds." - Chinese Proverb.

The geographic will of God.
The spatial context of a memoir shows the relevance of mobility. Mobility is important. If all we did was sit, there might not be much of a story.

God has a geographic will for us as He does a positional will where we are to reside in Him and Him in us. In His geographic will He wants us to be somewhere at a certain time.

Scripturally we know how Stephen, one the seven original deacons, met the Ethiopian eunuch in Acts 8:26-40.

We know the Macedonian call for the Apostle Paul in Acts 15:39-18:22.

We know that before Elijah could face his enemies on Mount Carmel, he had to go to the brook Cherith. Later, he then had to walk from the brook, about 85 miles, to meet the widow of Zarephath in I Kings 17.

I picked up a hitchhiker in Vermont who told me he was "into movement" and planned on the rest of the winter skiing every day. Perhaps that young man was in a place to minister to me. Missionaries Peter and Carol, in their book, told of my gift of travel, or mobility. I have always gotten to wherever I needed to go. I have gotten there on time, sometimes in luxury, often not. There has always been some dated task to accomplish.

Charles McCartney, the " Goat Man," understood the value of mobility.
When I was growing up in the south the Goat Man was well known as an itinerant preacher. I saw him near our homes and while traveling with my parents. I talked with him a number of times. He had an impact on my life in a number of ways.

I am not sure of the origin of this material, that I had in my file, about the Goat Man:

"Charles McCartney was born on July 6, 1901. In 1915, at age 14, he ran away from his family's Iowa farm. He eventually wound up in New York, and was soon married to a Spanish knife-thrower. When she got pregnant they tried to make it as farmers, but bad weather and the Great Depression wiped them out.

About the same time, he experienced a religious awakening. A man on a mission, he hitched up his team of goats to a wagon and took to the open road with his wife and son. His wife made goatskin clothes for him and his son to wear as a gimmick during their travels, but she quickly grew tired of the road and returned to Iowa, taking their son with her."

"Charles McCartney looked like a goat. He smelled like one, too because he rarely took a bath. You take a fellow who looks like a goat, travels around with goats, eats with goats, lies down among goats and smells like a goat and it won't be long before people will be calling him the Goat Man. And that is exactly how he got his name. Someone would spot the Goat Man and his goats coming down the highway, his wagon piled high. Word would get around and pretty soon parents would be driving their children out to meet him."

"For decades he traveled the back roads of the southeast. Sometimes there were as many as 30 goats. One team would pull a large wagon while baby goats and nannies rode. Great big billies walked behind to push the wagon up hills and to act as brakes."

"People are goats, they just don't know it," he would often say.

"The old iron-wheeled wagon was piled high with garbage, lanterns, bedding, clothes, an old pot belly stove, and plenty of scrap metal that McCartney gathered and sold. McCartney would wander 10 miles or so along country roads each day, then pull over into a field in the late afternoon. He'd light a bonfire, which was never complete until he hurled an old tire on top. Curious townspeople would see the black smoke and wander to his campsite. There he would preach the Gospel, drink goat's milk and sell picture cards of himself."

"Eventually settling in Jeffersonville, Georgia, he established the Free Thinking Christian Mission. From the mission he journeyed out with his goat-pulled wagon to preach his message of impending and eternal damnation for sinners. His path through the countryside was easily traceable from the distinctive wooden signs he tacked on trees by the roadside, signs bearing such harsh messages as PREPARE TO MEET THY GOD with the fires of hell painted underneath."

"Occasionally, McCartney was attacked and mugged during his trips around the country. During one such attack in 1969, three young men assaulted him while he slept in his cart. He suffered three broken ribs, and two of his favorite goats were killed. Following this incident McCartney retired to his mission in Jeffersonville. In 1978 that home burned down, after which he purchased a bus and lived in it. "

"In 1985, during one of his final journeys away from Georgia, McCartney set out on foot to California, hoping to meet the actress Morgan Fairchild, whom he wanted to marry. En route to California, he was again mugged and hospitalized for his injuries. Following his return to Georgia, he left the road for good in 1987. He spent his final years as a local celebrity at a nursing home in Macon, where he died at the age of 97 on November 15, 1998."

Family trips.
When I was growing up, there were family trips to all kinds of places. Going to visit my mother's family, when we lived in the Atlanta area, was an all day trip, leaving early in the morning.

At that time there were still a number of people that used mule-drawn wagons to get around.

One time I was waiting in the car with my uncle Hugh Dorris. I was about three years old. It was cold and there was steam coming from the mule's mouth and nose. My uncle never let me forget that I said: "That horse is smokin'."

Cheri and I made road trips before and after having children and grandchildren.

I learned something that played a most important part in being able to be somewhere on time, especially when it was a long distance away.

With just me I could average 62 miles per hour. With me and one other, adult or child, I could average 54 miles per hour. With me and two or more others, I could average 48 miles per hour if I was lucky.

I did get to be pretty good at predicting arrival times.

The trip is what is important.
When we travelled we viewed that the trip was more important than arriving at the destination. My goal was to teach the children.

There were things that they would not see on their own. There were people to meet, things to learn, and chances to make a difference.

Along the road heading from Stovepipe Wells, in Death Valley, in the direction of Ridgecrest, California there is a ghost town called Ballarat.

At the entrance to Ballarat is a crudely made sign that says with this spelling:

"You LEARN NoThing by SiTTing IN The CAR."
Yet the trip experience is not just out of the car.

As our one of our sons had gotten older and more literate he would preach to the rest of us in the car while we travelled. He was also the habit, from an early age, of wearing a coat and tie.

One one occasion that we were getting onto the New Jersey Turnpike, we were going around the curve of a cloverleaf intersection, he said:

"This really is a turnpike."

In New York City, one daughter had an experience at Tiffany Jewelers. She was somewhere between 10 and 12.

A salesman asked her if she wanted to try on some jewelry. She got to wear some very expensive bracelets. I happened to find out a few days later that Tiffanys had a conscious plan to involve young people with Tiffanys in order to build customers for the future.

A camping trip is nice, for the first hour and a half. After that it is for the birds, literally.

Cheri, I, and my brother, who was about nine years old, went camping at Clingmans Dome, 22 miles from Gatlinburg, Tennessee. I left the car lights on so the battery was dead when we came back. The Jaguar was a straight shift which means it can be push started. We went miles down the mountain until we got it to start.

"Of course it would be raining, just like in Narnia." A quote from somewhere.

British cars in rainy weather often did not respond well.

I was most blessed and thankful that I had an independent job and could take children with me while traveling, not having to wait for off-work times like those with regular jobs. Cheri was also independent like that, with no regular job, except for a short time after we moved to Wyoming where even then she worked for me.

So when I was traveling, any children who were not with Cheri, were with me.

Throughout our child-rearing years, we stopped at playgrounds when we were on any driving trips. Just watching the kids play was a hit of the trip.

Travel involves doing things.

I have done a lot. To use an old Wyoming saying: "If it's true it ain't braggin!"

How could I have done all of this? Certainly not by being a career employee of one company or by being a man who lacks faith.

How I got to New England.
I was on business at a fish dealer client. I had arrived by air and was without a car. From Logan Airport in Boston, I had taken the subway to North Station and from there the train. I walked to my hotel and walked to my client's location in the morning.

How I got to Rye, New York.
In the early evening, one very rainy day while I was at the fish dealer, I got a call that I needed to be in Rye, New York as quickly as possible. There was no suitable flight or train to get there.

I found a trucker who could get me to southern Rhode Island near the Connecticut border.

From there I hitchhiked on I-95 in cold rain and snow. When the folks came in to work the next morning in Rye I had already been there and fixed their problems. Having keys to my clients offices made a difference.

It is good to know the paths to get from here to there.
I-95, as opposed to predecessors such as U.S. 301 and U.S. 1, is a travel of stress and excitement. There is heavy traffic 24/7 on I-95 especially south of Jacksonville, Florida. Travel between North Carolina and New York means the New Jersey Turnpike.

Going south I almost always got off at Exit 7 that connects to I-295. I-295 is toll free, runs parallel to the turnpike and connects to I-95 at the end of the New Jersey Turnpike.

That bypass meant not just saving tolls but meant avoiding traffic at the toll booths at the end of the turnpike. In the summer the southbound traffic backed up for miles.

I-80 is quite a bit different from the other east-west interstates and from the Trans-Canada highway. I-80 can be boring especially in crossing Nebraska and the truck traffic is heavy.

Much could be written of travel experiences on different highway numbers, directions, and time of the year. In traveling we make memory points, often small seemingly insignificant things that help build our own world.

My traveling has always been without access to GPS and mostly without a cell phone. Printed road maps and memory have sufficed.

To me the worst thing was loss of access to pay phones to be able to make contact with home. Otherwise I would have not gotten a cell phone.

The ability to receive calls from home or elsewhere did not make any difference. My clients and family knew I would be in touch as soon and as often as I could.

In one long ago Bob and Ray radio program, the possibility of receiving a call, while common today, was a point of humor. While getting gas for their car, the nearby payphone rings. One of the two answers. It is a call for them. It is treated as if it was not an unusual event at all.

Incidentally, I have noted that with all the technology, most people today cannot readily point to the north from where they are standing.

It is good to use alternate modes of travel such as ferries.
I have taken ferries wherever possible. The ones I remember are:

1. The Sans Souci Ferry, a cable ferry that provides access across the Cashie River in Bertie County, North Carolina.
2. The Cedar Island to Ocracoke ferry in North Carolina.
3. The Hatteras to Ocracoke ferry in North Carolina.
4. The Swan Quarter to Ocracoke ferry in North Carolina.
5. The Cape May-Lewes Ferry that connects New Jersey to Delaware.
6. An aluminum rowboat from Big Bend National Park across the Rio Grande River to Boquillas del Carmen, Coahuila State, Mexico.
7. The seasonal Peel River ferry near Fort McPherson, NWT, Canada.
8. The seasonal Mackenzie River ferry near Tsiigehtchic, NWT, Canada. Tsiigehtchic is spelled correctly.
9. The overnight ferry that connects Piraeus, Greece, close by Athens, to Chania on the island of Crete.
10. The train ferry that connects Denmark and Sweden and passes by Kronborg Castle, Hamlet's Castle, called Elsinore by Shakespeare, as it leaves Denmark.
11. Temporary ferries when bridges are out.
12. The ferry across Long Island Sound from Bridgeport, Connecticut and Port Jefferson, New York.
13. The Scotia Prince, the all night ferry connecting Portland, Maine with Yarmouth, Nova Scotia. Sadly, this ferry is no longer running.
14. The seasonal George Black Ferry crossing the Yukon River in Dawson,

    Yukon, Canada.
15. The Staten Island Ferry in New York City.
16. The Bainbridge Island Ferry connecting Seattle Washington and Bainbridge Island.

Kannapolis, North Carolina.
On one family trip, we spent the night in Kannapolis, North Carolina.

Cannon, the towel maker had been in Kannapolis since the company was founded in 1888. Cannon went bankrupt in 2003 and there was actual demolition of all of their buildings.

On that trip, it was not by plan that we stopped in Kannapolis. We did not have any planned stops. We just stopped for the night when we got ready to stop.

In Kannapolis, I noticed that we were getting the evil eye from the desk clerk at the motel and by people at the restaurant.

I remembered that Ralph Nader had recently done a documentary on Cannon being a paternalistic company and how it controlled everything not just in Kannapolis but in all of Cabarrus County.

I remember in the documentary a policeman walking down the street. The documentary said that the police were just as much employees of Cannon as the mill workers.

Cannon was the main taxpayer in Cabarrus County. The people and their homes were all effectively, if not directly, owned by Cannon.

A union could not find a meeting place to talk about organizing anywhere in the county.

Were we there as Nader troublemakers?

There we were, in a Volkswagen beetle with a northern state license plate.

I did not sleep well and was glad to be out of Kannapolis the next morning.

The Delmarva peninsula.
The Delmarva peninsula, the name an acronym of the three states of Delaware, Maryland, Virginia, is quite a place.

The Delmarva peninsula ends at the Chesapeake Bay Bridge Tunnel, a 23 mile connector bridge with two tunnels to allow ship traffic to pass over. Smaller vessels can go under the road spans. Virginia Beach, Virginia is directly across the mouth of the Chesapeake Bay, next to Norfolk.

On one trip to, or through, the Delmarva peninsula we had been to Assateague Island to see the wild horses. Assateague was made famous by the book and movie *Misty of Chincoteague*. Chincoteague was the larger of the two islands and is inhabited.

We got a motel room, then went to dinner. I looked at the menu in the restaurant. I wanted flounder but the price was way too high. I even made a comment about that to the waitress. I had an idea.

How I turned a sandwich meal into a dinner meal.
I ordered two flounder sandwiches and an order of french fries. When our food arrived I asked for a large dinner plate. The waitress brought one. I put the french fries on the big plate. I put the sandwich bread on the french fries plate. I put the two fish fillets on the big plate. I put the lettuce and tomato from the sandwiches on one of the sandwich plates.

I did this rapidly while the waitress was still there. Her eyes got big.

"That's more than you get with the fish dinner," she said.

"And $5 beats $15," I replied.

Barbecue on the Delmarva peninsula.
In the summer the volunteer fire departments had chicken barbecue cooking over fire pits in the wide, park like areas of the highway median. Even though Route 13 was a four lane, customers would simply park off the left side of their lanes.

I have never missed a stop in Painter, Virginia, near the island of Wachapreague, at Formy's Barbecue, when I passed during opening hours. Really great barbecue. And some really great conversation with Formy, the owner. James Formyduval was his full name. He was also a real estate agent.

Cheri and I have been to many "bobecue" joints.

We meet Dr. C. M. Ward.
One day, Cheri and I were at the Morrison's Cafeteria in Virginia Beach, Virginia. As we were looking for a table, I thought I recognized C.M. Ward, one of the last of the old time pentecostal preachers. It was in fact Ward. He invited us to sit with him. Dr. Ward was a prolific writer and lead a daily radio program of the Assemblies of God, called Revivaltime. He had started on

Revivaltime in 1953.

After dinner we went with him to The Barn, a non-denominational church, where he was preaching.

Dr. Ward asked me to join him and the church pastor at the altar in front of the church to pray for healing of those that came forward. There is much involved in the ministry of healing. At that time I did not know a whole lot. I still don't.

Rev. R. W. Schambach.
On another occasion while we lived in North Carolina we went to Raleigh, to hear the Rev R. W. Schambach preach. Another great old time pentecostal preacher. C.M. Ward had led Schambach to Christ. One uniqueness of Rev. Schambach was his pithy sayings.

"Some people have asked me if I'm a Seventh Day Adventist. I tell them no but that I'm a SEVEN Day Adventist."

"There has been criticism of Jesus bumper stickers, and pins, and whatever. I'm glad about them. With a lot of people that's the only way you know they are Christians."

"The Bible tells us we should cast out the devil, raise the dead, and pray for the sick. We've got it all backwards. We cast out the sick by putting them in hospitals, pray for the dead, and raise the devil."

Pseudepigrapha in New Hampshire.
At an antiquarian book store in New Hampshire, there was a copy of *The Sixth and Seventh Books of Moses*. This book, among other things, supposedly tells how Moses parted the Red Sea, changed a staff into a serpent then back again into a staff. It tells how Moses did so many other things.

I did not even look through the book.

Christians should not have anything to do with what is known as pseudepigrapha, writings that sound biblical yet are not and which are falsely attributed to certain authors.

I told the man at the register about the book, what it contained, and my views about why Christians should avoid it. I asked where he got the book. He did not know. I continued my shopping though ended up not buying anything. Antiquarian books can be quite costly.

Just before I left I walked by the shelf where I had seen the book. It was gone.

Root working.
The root workers in North Carolina use *The Sixth and Seventh Books of Moses* as do some of the Pennsylvania Dutch. Root working magic and spells is still widely believed in parts of the south, particularly in North Carolina and Louisiana.

I remember a lawsuit against a community hospital near where we lived in North Carolina. I mention community hospital because that is a hospital that is owned and operated with tax money from its community.

A root worker claimed that she was given a CAT scan and that the procedure took away her spell powers. The jury was out for quite a while.

Then the jury had a question for the judge. Could they give the plaintiff more than was asked for in the suit? The answer from the judge was yes. The jury unanimously awarded her double damages.

Lake Chargoggaggoggmanchaugagoggchaubunagungamaug.
Our of our sons could spell and pronounce the original name of a lake just south of Webster, Massachusetts that we had discovered while driving around. The lake is also known as Lake Webster. The long name is on a round sign by the lake.

Larry Glick.
He called Larry Glick on his WBZ Boston radio talk show and told about this long lake name that means:

"You fish on your side, we fish on our side, and no one fishes in the middle."

David Brudnoy.
It was David Brudnoy, the famed talk show host in Boston, that was asked why with so much knife and gun violence in inner city Boston schools that metal detectors were not used at the door. Brudnoy said that:

"When people with authority to solve a problem don't solve the problem it is because they don't want to solve the problem."

Brudnoy pointed out that "There are many whose jobs depend on dysfunctional inner city schools. "

The woman with a CAN do attitude.
One of our sons graduated from Crestmont College, at Rancho Palos Verdes California. His first Salvation Army assignment was at Redondo Beach,

California. I went to visit him.

There was a shiny red Corvette in the parking lot. I found from him that the car belonged to a lady, mid-nineties in age, who lived in the senior apartments.

"Dad, you've got to meet this lady."

She was tiny, had long gray hair, and wore a baseball cap backwards. She seemed in perfect health and had a great attitude.

"I don't subscribe to the theory of aging," she said. "And I haven't been to a doctor since 1948," she added. "I figured that if I hung around those guys then I would not live very long."

The woman with a CAN'T do, no mobility, attitude.
I had a long term project with a company in Rye, New York. I was there frequently. The receptionist was a young, single, woman, seemingly well educated though I did not know any details. She did have a nice and fairly new car. One day as I was leaving the office she said,

"Where are you headed now?"

"Connecticut," I replied.

"Ohhhh Connecticut," she said. "I want to go someday."

"You could go there today right after work," I told her.

Byram, Connecticut was three miles away on the interstate. It was maybe a mile to the state line.

"You could drive all the way through Connecticut and back before dark," I added.

It was summertime and the days were long.

"I couldn't go during the week," she said. "I have to fix my dinner and get ready for work the next day."

"The weekend is coming up. And the weather looks to be good."

"On the weekend I have to clean my apartment."

I have run across many people with this same CAN'T do attitude. Getting into mobility is the first step of attitude change.

I stay at cheap hotels.
In my travels, the cheapest place has been fine for just me. Even when I have gone to a conference, with all costs paid by my employer, I have still stayed elsewhere than the conference venue whenever I could save money. I have often stopped at a motel for just a couple of hours for some sleep and a shower when it was just me.

Along I-95 there are plenty of motels from the 1950s and 1960s, built for the New York to Florida tourist trade.

Those motels now seem to all be owned by people primarily from Gujarat State in India or Indians from the diaspora in east Africa when they were expelled from Uganda in 1972 by Idi Amin.

The prices are cheap and waking the proprietor at 3:00 AM is not a problem. There is the usual negotiation for the price that often ends with simply removing the amount of sales tax.

When I was working in the area, I regularly stayed at an old Post Road motel with tiny rooms where the cost was exactly $19.

No matter what time or day of the week I got to that place, the window clerk was the same Indian woman.

I think she was the owner.

How someone can stay in one place for years and do the same thing is most baffling to me.

One of my regrets was in taking Cheri and several children to that motel. A nicer place close by had no vacancies. I should have kept looking.

Our son that was with me with me on one trip, I forget his age, where he made the statement that he wished we could stay there at the Post Road place all winter. It was a cold and snowy day, the room was compact and warm, and we were unstressed. Maybe that was a clue about the window clerk.

At one motel in northern Wyoming, where the only hotel choice is an old cheap place, the owner offered a dinner for $5 to his motel guests. I took him up on it. I had antelope stew in the shop back of the motel.

I sat on a stool, pushed the tools and other stuff away, and chowed down.

There was good conversation with the owner and with a couple of other guys who were staying there while they were on a job in the area.

Ironically I have known of people who would either not go to an area or would travel a great distance to get to a modern chain hotel.

I knew where to eat.
A frequent traveller knows where to eat. These restaurants become mid-trip destinations.

I know a small place on Route 83 not too far south of Liberal, Kansas, in the Oklahoma panhandle. Nothing special. A stranger can go in and be treated like a regular.

I knew an old restaurant in New Orleans with only one table. Great fried chicken. I'm sure that place was gone with hurricane Katrina.

In Baltimore, near the tunnels, there was a great all night barbecue restaurant.

In Richmond, Virginia there was another barbecue place right by the interstate exit.

At Pocomoke City, Maryland on Route 13 there is an old restaurant that has been given the nickname Pocomoke Smoke 'em Up and Choke 'em Up. It is always busy.

At Salina, Kansas is the Cozy Inn, an iconic hamburger joint.

These type places, all single unit, are going away. That is all too bad.

On I-95, there are plenty of Waffle Houses, all 24/7 and with a counter. In the south there is a Waffle House at almost every exit. I always like stopping in at 2:00 AM for some coffee and a double hash brown, scattered on the grill, covered with onions, and chunked with small ham cubes. Other options are Diced with tomatoes, Peppered with peppers, Capped with mushrooms, and Topped with chili. I never picked those options.

In the north there is White Castle; in the south, Krystal. In Nashville, Tennessee there are some of each. They are the same but they are different. Small hamburgers with thin steamed patties. Krystal uses mustard. White Castle is now plain but used to have catsup.

My teacher.
A teacher of mine in Colonial Heights, Virginia often mentioned that she was

planning on taking her children to Washington, D.C. though wanted to wait until her children were old enough to appreciate it. I once told her that by then they might not want to go.

I was respectful enough as a child to not ask her a certain question that was on my mind.

Since when, with cheap gas and interstate highways, is it a once in a lifetime trip to go to a place that is 130 miles away?

Athens, Greece to Delphi, Greece by way of Arachova, Greece.
One of our daughters took me 130 miles, same distance as Colonial Heights, Virginia to Washington, D.C., though from Athens, Greece to Delphi, Greece. We went in a car, with an overnight in Arachova, a picturesque ski town on Mount Parnassos.

Years ago there were people who walked from Athens to Delphi to get an answer from the Oracle. They would return to Athens with the answer, pick up a new question, and head back on foot to Delphi.

I never got a good answer from her if these walkers carried a spare sandal on their back, in case a sandal went out, like a flat tire, on the lonely mountain road. Even today there is not much along the road to Delphi.

Trips through Washington D.C.
My standard route through Washington D.C. from the north was I-95, to Baltimore-Washington Parkway, to New York Avenue, to I-395, and back to I-95. I took the reverse path from the south.

I-95 around Washington D.C. was always bad. Even if it wasn't traffic, the mileage on I-95 is more, I-495 way more. In traveling through Washington, D.C. I might also detour through some city streets. At any time of the night or day we would go past the major sites for whichever kids were along.

"Wake up, we're going past the White House," I said one night to one son that was sleeping on the back seat.

"I've seen it thousands of times," was his reply. He still got up, albeit reluctantly.

New York City.
Driving to or through New York City from the south meant the George Washington Bridge. Traffic was to be expected until one morning. Where was everybody? I went over at the same time as usual yet with no stop and go. I

found out later that it was Rosh Hashanah, the highest Jewish holiday.

For a number of years the toll was $1.50. I would tell whichever child was with me that in honor of George Washington we would give the man in the booth two pictures of George Washington. To show his good spirit he would give us two pictures of George Washington. Our gift was two paper dollars. The toll taker return gift was two quarters.

We frequently sang the Sesame Street song *George Washington Bridge*. The lyrics are simply "George Washington Bridge. George Washington Washington Bridge" with a simple tune. For the sad part it is sung slowly and sadly. For the happy part it is sung faster and cheerfully. Still the same lyrics.

I set my career goals at age 16.
I intentionally planned periodic reinventions of myself. I remember telling a group of my friends in my first quarter at Georgia Tech that I saw my future in ideas and information. We were standing around at the campus post office sharing our plans. I was 16.

Little did I know at that time where ideas and information would carry me.

Baby boomer careers.
Many baby boomers came from factory worker families. The day shift in the factory was 7:00 AM to 3:30 or 4:00 PM. The parents saw the bosses come to work at 9:00 AM.

What the parents did not see was the managers working late, then taking work home, all with no overtime pay.

Parents sacrificed current consumption, saved up so their children could go to college, then get a cushy job that started at 9:00 AM. A college degree was believed to mean a life of ease with little or no work.

Real life set in for the baby-boomer college graduates.

They went back to school at night and on weekends thinking that a masters degree would open the door. Instead they ended up divorced or out of work when their job went overseas.

I passed out copies of *A Message to Garcia* by Elbert Hubbard, no relation or connection to L. Ron Hubbard.

I referred them to *The Strangest Secret* by Earl Nightingale.

The Strangest Secret.
Earl Nightingale was most noted for his speech *The Strangest Secret*. It was first presented on his radio program. It has been sold on recordings millions of times. It is available free on the Internet. In short, *The Strangest Secret* is that we become what we think about.

The aim of education.
So many of my baby boomer associates did not know that the purpose of education is to learn how to learn.

When they graduated they said: "I'll never open a book again."

They were correct. I remember visiting baby boomers' homes where there were no books and no newspapers, except maybe a copy of *The National Enquirer*. Always there was the ever-on television.

Cheri and I never had a television and not much living room furniture. We did not have time to sit.

Herbert Spencer, the 19th century British radical said: "The aim of education is not knowledge but action."

Henry Ford goes to court.
In 1916, Henry Ford sued *The Chicago Tribune* for calling him an ignorant idealist. In eight days on the stand efforts were made to prove him ignorant.

"What was the United States before?"

"Land, I guess" said Ford.

"Do you know anything about the revolution, Mr. Ford?"

"Yes, sir," Ford answered.

"What revolution did you have in mind, Mr. Ford?"

"In 1812," Ford replied.

"How many British soldiers were sent over from England?

"I don't know but from what I've heard is was considerably more than ever went back," said Ford.

Ford thought Benedict Arnold was a writer. Ford was asked to read various items and he could not easily do it. He got fed up with the questions and said to the lawyer:

"Young man, I can't answer most of your questions but if we go back to my office I have a row of buttons on my desk. I can push a button and a man with a college education can come in and give you the answer."

Ford was viewed by the public quite favorably. Knowing an answer was not as important as knowing where to get the answer.

Mike.
We used to kid Mike, one of our little group at Georgia Tech. Mike had dropped out of high school to join the Marines at age 16. After the Marines he was accepted at Georgia Tech.

We told him that he would have to have a high school diploma to get a good job and that he should go back and finish.

We could kid Mike because we all realized that high school diplomas and college degrees might become worth less and less in the future as new options for work and making money opened up.

Little did we know how true this would become within our lifetimes.

Two unemployed men made $19 billion in two years.
Two young men, one of Ukrainian birth, both applied for jobs at Facebook as programmers. Both were turned down. I'll bet they tried going through the human resources department. They decided to start a business.

Four years later they sold WhatsApp to Facebook for $19 billion, not million, mostly in Facebook stock. Both of them began selling their shares in large chunks as rapidly as they could. These type sales of stock do become public knowledge. It is not a good idea to have all of your assets in one stock. I'm sure they have diversified their investments.

They succeeded not because jobs have changed. but because of the way that ideas are monetized. Services are free because the customers have become the products. People are not customers if they are not paying for something.

My choices.
I made the decision in 1976 to get out of the corporate rat race and have never regretted it. I have devoted a lot of time to volunteer activities. Over time we see our experiences in ways that are different from when we had them.

Bob Dylan may have expressed it the most succinctly in his song *My Back Pages*:

"Ah, but I was so much older then, I'm younger than that now."

The context for Dylan was his disillusionment with the 1960s protest movement. I also had cause for disillusionment.

I think one of the saddest things about getting older is looking at young folks, especially of one's own family, children, and grandchildren, seeing things they don't see and knowing that it is pointless to tell them.

I have chosen to use humor in all types of situations and subjects. Penguins have been good examples on many occasions though thinking is required for the application.

Penguin Jokes Part 1.
The best penguin joke of all came from the radio show *Prairie Home Companion* with Garrison Keillor, that was a favorite when when we travelled and over the entire lifetime of the show.

Two penguins were on an ice floe. One says to the other: "You look like you are wearing a tuxedo." The other one replies "What makes you think I'm not?"

A penguin has a camera and is taking pictures of other penguins on the ice floe. One of them says "Why do you pay extra for color film?"

What do you get when you cross an alligator with a penguin? I don't know but don't try to hug it.

Why is that no matter how hungry an Eskimo gets, he will not eat a penguin egg? Eskimos are at the North Pole; Penguins are at the South Pole.

Where does a penguin keep his money? In a snow bank.

The Gospel Message.
H Clay Turnbull was an American clergyman and author. He played a big part in the Sunday School Movement. He wrote a book called *Individual Work for Individuals* in 1901.

Turnbull was on a train in western Connecticut. He sat next to one man that he knew from a church meeting. Here is the main excerpt of that story:

"He seemed glad to be spoken to, and I said I hoped he would enter into

Christ's service. He said he wished it were so. "

"Then why isn't it so?" I asked. "You have nothing to do but to commit yourself at once to the loving Savior as his servant and follower. He is more willing to accept you than you are to offer yourself."

"Do you mean, Mr Trumbull, that here on this car-seat, just now, I can give myself to the Savior, and he will accept me without any further preparation on my part?"

"I mean just that," I said. "The Savior is ready when you are. There is no gain in your waiting; and no farther preparation is needed than for you to give yourself to him and to trust him, unhesitatingly."

Important related verse From I Corinthians 6:2:

"For he saith, I have heard thee in a time accepted, and in the day of salvation have I succoured thee: behold, now *is* the accepted time; behold, now *is* the day of salvation."

CHAPTER 2: VERY EARLY DAYS

"WHETHER I shall turn out to be the hero of my own life, or whether that station will be held by anybody else, these pages must show. To begin my life with the beginning of my life, I record that I was born." From the opening lines of David Copperfield, by Charles Dickens:

I, David, was born.
My parents were in Hinesville, Georgia prior to my birth, from August 1944 to March 1946. My father was the pastor of Hinesville Baptist Church. He had just graduated from Mercer University, in Macon, Georgia.

They moved to Savannah Georgia. From March 1946 until May 1947, my father was Associate Pastor of Bull Street Baptist Church.

During that time, I was born, David Newton Sneed. My middle name was from my maternal grandfather Simeon Newton Dorris.

From May 1947 to May 1948, my father was the senior pastor at Jasper Springs Baptist Church in Savannah.

I have three brothers and no sisters.
I have three brothers. I am the oldest.

With one I was closest when growing up. One was a competitor and in late teens we became separated geographically. The other was like a stranger because I was gone before he was born.

The same is somewhat true with our children. The birth years between the oldest and the youngest is 25 years.

Toccoa Falls and Dr. R. A. Forrest.
My parents met while they were students at Toccoa Falls College in Toccoa, Georgia. My father sold tickets to see the Falls. My mother's dorm was Gate Cottage at the entrance to the path to the Falls where tickets to the Falls were sold.

One daughter attended and graduated from the same college, now named Toccoa Falls University.

I have a photo of me at about age 18 months being held by Dr. R. A. Forrest the Founder of Toccoa Falls College when he visited my parents in Savannah. The story of Dr. Forrest and Toccoa Falls is miraculous.

Achieving the Impossible with God is the biography of Dr. Forrest and *A Tree God Planted* is the history of Toccoa Falls College. Both books are required reading for students at Toccoa Falls.

What has amazed me is how many used copies of both books are available in the bookstore that students have sold back.

I wonder if they really read them at all. Those two books are a college education unto themselves.

Bridging the gap from early days to late days.
I have learned that the best way of keeping up with the past is not to keep up with it. Remaining memories are probably the best way. Various media just clog things up.

So much change in my lifetime.
There is so much change that has occurred in my lifetime. Not just in one arena. Everything has changed. Some may say that an airplane is just a bus with wings, but look how far we can go, so quickly, on an airplane.

I remember at age three standing in the front seat of the car. That was standard in all families. There were no seat belts at that time. I also remember sitting in my dad's lap while he was driving.

A typical middle class home was like what my uncle Buck and my aunt Katherine had in Fort Walton Beach, Florida for many years. Two bedrooms. About the size of a small apartment. When air conditioning became available they got one small unit and put it in their bedroom. It ran full blast 24/7. Nothing for the rest of the house.

It has amazed me that places that were run-down and poverty-stricken, in the United States as well as in other countries, have become so advanced.

Hotels and motels, have gone through vast changes that have kept occurring faster and faster. The simplest and cheapest motels have better rooms than the fanciest hotels of days gone by.

CHAPTER 3: I LIVED IN MANY PLACES

"This morning I saw a coyote walking through the sagebrush right at the very edge of the ocean - next stop China. The coyote was acting like he was in New Mexico or Wyoming, except that there were whales passing below. That's what this country does for you. Come down to Big Sur and let your soul have some room to get outside its marrow." -Richard Brautigan, A Confederate General from Big Sur.

Why I moved so much.
I lived in a number of places while growing up.

Baptist pastors years ago did not stay long at a church. Two years would be pretty much an extended term. I think the reason was that the pastors were more of evangelists unlike the administrative pastors of today.

I have jokingly said that Baptist pastors were treated like the scapegoat, a King James Bible word in Leviticus 16:10, from the ancient church of the Jews in the Old Testament. The sins of the congregation would be symbolically placed on a goat that was then sent into the wilderness.

Everything these pastors could do to win the lost in a neighborhood, through what the Apostle Paul called "the foolishness of preaching," could be done fairly quickly and it became time for someone else.

Pastors would preach at other churches, exchanging with other pastors.

Though in a segregated society, I can recall my father and other white pastors exchanging with black pastors. While today it might be hard to understand, while I was growing up it was not.

The pulpit exchange of pastors, and even choirs, black and white, was not strange in years past.

The Rev. Arthur Price Jr., pastor of the historic 16th Street Baptist Church in Birmingham, said his church often carries out pulpit swaps with neighboring congregations.

"Heaven is not going to be a place where we're all going to think alike, sing alike, and worship alike," he says.

Pulpit swapping "gives us a chance to demonstrate unity in the body of Christ and also demonstrate diversity."

Middletown, Kentucky.
I lived in Middletown, Kentucky from May 1948 until January 1949 when my father was at seminary. Evangelism was a top priority.

Pastors did not need to know administration, human resources, psychology, counseling, fundraising, budgeting, and long range planning.

It has been my observation that the goal of seminaries is to teach, at the lowest possible level, the differences in their denomination and how to defend these differences.

Perhaps in humor, it has been said that the goal of the Dallas Theological Seminary is to teach how to preach with a southern accent.

St Marys, Georgia.
I lived in St Marys, Georgia from January 1949 to September 1951 when my father was the pastor at St Marys Baptist Church.

St Marys was a shrimp fishing community as well as a paper mill community.

Gilman Paper Company operated there from the 1940s until 2002.

The parsonage was a nondescript house next to the church.

My aunt, Ruth Dorris, my mother's sister-in-law, came to visit. She brought me a WWII leather pilot's helmet with goggles. I treasured the gift.

I remember the time my father and I rode a locomotive to either Kingsland, Georgia, eight miles away, or Brunswick, Georgia, 44 miles. I don't know which.

Brookhaven, Georgia.
I lived in Brookhaven, Georgia from September 1951 to January 1953 when my father was the pastor of Doraville First Baptist Church. I started first grade in Brookhaven.

Davids Island at New Rochelle, New York.
I and my brother and our mother lived with grandparents in Georgia while my father was at the U.S. Army Chaplain School at Fort Slocum though we did visit and stayed in guest quarters.

Fort Slocum was on 78 acre Davids Island in the western end of Long Island Sound in the town of New Rochelle, New York. The island had been used by the military since 1857. Uses have included the largest military hospital and a Confederate prisoner of war camp. Fort Slocum has been gone since 2002 though the rare Kemp's Ridley turtles are still there.

Fayetteville, North Carolina.
I lived in Fayetteville, North Carolina from March 1953 to August 1953, when my father was at Fort Bragg.

Years later I remember I was driving on the highway close to Fayetteville.

Across the median in the other direction a small crowd had formed. I stopped to see if I could be of any assistance. Two elderly ladies were in a car that had run off the road and hit a large tree. The car had then moved around the tree and was facing in the opposite direction. I went over to the car. It was heavily damaged in the front from the collision with the tree. Both ladies were sitting though I could tell they were both dead. I observed that they had been eating their lunch from McDonald's. Food and wrappings were all over the car.

A moment's distraction is all that it takes for disaster.

Coral Gables, Florida.
My mother had elected that we move to Coral Gables, Florida, where we lived from August 1953 to February 1955, while my father was an Army chaplain in Korea.

My father served though he was not required to do so as he was a sole surviving son. His only brother was killed during the bombing of London during WWII. He had two sisters.

The duplex where we lived in Coral Gables is still there though what had been a quiet residential area is now a bustling Cuban commercial area with some housing.

Where my brother and I sold lemonade is now a row of stores directly on the roadside and sidewalk. Sylvania Heights Elementary School where my brother and I went to school is still there and is still a functioning school.

I accepted Jesus as my Lord and Savior.
I accepted Jesus Christ as my Savior at home in Coral Gables, inspired by Revelation 3:20: "Behold I stand at the door and knock: if any man hear my voice, and open the door, I will come in to him, and will sup with him, and he with me." I went to my mother and asked her what to do when Jesus is knocking on your heart. She led me in the sinner's prayer. Later I got a letter from my father who at Camp Casey in Korea.

My brother and I run away from home.
One day, I was seven, my brother and I got fed up with something and decided to run away. We loaded up our wagon and took off. We went a few blocks and then set up camp. Later in the day our mother came looking for us, found us, and took us home.

I move away from being just with close family.
In second grade, I had a good friend named Bill. This was my first move from just being with close family.

Bill lived close by. He and I in our explorations moved further and further away from our homes.

Hurricane Hazel.
In October of 1953, we were in Florida when hurricane Hazel hit. How well I remember that storm.

I don't recall why but my aunt Kat and my uncle Buck, Kat being my mother's sister, were there. I remember some of my uncle Buck's humor:

"We'd better get to the store and stock up before the hoarders get there."

My mother helped the needy.
My mother was big on helping the poor, primarily Cubans, though also blacks.

She would buy groceries and other things and take it to their homes.

I don't know how she decided where to go. I know that there were frequent repeats.

She would stay and talk about Christ to the people she served.

Again, Fayetteville, North Carolina.
We went back to Fayetteville, North Carolina from February 1955 to September 1955 when my father was again at Fort Bragg after returning from Camp Casey in Korea.

While we were at Fort Bragg, North Carolina, I got a job bagging groceries at the Commissary. The pay was only the tips and we had to take the groceries to the customers' cars. The tips were not bad.

On payday the store was really hopping. Each customer often had two grocery carts. Payday was once a month so they stocked up while they had money.

My fondest memory was time with the Bragg-Pope Little League. Pope was Pope Air Force Base, also at Fayetteville.

I remember one day playing in the woods with some other kids. I happened to notice that there was a man hiding in the bushes. I got behind and herded the kids toward the apartment complex.

When we were some distance from the man, I shouted for everyone to run. I took off running. They followed. Later I told them why.

Several did not believe me.

Ocean Drive, South Carolina.
We moved to Ocean Drive, South Carolina, to a house right on the beach, while the parsonage at the rural Horry County church was being built.

Ocean Drive, along with Crescent Beach and Cherry Grove Beach became North Myrtle Beach in 1968.

Living in a house on the beach was great.

There was a nearby fishing pier. Fishing was so good then that we put four baited hooks on each line and could catch several fish at once.

On the beach outside our house, fishermen with a large net would go fishing.

Some would hold the net while a row boat took the other end and made an arc bringing that other end to the beach where other men would hold that.

Then by hand each team would pull their end of the net. Thousands of fish of all sizes were brought onto the sand. Who knew when swimming that we were sharing space with all of this?

There was an abandoned two story hotel on the beach near our house. We kids had lots of fun playing hotel.

I took piano lessons. I would ride my bike on the beach road to the teacher's home at Cherry Grove Beach.

Horry County, South Carolina.
My father was the pastor of a rural church in Horry County, South Carolina, from September 1955 to September 1956.

We moved into the new parsonage.

I quickly got used to enjoy exploring the swamp near the parsonage. I learned to watch out for snakes and other wildlife.

I did not have a boat as there was plenty of reasonable solid ground for walking. Much of that swamp is now gone as The Army Corps of Engineers built a concrete waterway for some reason. Maybe flood control.

I was in charge of setting up a cookout for the youth group.

Since there was only the one general store I could not price shop for hot dogs and buns. I did get a small discount.

I wrote a full report with details of the items purchased and cost of each. I don't have a copy of the report but I remember the first line I wrote was "The cookout was a success."

In good weather there was dinner on the grounds after the worship service.

Rural churches had saw horses covered with boards in the back or to the side of the church building.

People would bring something. Always plenty of fried chicken and cake.

Those were great meals.

On bad weather Sundays and sometimes on weekdays, we would get an invitation to go to someone's home for a meal.

We kids got to catch a chicken or two. Chickens were loose in yards during the day and went into their coops for the night.

There was a unique food item known as chicken bog. It was a favorite in the small, low-population area centered in Loris, South Carolina. Chicken bog consists of chicken, sausage, rice and onion. It is a cross of casserole and stew.

I attend a two room schoolhouse.
School was an old two room schoolhouse, one room being the lunch room. We at least had milk and pinto beans. Around the walls of the lunch room were burlap bags of government issue pinto beans. Sometimes we also had bread and butter. Though rarely, there were other items that we all enjoyed.

There were two outhouses.

There was a hand water pump outside. Heat was from a large coal stove in the center of the classroom. There was much competition to be good enough to be able to go get more coal.

There was one teacher for all eight grades in one room. He used a long switch liberally. I saw him not just on school days but on Sunday as he was a deacon at our church.

I was in third grade but pretty much learned all eight grades as I could hear all of the lessons. The next year, in another school, I skipped fourth grade and went into fifth.

My friend Cecil, who was older and bigger but more experienced as a student at that school, and I would often go out the window at the back of the classroom and go to the general store for an RC Cola, Royal Crown, and a Moon Pie.

I don't think the teacher, an elderly man, could see to the back of the room.

Visits to Florence, South Carolina.
I think it was weekly though it could have been monthly that my father had Army Reserve meetings in Florence, South Carolina.

The trip took about an hour and a half each way on a busy two lane highway with plenty of log trucks.

There was a really great drive in barbecue restaurant. I can still taste the sandwich and the fries.

This was in the day that barbecue was always on a hamburger roll and there was not a lot of meat. I still prefer that type of sandwich.

Change came to Horry County.
When I lived in Horry County,, the people were mostly tobacco and cotton farmers. I picked cotton and I tied tobacco leaves onto the long sticks that would be hung up in the barns for air drying.

After the tobacco drying process where the leaves turn brown the tobacco went to an auction house. These auction houses were quite common so there was not a great distance to carry the tobacco.

That whole area just before the turn of the 21st century had become filled with multi-million dollar retirement homes.

Suburban Atlanta.
I lived in suburban Atlanta, from September 1956 to September 1958.

I cut grass with a reel lawn mower, during the season. I saved up and bought a new power mower for $65, with a three horsepower Briggs and Stratton engine. That would be $553 in 2017 dollars. Yet that with a few improved features could be bought in 2017 for only about $130.

I tried various ventures such as making window wash and doing printing on a small letterpress.

I worked at 7-11 when the stores were open front with long garage type doors.

Boys like me would take orders and money, make the purchase, and bring items to the customer in their car. The pay was tips though some people did not tip.

There was an adjacent 7-11 ice house and people bought blocks of ice. On hot days it was great to get an order for ice. We could linger in the cold.

I was a school crossing guard at a busy intersection a few blocks from the school.

After school, some kids, I was one, usually went to the soda fountain at a nearby drug store.

Smitty was an older guy that was a career soda jerk.

Pepsi Cola had become popular. At the soda fountain a big glass with flake ice went for five cents.

Destin, Florida.
Somewhere around this time my closest in age brother and I went camping on the beach at Destin, Florida. We were in the area with our parents to visit my aunt Kat and my uncle Buck that lived nearby.

The most notable feature was the nothingness. Miles of vacant beach. No lights visible anywhere. Today, that area is known as the Redneck Riviera. Not a vacant space left. Solid hotels, condos, restaurants, and gift shops.

I was a troublemaker in seventh grade.
In seventh grade I did not behave well. I knew all the material. I got 100% on tests and an A on papers.

The school librarian only let me take out one book a week.

I got bored. A bored student is a troublesome student. Suspension did not work so I ended up being thrown out of school for most of the year.

What I had to do to be able to read books.
We went to a large church in Atlanta.

During Sunday church services, I would sit in the balcony and read orange biographies from the church library, that had no book limit like the school.

I believe most baby boomers know the orange biographies published by Bobbs Merrill during the fifties. There were about 200 titles.

I could read three of the books during one church service. They were really well written just for younger readers.

Take care of what you get.
Christmas 1957 I got a Papermate ballpoint pen. Ballpoints had just come out and were not cheap.

I accidentally dropped mine in the floor heater register early on Christmas Day. I was most upset.

My parents gave me the money to go buy another one.

That may have been the last time they bailed me out from a mistake.

I start making rockets.
Seventh grade was the the time of Sputnik. Many kids my age were into rockets.

To make solid fuel we could buy potassium nitrate and sulfur at the drugstore until drug stores quit selling to kids. We would break up charcoal briquets. With the right mixture we would have great black powder for fuel.

I got a school suspension for launching rockets at recess. Later, though not at school, I tried liquid rockets with gasoline.

Didn't work!

Motor scooters and Mopeds.
One of my friends had a utilitarian motor scooter. Nothing fancy in looks. The chain and rear wheel was fully covered. The starter was a foot pedal. I envied

my friend's mobility. Sears Roebuck, under their name Allstate, came out with some really good mopeds, made by Puch. I wanted one but never got one.

I had learned that living in the country you might not have things, but you might not know that you were missing anything. In the city you knew what you didn't have but that didn't mean you could have it all.

A missionary from India came to dinner.
Our church had a dinner on Wednesday nights. It was a big event in a really big room. Hundreds of people attended. Each week there was a speaker.

One week the speaker was a missionary from India. As there was no head table the speakers sat in the audience. The speaker from India was sitting at our table.

As the plates were being served, I could see that dinner was beef and potatoes with gravy.

I was most anxious to see what would happen when the servers got to our table.

Would they have a suitable plate for the Indian speaker? They did not. She was served the same dinner as everyone else.

When she saw the plate she got up and left, perhaps feeling nauseous. A lot happened at once and a number of people got involved. She came back to the table. The beef dinner had been removed.

About the time everyone else had eaten, the guest from India was given a big plate with nothing but rice. Rice was not on the menu so someone in the kitchen had quickly cooked a batch.

Racial segregation.
When I was growing up, racial segregation was standard nationwide though in ways that people today do not understand.

It has been said that in the north people loved the race but hated the individual while in the south people hated the race but loved the individual.

I saw both of these viewpoints, having grown up in the south and in the north.

In the south, segregation was de jure, meaning by law. There were separate public restrooms, water fountains, separate entrances, separate schools, and places where black people were not allowed.

Sometimes de jure meant black people could cut grass or clean houses in town yet had to be out of town by dark. "Sundown town" was the term.

In the north, segregation was de facto, meaning it happened by circumstances.

Black people and white people did not live in the same neighborhoods together so schools and other places were naturally segregated.

The last schools to be integrated, this by court order, a generation after Brown vs Board of Education, were in Boston.

Most tourists are not aware that there is even today a black section of Boston.

This does not mean the south was better. At an early age I was aware of de jure segregation and found it reprehensible.

A black woman that worked for my mother also worked for my grandmother from the time of my father's birth. Her relationship with us was something not likely to be seen in the north.

She and my mother were like partners. Each would do the same tasks with the same goals. At lunchtime all at home would eat together at the same table. If this lady had something else she needed to do on a given day, there was no problem. Often my mother would drive her to a doctor's appointment or wherever.

Yet my mother would often talk about the black people, always using the N-word.

I have never had any problem with race relations though I have had many disappointments.

I was one of many that worked on legislation and community activities involving voting rights and civil rights.

Culture change is still needed for equality to take place.

I can give what may seem to be an extreme example.

A young black woman came into our office in and asked if we had any job openings.

She had a resume. I noticed that she had not completed a degree in accounting.

It turned out that she missed the last semester because the money ran out.

"What do you mean the money ran out?" I asked.

She explained that she had been living with her grandparents who lived within walking distance of the college.

The grandparents were on social security. As a dependent, under age 23, since then changed to age 18, and still in school, she was qualified to receive a social security check based on the income of the grandparents when they were working. She had turned 23 so the checks stopped.

The cost to attend the college was zero. Her living expenses were zero.

Yet with no free money coming in she saw no need to continue in school, even that close to a degree.

Why was there no one that could get through to her that she should finish the program?

Church and segregation.
During Jimmy Carter's term as President of the United States, his church in Plains, Georgia split over the issue of whether or not to allow blacks as members.

I know of times, once at one of the largest and most prominent Southern Baptist Convention churches, when my father was preaching, he was told that when he gave the invitation, that if any blacks came forward that he was to tell them that their application for membership would be referred to the deacons.

Sermons by southern pastors.
There are a number of types of sermons given by southern pastors. They differ from the sermons of the scholarly pastors in the north.

I had a series of books of sermons by Phillips Brooks, author of he Christmas hymn *O Little Town of Bethlehem*. I don't know how the congregation could sit through his sermons.

Holy Ghost preaching has no preparation. The minister may not even have a scripture until he gets into the pulpit. These sermons are generally always from the King James Bible. Holy Ghost preaching assumes a goodly amount of memorized verses and passages.

The minister cannot bounce around different translations as do those that spend much time preparing a sermon to read, with verses that best say what that minister believes. I have tried counting the number of transactions used in a given sermon.

I wonder how a southern accent would work with an NIV?

There were short visiting pastor sermons. My father's visiting pastor sermon was called *Faith's Certainty* that I had pretty much memorized. He got to be quite good at presenting it. The intent was to have a gospel message for the unsaved that might be in attendance as well as to grow faith among the saved. *Faith's Certainty* was a series of examples of faith in practice from the Bible as well as from personal experience.

I remember hearing of a pastor that gave a good sermon when he was a candidate for pastor at a certain church.

His first Sunday as pastor he gave the same sermon. The deacons figured he had just forgotten.

The next Sunday was the same sermon. And the next.

The deacons called him aside and asked him if he had any other sermons.

"Yes," he replied, "and when you learn this one I'll move on to another."

In another case, a new pastor gave his first sermon on the evil of cigarettes.

After the service the head deacon told him that many members were tobacco farmers.

The next Sunday he preached on the evil of drinking.

The head deacon told him that many members worked at a nearby brewery.

The third Sunday was about gambling. The head deacon told him that many members worked at the casino in town.

The fourth Sunday, hoping to stop the offenses he was making, he preached against foreigners fishing inside the 200 mile limit.

The church today is nominalist rather than realist.

A sermon can be given in the morning and in the afternoon the same people that attended the morning sermon will vote something just the reverse.

What is needed is to understand that God is real and that He plays an active part in the world and in our lives.

I become disillusioned with church.
I got used to contentious meetings at the parsonage with deacons and other church groups. Petty things became big issues. This was the beginnings of my disillusionment with the formal church.

When I talked with my mother about it, she seemed to take it all in stride. She said those meetings were nothing compared to meetings of preachers.

She said that you cannot know jealousy until you see it between two preachers.

It was around that time that I saw a print of a drawing of a man in a coat and tie going into a place of business. He was shaking hands with Jesus.

"Well, goodbye for now. I'll see you next Sunday."

In a bigger picture, Michael Gerson said:

"This is the result when Christians become one interest group among many, scramble for benefits at the expense of others rather than seeking the welfare of the whole. Christianity is love of neighbor, or it has lost its way."

The book In His Steps.
I had my introduction to the book *In His Steps*, by Charles M Sheldon. The book was first published in 1896. It has become one of the best sellers of all time with over 30 million copies sold.

The story involves a pastor that challenges his members to commit a year before doing anything to first ask themselves: "What would Jesus do?" Only a few members agreed to do it. There are stories of what happened to each of them. Commonly it meant a loss of income, or fame, or position. It is a work of fiction so there of course can be no proof of what would actually happen to those who practiced Jesus teachings. Yet it is a most thought provoking book.

Elbert Hubbard.
Elbert Hubbard, of East Aurora, New York, the writer, philosopher, restaurateur, maker of handcrafted books, jewelry, lamps, art, furniture as well as conference center owner, and artist was a speaker on the Chautauqua circuit.

He would often debate Christian pastors. Reporters asked him why he was so against Christianity. He said he was not opposed and thought it was the greatest idea that had ever come along. He said:

"Someday, someone should give it a try."

I leave the south and move to South Jersey.
I lived in Sourh Jersey from September 1958 to January 1960, when my father started a church at Levittown, now Willingboro, Pennsylvania.

My best memory of that church was when I caught my right thumb in the back door of our 1959 Chevrolet. The thumbnail has never completely healed.

There was good fishing off a bridge in a creek near our house. Bream, pronounced brim, easier to say than acanthopagrus australis, and sunfish.

Eighth grade in New Jersey.
I went to school in South Jersey for eighth grade. I think that school is now an elementary school.

Since I had skipped fourth grade and had started school early because of my September birthday I was as much as two years younger than my classmates.

I was tormented for my souther accent. My teacher even said to me in class one time "I'm going to hit you real slow," and illustrated with his fist in the air.

I worked hard, and succeeded, to get rid of the accent.

I did not have the advice, not yet given, of Sam Ervin, Senator Sam, of North Carolina, or I might have kept the accent.

During the Watergate hearings we got to know Senator Sam Ervin. When asked about his success in life he replied:

"Being a graduate of Harvard Law School and not looking or sounding like it."

We learned how to read a newspaper.
At school we studied a book called *How to Read the New York Times*.

It was a most impressive lesson that applied to most newspapers.

I had not known that a newspaper headline tells the story in short. Reading down, the article gives more and more detail. The first sentence tells more. The first paragraph even more. Quit reading at any time the reader knows enough.

Books that were important in my education.
There were two publications, one a single book, the other a set of books that were most important to me.

High School Subjects Self Taught, 28 Subjects in One Book, 1,442 pages, published by Garden City Books. In 2017, I gave that book to one of our granddaughters.

Mathematics for Self Study, a five volume set, hardbacks with red covers published by D Van Nostrand Company. The books were titled:

- *Arithmetic for the Practical Man*
- *Algebra for the Practical Man*
- *Geometry for the Practical Man*
- *Trigonometry for the Practical Man*
- *Calculus for the Practical Man.*

I had suggested to my mother that it might be great to get the math books for Christmas. That happened because in looking around I found the books under my parents bed. They had already opened the box so I had a sneak peek. I still have the books.

I bought several large encyclopedia type books that were sold in pieces at large grocery stores.

Every week I rode my bike to a town two and a half miles away to get that week's installment. There was a binder with a screw closure for the entire book.

I learn about public school education.
I could not wait for Christmas the year I got the math books. That day, I started with the arithmetic book and was fascinated. It contained material that I had never seen in school. There was a whole chapter on compound interest, a most important subject for money management. The teaching method was much simpler and easier to comprehend than what I had learned in school.

The arithmetic book played a big part in my overall understanding that the purpose of public schools is all about making full time government jobs for union member teachers and to keep children supervised while parents are at work.

Education is not the top priority.

Marya Mannes did not go to school.
My favorite quote from the American author and critic Marya Mannes,

1904-1990, is that: "My mother wanted me to have an education so she kept me out of school."

According to the Encyclopedia Britannica, Mannes "was educated privately and benefited from the cultural atmosphere of her home and from European travel."

Perhaps ahead of her time she said "The earth we abuse and the living things we kill will, in the end, take their revenge; for in exploiting their presence we are diminishing our future."

I get a job serving afternoon newspapers.
As soon as I turned 12, I got a job serving 110 afternoon papers, Monday to Friday;*The Philadelphia Bulletin, The Camden Courier, The New York Times, and The Woodbury Daily Times.*

I had to roll papers and tie them with a tying machine. In bad weather I would first wrap each in a piece of brown waxed paper.

I was paid $4.00 per week, equivalent to $33.00 in 2017 dollars. Often I would spend all my pay at the newsstand.

I had to ride about three miles on my bike to town to pick up my papers. Deliveries were in town. In cold weather my hands would almost be frozen to the handle bars. When I got home I would eat a dozen fried eggs plus sides.

Many years later, after moving to Wyoming, after joining a network, I knew the Executive Director of a New Jersey non-profit. I found out that he had lived in the apartment above the newsstand when he was first married. His landlord had been my boss.

A small world indeed.

I get a farm job.
I worked at the farm in South Jersey where our house was located. The farm was a combined truck farm and plant nursery. All of the workers but me were migrant Puerto Ricans that would go home after the season.

Ford 8N tractor
At age 12, I learned to drive a Ford 8N tractor. The 8N was the all time best selling tractor.

It had a clutch on the left side and the brakes on the right. It was the first four speed tractor.

With that tractor, if I was just traveling and not plowing or hauling a trailer, I would skip first gear. I would get chewed out for that by Juan, the Puerto Rican team head. The few feet in first, that I thought was too much trouble, did get the tractor in motion with less strain on the engine.

Almost 60 years later I saw an 8N at a county fair in Wyoming and showed it to one of our daughters. I showed her where the 8N is cast right into the left side of the engine block. I showed her the configuration for the four speed shifting that starts in the upper right and ends in the upper left.

At that farm, I hoed vegetables. Taking out weeds in a vegetable field in a South Jersey truck farm in the summer has to be the most miserable job that there is.

I cut and planted leaf and stem cuttings for vegetative propagation of plants.

I cut off new growth on shrubs and flowers such as geraniums and chrysanthemums. Four inches or so. Often large leaves are suitable. I removed about two of the four inches of leaves. I made a 45 degree cut, dipped the ends in water, then into the hormones. The two main brands at that time were Root Tone and Hormodin. Both brands are still around, at Walmart, Lowes, and Home Depot and, no doubt, other places. There are now other brands also.

I made little cuts into sand and planted the cuttings one to one and a half inches deep. Planting in the cut in the sand, like a trench, kept the hormone powder from rubbing off. I packed the sand tight and kept it wet. In as little as two weeks, sometimes a month or so, there were be plenty of new roots. I transplanted to soil in pots or ground.

Other things to do in South Jersey.
In warm weather I went to a nearby pond nearly every day and rowed around in a row boat.

There was no garbage collection where we lived. Homes had fire pits in the backyard. Everything was burned.

There was no heat on the second floor of our house. It got quite cold in the winter.

I wired my bedroom with low voltage lights and switches from batteries. I had a radio antenna made by stringing a long horizontal wire from my second floor room down to the detached garage. I would stay awake at night listening to Jean Shepherd monologues on radio station WOR through headphones.

My brother and I rode our bikes to the Delaware Memorial Bridge. We had planned to go farther but bicycles were not allowed on the bridge. From our house it was about 15 miles though it did not seem anywhere near that distance.

It was easy to take the bus to Philadelphia.

I start high school.
I went to the a new high school. I had to change school buses en route each way. It was only nine miles but it seemed much farther. I read a lot of books from the library. I wrote reviews of Charles Dickens books for the school newspaper.

Colonial Heights, Virginia.
When my father started Western Heights Baptist Church in Petersburg, Virginia, I lived in Colonial Heights, Virginia. That was from from January 1960 to March 1962. Colonial Heights is directly on U.S. Route 1, beside the Appomattox River, that separates Colonial Heights from Petersburg.

Around this time the evangelical church began a rapid decline. Where it had been that Christians did not have a television or go to the movies, it became so that only the pastors could not have televisions. Next, anyone could have one.

Good News for Modern Man, a paraphrase rather than a translation, became the Bible of choice. The King James had become harder to read as educational standards declined. People were becoming functionally illiterate.

I had an experience that turned me from God. A gas station in Colonial Heights was having a drawing for a sailing board boat. I filled out as many entries as I could until they told me to stop. I prayed that I would win. I did not win either with God or with all of my entries.

I went to summer camp at Eagle Eyrie, a family conference center in the mountains out from at Lynchburg Virginia. One day I escaped in the truck that picked up and delivered laundry. I don't remember the details of what I did and where all I went.

Library cards for whites only.
As a white, I could have a free library card from the Petersburg Public Library, a separate city across the Appomattox River from Colonial Heights, even though I was not a resident.

Black residents of Petersburg, Virginia could not get a library card at all nor could they even enter the library.

This bothered me but it was the way it was.

While we lived in Colonial Heights the lunch counter sit-ins began in Petersburg. I began to think there was a solution but it would be almost another two years before I began to do something for equal rights.

No money down and 50 cents a week.
I bought various tools, like an electric drill set, at a jewelry store in Petersburg. No money down and 50 cents a week. I always paid on time.

The city dump.
I spent large amounts of time at the city dump in Colonial Heights. Dumps of that kind were large areas where people could dump anything. To burn the refuse, there would be fires set by City employees running the dump. There were good pickings of all kinds of things.

Water sports.
I spent a lot of time by the Appomattox River fishing and digging crawfish and catching frogs. I supplied the Biology Department at Colonial Heights High School. One time in the winter I had made a raft with a 55 gallon drum. I attached five foot long logs on each side. In a snowstorm I went out. The raft was not stable and it rolled into the water. I was ok though wet and cold. I later found an old john boat in Swift Creek, a smaller river and swamp. I had a lot of fun with that boat. It leaked some at the front but that was not a big deal. The point was that I had mobility on the water.

I was a teenage archaeologist.
A friend had a metal detector. We would often go out and find all kinds of Civil War items. When we found unexploded shells from a parrot rifle, a type of artillery gun, we would call Fort Lee and they would come and detonate them. The vast majority of what was found was not explosive. A good place to go was the large shopping center construction sites where digging had already been done.

I work at another farm.
One job that I had in Colonial Heights, Virginia was at a flower farm that grew long stem chrysanthemums. That was focused work with a perennial plant. There were different lengths of cutting. It was a wholesale farm and there was some packaging to be done.

Optimist Club oratorical contest.
I came in third in a field of three for the Optimist Club oratorical contest in Colonial Heights, Virginia. I still got a trophy. Most importantly I was a speaker.

The speech was re-written. The first line was "The speed of the leader is the speed of the gang."

I learned plenty from the speech and from participation.

Central Massachusetts.
From March 1962 to April 1963, I lived in central Massachusetts. My father started the Nashoba Valley Baptist Church, now Calvary Baptist Church, primarily for Baptist soldiers at Fort Devens.

I don't remember how it all happened but I would regularly have breakfast at Fort Devens with my father, either in the enlisted mess hall or at the Officers' Club. Copies of the *The New York Times* were available free at the Officers' Club. I began to read that paper on a regular basis.

I remember one time when a man at the mess hall called another man by name but prefixed it with "Jesus Christ."

I heard my father say: "Why don't you make up your mind what his name is?"

The man apologized.

I was one of the few at school that had a car. It was a black 1953 Ford Crown Victoria Sports Coupe with leather seats and a flathead eight cylinder engine.

I had bought it for $125, a little over $1,000 in 2017 dollars, and never had any trouble with it.

One of the teachers at my high school had a French sedan, a Facel Vega HK500, like the one that Albert Camus was in as a passenger when he and the driver were killed in a crash.

Another teacher had a Nash Metropolitan.

The Cuban missile crisis occurred while I was there.

We had practices where we would hear the bell and get under our desks.

One of my teachers said that if an attack became real, if any of us tried to run out, that he would break our legs. Fortunately it never became real.

I get a job in town.
I was janitor for the health department. I set my hours and work priorities. I was paid $100 a month.

I would cash my check and deposit most to savings. I would go to a restaurant a few blocks away near the railroad station and have a sit-down dinner, always of a hamburger, fries, and a milkshake. So much better than a fast food restaurant.

I also picked apples.
I am glad that I can add apple picking in orchards around Ayer to my resume. Good honest work where pay is directly related to production. The tally man kept a card for each picker and the number of boxes picked. The ladder gets rested against out branches and the ladder bobs as the picker runs up the ladder without holding on. A balancing act. There was a canvas basket around our necks. The bottom could be dropped out for the apples to go into the box. Everyone worked hard and fast. No time to mess around.

My brother gets lost.
I was doing some work for a contractor that was building more houses on our street. I was helping at one that was two houses away.

Our street was a dead end and had only a few houses on it.

My youngest brother at the time was maybe four years old. My mother told him he could go and be with me.

He was thinking of my janitor job in town.

He took off to town walking on the railroad track. He had walked with me before. It was not a busy track as it was only used by a commuter train at certain hours.

No trains were running at that time yet it was an active railroad track.

Later, I came home alone after work and Mother and I both panicked.

We went looking for him. He had gotten to town and had been found by the police. They asked him where he lived and he said simply "Massachusetts."

I forgot how we all got together but it ended well.

Henry George School of Social Science.
I took a mail order course from the Henry George School of Social Science in New York City.

The main textbook in use was George's *Progress and Poverty*. This all-time best selling book on political economy was written in 1879.

Winston Churchill, Leo Tolstoy, John Dewey and Albert Einstein were among the influentials who endorsed George's proposals.

This study was perhaps the greatest secular influence on my ideology.

I felt that the ideas of *Progress and Poverty, Protection and Free Trade,* and other books by Henry George made too much sense to ever be implemented.

From the publication *Dollars and Sense,* here is a summary of the single tax that Henry George proposed:

"To summarize George's political-economy: George began from the premise that the land, along with all other natural resources, is the common inheritance of all. No persons or firms should own land; they should only be able to rent it. Furthermore, that rent should be paid to the public, as the rightful collective owner of all land."

"Individuals and firms should own entirely whatever results from their efforts to make the land productive, however, whether by farming it or building a factory on it. They should also own entirely whatever profit they can create through the investment of accumulated capital. In other words, George was not a socialist."

"The single tax program was George's plan for implementing this view.

The single tax was to be a property tax, on land but not on improvements, at a rate high enough to provide adequate revenue to the government.

These tax payments would represent the rent those who use the land owe to the public.

At the same time, taxes on labor income and on capital earnings would be eliminated."

Quotes from Henry George.
"There is danger in reckless change, but greater danger in blind conservatism."

"Let no man imagine that he has no influence. Whoever he may be, and wherever he may be placed, the man who thinks becomes a light and a power."

"He who sees the truth, let him proclaim it, without asking who is for it or who is against it."

More on Progress and Poverty by Henry George.
I want to say the Bible rather than *Progress and Poverty* was the greatest influence on my ideology. Unfortunately, my early study of the Bible was heavily influenced by Bible teachers and pastors, that, sad to say, were really not believers in the Bible.

These folks would start teachings and sermons with

"What the Bible really means…",

"Now in the Greek the Bible really says…",

"What Jesus meant was…".

They negated what the Bible said. For a long time I believed them.

A peculiarity of Bible teaching is that the person that does not believe a doctrine is the expert in why no one should believe it. Wouldn't it seem that the expert should be the person that believes doctrine and has benefitted from it?

Dedham Kayak Company.
I washed dinner dishes at home for my mother for small pay, saved up, and bought a kayak kit for $19.00 from the Dedham Kayak Company in Dedham, Massachusetts, near Boston. Dedham Kayak Company was at a farm. The factory and warehouse for the kayaks was in the large old barn. The farmer put all the parts into brown paper grocery bags. The frame was to be assembled and then covered with canvas and waterproofed with airplane dope, that smelled like bananas and was toxic.

There was a vernal pool in the woods next to our house where I tested my finished project for leaks.

I used the kayak in rivers and in the ocean between Plymouth and Cape Cod.

I especially remember traveling the 16 miles of the Squannacook River starting below the dam in Townsend, Massachusetts.

It was a most miserable trip as I had to portage around an incredible number of fallen trees that blocked the river.

When we moved, I took the kayak to Georgia. The moving company tied it underneath their semi-trailer.

The last I saw of it was in my grandfather's garage in Georgia.

I took a bike trip.
I took a bike trip around New England when I was 15.

It was a great trip in great weather.

A typical hotel rate was $2.00 a day, in the old wooden two story buildings typical of rural hotels. Those hotels had a front porch with rocking chairs. No air conditioning. No fancy designs or private bathrooms. I would guess that all those hotels were at least 100 years old.

I took trips to Boston on the train.
I enjoyed walking around the waterfront area in Boston. At that time there were plenty of old buildings and stores.

James Bliss and Company was a nautical supply business. I always went there and always bought something.

I win an essay contest.
While attending high school in Massachusetts, I won the local Women's Club essay contest.

My paper was called *What Makes a Man the Best?* based on Owen Wister's *The Virginian,* the quintessential Wyoming book about equality.

My mother said that I won because I was a white southern boy that had moved north and was writing about racial equality.

Elsewhere I have written of my mother's actual practice that exceeded what most northerners would do.

The Virginian.
The Virginian was an unnamed cowboy, that I believe was one of the black farm workers that left the south after the Civil War.

I have read that during the heyday of cowboys that about 30% of the cowboys were black.

There was one point at a party in Johnson County, Wyoming where Molly Stark Wood, in the book to represent aristocracy, said:

"Who is that black man over there?"

"Well Ma'am he ain't exactly acknowledging that he is one."

Wyoming was the place where you could go and it did not matter who you were or what you did before you got there.

All that mattered was who you were and what you did in Wyoming.

How I transitioned from high school.
My parents moved to Georgia from Massachusetts.

I had gone first and my address was my grandparents' home.

I graduated from my father's high school alma mater, after attending just three weeks. Credits transferred.

My parents gave me a 1952 Chevrolet coupe. I fixed it up and used it for drag racing at the Houston Brothers Drag Strip at the airport in Fairburn, Georgia. That car met its end when the clutch was gone.

It was cheaper to buy another car than to do the bigger repairs.

Yet at that time it was cheaper to repair a tv set than to buy a new one.

There were plenty of people whose job was to repair tv sets.

A cabin at Lake Burton in north Georgia.
My paternal grandfather, Henry Alfred Sneed, Grandpa to me, built a cabin on a lake when the lake was formed with a dam.

I have found that it seems most Georgians do not know that the lakes in Georgia are man-made, by the power company.

The lot at was on a 99 year lease from Georgia Power.

I don't know what has happened since then except that the houses up there now are all large and have multi-million dollar values.

Today it is easy to get there.

Back when the lake was formed the accesses were all narrow, rocky, clay and dirt roads that were quite slippery and muddy in wet weather.

Grandpa was the contractor for the land clearing, house construction, and boathouse construction, and well-digging. I helped when I was there.

The day that my grandfather announced he was starting work on building a boathouse, I asked him about the plan drawings. He did not have any. I expressed shock at this oversight. Without plans he built a fine boathouse.

We dug the well in the red clay, me and Grandpa. I was 10 or 11 at the time.

Grandpa had cut off most of the handle length of shovels so they could be used to dig in the narrow width of the well hole. Miners called those shovels banjos.

We started at the surface and dug a hole about three feet across.

The digger put the red clay in a bucket and it was hoisted up by the other who was taking a break from the digging.

There was a crude ladder for entry and exit.

While we dug, the ladder was out of the well.

I think we went down about 20 feet.

The lake house was a good place to go.

The lot and area was well wooded and shaded. There was fishing from the boathouse dock. There was a boat with a forward deck, forward facing cushioned seats, steering wheel, and an outboard motor with electric starter for cruising or for going to a grocery store several miles away.

Sneeds Nursery.
I worked at Sneeds Nursery, my grandfather's landscaping business that was in the area at the bottom of the hill from the house in East Point.

The total land including the house was at the end of the block and bordered on three streets. At the house level, there were nice homes on the street.

Turn left out of the neighborhood, then turn left at the stop sign, then it was like partially wooded farmland where my grandfather grew trees and shrubs.

The hill was quite steep. From the house it was at tree top height of the big trees below.

Early in the morning, Grandpa would shoot squirrels with a .22 caliber rifle out the window of the house. The squirrels were a nuisance to his business by eating young plants.

Grandpa bought coke, "co-cola," by the case, 24 returnable glass bottles in yellow wooden cases.

The Coke truck would come to the house, pick up the empties, and replenish stock.

At break time, Grandpa would match each worker for a drink. Free if they won, retail price of five cents, if they lost. He actually always won because his cost was wholesale.

My grandmother was most frugal. At lunch or dinner, only one glass of iced tea.

I worked in the dirt yet could only have a bath once a week.

I did get paid the going wage.

Grandpa died one Saturday morning at the age of 72.

He was sitting in his truck down the hill at the Nursery waiting for a customer.

His bottle of nitroglycerin pills was in his hand. I don't recall when or how my grandmother died.

The Sneeds Nursery land.
There was a touchy situation after my grandfather died.

The land used by the business was to be sold. My father's sister was the executor. Her husband, my uncle, was willing to buy the land at the full price that the real estate agent was to offer it for sale. My uncle announced this to the family and said that if any of them wanted it they could have it. He only would buy it if no one else would.

My father called me and asked what he should do. He said he had some knowledge that led him to believe the land was worth much more than the asking price.

I told him that in cases like that the real estate agents would buy the property themselves. This agent did not want to buy which led me to believe it was not a bargain.

I suggested to my father that he buy the land. He said he did not have the money. I told him that if it really was worth so much that he could probably borrow the purchase price and then sell for a higher price.

He ended up doing nothing though some bitterness developed. I told him that his brother-in-law had no use for the land and would attempt to sell it for a higher price but would have to take the risk. He would have to do the work and the waiting that could take years. In the meantime he would have taxes and opportunity loss on his investment.

For my uncle to make whatever profit would not be cheating the family.

I get a job at McDonald's.
The summer before starting college, I worked at McDonald's for 55 cents an hour.

Hamburgers sold for 18 cents so I could buy three hamburgers for an hour's pay.

Many years later when the same hamburgers were selling for $1.00, pay was $9.00 an hour. A worker could then buy nine hamburgers for an hour's work.

Hamburger meat was sourced locally and was fresh, never frozen. Patties were made by the supplier and separated with a square of paper.

French fries were made from potatoes at the store.

There was no breakfast.

A setup person would come in at 5:00 AM and start with peeling potatoes and cutting up fries in the basement.

Potatoes were delivered in 50 pound bags. The peeler was like a washing machine with a rough inside that would remove the peels. Cutting was one potato at a time. The fries were then pre-cooked and the baskets placed in racks next to the fryers. The finish time was then only a few minutes.

Milkshakes would be made in advance by the setup person.

Chocolate, vanilla, and strawberry. Each had a different weight. The was a scale but none of us used it.

We could sense the right weights and did not take the time to weigh. The manager and the district manager, if he happened to be there, would sample weigh some shakes. Never a problem.

There were no headsets or other electronics. No drive thru.

The registers were just registers. All of us could add things up in our heads and keep several orders in process at once.

Most of the time either two or three employees could handle long lines at the windows.

No inside dining rooms.

No 24/7. Open at 11:00 AM and close at 11:00 PM.

Many people always had the same order. We could see them coming and could have their order ready when they got to the window.

The menu was simple. Hamburgers and cheeseburgers, one type only. No doubles or whatever. One size fries. One size drinks. One size of three milkshake flavors. Milk in a carton. A total of eight products.

Maybe I should say nine. There was a ninth item that was never listed but would be made to order if someone asked. Cheese Delight.

A hamburger bun, both sides upside down, pressed flat, and grilled with two slices of cheese.

Sometimes we employees practiced a variation of Cheese Delight to make a different hamburger. Taste changed when we reversed the halves of the buns and flattened them.

One cook could prepare 24 hamburgers in four minutes.

Mustard and ketchup was dispensed in precise quantity with portable dispensers and had to be consistently placed on top or bottom of the bun.

A round tray would be set up on the divider between the grill and the front.

The counter people would wrap the hamburgers either direct for an order or to go into the warming bin that was on the back of the grill.

On the left side were the hamburgers with blue printed paper and on the right cheeseburgers with yellow printed paper.

There was a manager, an assistant manager, and a trainee manager.

Business in Action.
At an early age I began to learn about business.

I have noticed some things that seem to be universally true.

All of it is a subset of the workings of a fallen world ruled by Satan.

1. Most small business people do not want to make a profit.

2. Most small business people do not care if their business survives.

3. Most small business people do not know what business they are really in.

Note: If you look for the article "Marketing Myopia" from the Harvard Business Review in 1960 by Theodore Levitt you can learn about this.

An emerged phenomenon, of great impact to the future of business, is that to many, if not most, of younger people today, the Director of Human Resources is more important than the CEO.

CHAPTER 4: EDUCATION AFTER HIGH SCHOOL

"The schools ain't what they used to be and they never were." - Will Rogers.

Georgia Tech.
I had been accepted at several colleges.

For financial and other reasons I selected Georgia Institute of Technology, Georgia Tech, in Atlanta, Georgia.

My diploma from a Georgia high school, albeit one I attended for only three weeks, entitled me to in-state rates at Georgia Tech.

The fact that we were natives of Georgia was not relevant because we had moved away for a number of years.

The total cost was $75 per quarter for full-time in-state, almost $600 in 2017 dollars.

I began studies at Georgia Tech, also known jokingly as North Avenue Trade School, majoring in Industrial Management, also known as Jewish Engineering.

Looking ahead I could see that I would be in management, primarily because I liked working in the visionary and in the overview.

With Industrial Management I got survey courses to all of the major engineering disciplines. I learned the language of each discipline, its history, and its work.

Included was Ceramics, Textiles, Industrial, Electrical, Aeronautical, and other well-known names.

A great thing about Georgia Tech was that students could get free admission to cultural events.

We got a pre-punched IBM card in our mailbox that could be exchanged at the box office for an actual ticket.

The floor at the post office was littered with cards as most students, philistines if you will, had no interest in culture.

I took all of the liberal arts courses available at Georgia Tech.

I enjoyed writing and I liked doing parodies of poets and writers.

A piece I did in the style of E.E. Cummings was returned by my professor with "WHEE-EE" and with an A+ grade.

My writing subjects included a lot of what I was learning in the engineering courses, tied into a story.

I tried out being an artist. I did some paintings and exhibited. I was not good and really had no interest.

ROTC was a required course. I selected the Army.

Thursday was ROTC Day. All the students wore their dress uniforms. We carried our assigned M16 rifles that we used for practice. We had to keep them clean. There were inspections.

We each got a quarterly check for $25.00.

Many years later I learned that my mother and my oldest brother had thought that I did not graduate from Georgia Tech because I would not take ROTC. I did not dislike the military. I loved ROTC.

What I disliked was the Vietnam War as did half the population.

Freshmen had to wear yellow rat caps.

Good grades always went to students of a class that used, and consequently required the purchase of, a textbook written by the professor.

On the first day of class, we would look around and see if there were many students wearing purple socks. Those students were the football players.

The class could be expected to be easier to pass. I did not attend football games even though I had a free pass.

I have never liked football.

That first quarter at Georgia Tech, a major event occurred.

The President of the United States, John F. Kennedy, was assassinated. I think that it could be that most people remember where they were and what they were doing at 1:30 PM Eastern Time on November 22, 1963.

Where was I when JFK died? I was walking in the rain to the campus post office when it was shouted out from someone that had just learned of it.

Unlike today, everyone was saddened. He was the President regardless of political party as was Eisenhower before him. Respect for the President was taught in school. There was unity behind the President.

I still remember my campus post office box number was 34493. Every time I have visited Georgia Tech since then I have found that the combination to the box is still the same.

Aunt Janie.
Initially when I started college, I lived at my parents home and commuted by carpool with other students into Atlanta.

Later, after I got a job, and drove on my own, I went through the West End close to the home of my great aunt Janie Hood and my great aunt Dora Jackson. I would stop in for frequent short visits.

My aunt Janie would lend me books but made sure that they were returned.

She was a character.

My memories of my aunt Janie was of a little tiny lady sitting in a wheelchair, a glass of gin in one hand and a cigarette in the other. Smoking killed her at the age of 103. She was smoking in bed and set fire to her bed.

Federal aid to education starts for the general public.
While I was in college, the Great Society of Lyndon Johnson came into being.

One aspect was a government funded way that everyone could go to college.

Tuition and fees went up. Students accumulated college debt. The professors quit teaching and sat back. There was enough money to pay them to be window dressing. The professors had to get out of the way of graduate students who needed work. The graduate students taught the undergraduates as teaching was a part of their financial aid package.

With easier admission, and with inexperienced less motivated teachers, teaching standards declined and quality of education was dumbed down.

Colleges began hiring all kinds of administrators. Government money drove the costs up. More money was needed.

Each new generation of politicians promised more government money. Much money was given.

A new cycle of hiring administrators and of lowering of admission standards began. A new round of tuition and fee increases. There was increased student debt.

In the world of K-12, improving education, then and now, means giving more raises, earlier retirement, and higher pensions to teachers.

All because of almost unlimited free money.

In April 2017, the former CEO of the near bankrupt Chicago public schools, as part of a plea bargain, was given a four and a half year sentence, to be served at so-called Camp Cupcake, a little supervised federal prison, where Martha Stewart served time.

She had made a deal with a former employer to steer contracts to them in exchange for a 10% kickback. $23 million was already paid out to the company.

Her part was to be paid as a signing bonus when she went back to work for them later.

In one email produced in court she had said that she had tuitions to pay and casinos to visit.

This from a woman who had built a reputation, and multiple pensions, as a savior of inner city schools that had denied children of color a good education.

The tuitions were college for her two grandchildren.

As for the gambling, she needed more and more money as she had no expectation of winning.

Why I worked and supported myself while I was in college.
I applied for a student loan but was turned down. Though my father did not make much, his income was viewed as enough to pay for college.

I would not be able to live in the dorm and would have to work.

I was able to borrow each quarter's tuition and fees from Georgia Tech. Books were not included. Repayment was due before the end of the quarter and before any more loans. There was no Pell Grant or other government or other aid, at least for citizens.

Around the time I started college President Kennedy ransomed a number of Cubans that were imprisoned after the Bay of Pigs invasion. I knew one of them. He worked at the bank where I worked full-time at night.

He only worked two hours on two nights a week as he could not afford taking time away from study.

While I as a citizen could not get a loan, this man had full tuition, fees, and books paid at a high priced private college.

He also was getting adequate living expenses for him and his family.

All with a grant and not with a loan.

Lester Maddox closes his restaurant.
I was at the Pickrick restaurant in Atlanta the day that the owner, Lester Maddox, said he had changed his mind and would allow blacks as dining room customers.

The press and many bystanders were there to see what would happen.

There were some black Georgia Tech students who had previously tried to be served after the Civil Rights Act was enacted.

Maddox had chased them out with a pistol. When they again tried to get in, he announced that he had again changed his mind and was closing the restaurant.

The Pickrick restaurant building became the Georgia Tech placement office as it was right at the edge of the college campus.

I get a bank job and meet Rufus.
As a first step, I worked at a bank in the afternoon doing various menial tasks.

My supervisor was Rufus, in his late 20s. Even at 16, I could see that Rufus might have already peaked and might stay in his present position until he retired.

Yet he was then buying houses and renting them out. He was not married but had a variety of girlfriends. He was diligent at his work.

I learned a lot from Rufus.

I later moved into other banks operations tasks before getting involved in programming. I did tasks such as counting money in the vault, taking loan applications, approving or declining credit, with the bank's own credit card.

Bank credit cards started as a way for merchants to have a bank buy and take over their customers' accounts. In many cases the bank could charge back, have recourse, if the debts were not paid.

Charges had to be phoned in to the bank for approval. Me, at age 16, could decide yes or no, or yes with recourse.

The part I really hated was when a tire dealer had already put new tires on a car and I had to decline the charge.

But the same thing can happen today when credit cards are presented after the tires are installed. Today, however, people often have multiple cards and at least one card has some credit left.

In some cases the account was so bad that we could not take it even on recourse.

I could have said yes but I viewed myself as the lending officer for the bank, which I was, and it was my job to manage risk.

The customers would get cards that initially were only good at the store where they had an account. At first merchants did not like the idea that their customers would have credit at other stores. Then they realized that they would be able to give credit to their competitors' customers.

I meet G. Raymond LeMan.
I remember in picking up outgoing mail that I had met G Raymond LeMan who was the cashier.

The cashier was the second highest position at a bank, after the president.

Today, cashier would be executive vice president or maybe CEO.

I asked Mr LeMan how to get authority and responsibility.

He laughed and said that was easy to do.

"Nobody wants it. Just take it. You will not be stopped if you are going to take over their work so they don't have to do it."

The bank president.
Mills B. Lane, the bank president answered the phone: "This is Mills B. Lane,

can I sell you some money?"

His family owned the bank and all of its subsidiaries in Georgia and South Carolina. Lane had an open door policy for anyone.

He told me one time that he drove a Rolls Royce because he could not afford a Chevrolet or a Ford:

"Those cars are worth nothing after three years. A Rolls Royce is worth more than it cost in three years and it keeps going up."

The bank executive with the Ferrari.
There was another notable executive at the bank. I don't recall his name or title. Unlike Lane, he did drive Fords and Chevys but only during the week.

On weekends he drove his Ferrari. Every Monday he had it in the shop for an oil change.

I move to proof transit.
I moved to a job at night in the proof transit department operating a machine processing deposits and sorting the checks into the 32 pockets of a big internal wheel. The pockets were selected with 32 square buttons on the left side of the machine. The name of the game was item count and count per hour.

The department was mostly staffed with women.

Jealousy was rampant.

High counts were believed to somehow be fixed. I was the only male operator and the supervisor was a man on the management training program.

My count was always high and was believed to be because the supervisor gave me, a man, the easy work, whatever that was.

A deposit with several hundred checks was believed to be the high speed work. Deposits with postal money orders were even better and faster because they were usually small even amounts. There was work that was hard, the deposits with only one check. That was because there was extra work for each deposit slip.

To be fair to all, the single item deposits were divided up and each operator got roughly the same size stacks. I grew tired of the complaints.

I came in a few minutes early one night and asked that I get all of the single check deposits starting that night.

The supervisor was reluctant to do so. It was only he and I so we could talk about it.

He agreed and I took all of it to my machine all at once. A big pile of work. I had to stack some of it on the floor. The first night my count was not so good.

In just a few nights I once again had my item count and count per hour at the highest in the department.

The bank job had a set start time but the end was when we were done with processing deposits for the day, when the machine totals equaled the total that had come in. Usually that was around 4:00 AM.

Initially, I would drive from work at the bank to a parking lot at Georgia Tech and sleep in the car until class time. After classes I would go home for a shower, study time and some sleep time.

The Atlanta Times and other investments.
There was a new daily newspaper called *The Atlanta Times*. I bought stock before it started.

After it got going there was a lady at the bank that let it be known that she wanted to buy all the stock she could get to invest for college for her children.

Her offer was good so I sold my shares to her. I felt somewhat guilty when the newspaper only lasted a few months. The stock was then worthless.

I did some more investing in later years including a no-load mutual fund but never got really excited.

I found one stock that appealed to me. A company called Fluor. A broker told me that it was probably the worst stock on the market. Over the years it has become one of the best.

I become a computer programmer.
While I was at the bank I became a computer programmer because I took an aptitude test and had the highest score of all the employees that took the test.

Ironically I failed programming in ALGOL at Georgia Tech.

I used Autocoder and SPS languages. In these languages there was one programmer instruction for each computer instruction.

The programmer had to designate exactly where in memory the data existed for each instruction.

Positions 1 to 99 was for card input. 100 to 199 was for cards to be punched out. 200-399 was for data to be printed. There were 108 spaces of the 400 unused, 20 + 20 + 68, but that's the way the computer was designed.

All of the remaining 15,984 spaces were for the programmer to do calculations, rearrange data or whatever. Early programmers had to do things manually that would later become automatic.

Multiply and divide. This feature did not exist on many computers at the outset. On some is was an option. Multiplication means multiple additions. Divide means multiple subtractions.

Rounding. To round a number to two decimals meant: add .005, multiply by 100, find the integer, the digits to the left of the decimal, then divide by 100. For some reason the integer function was usually hardwired.

Day of the week. There is a formula for this that I have forgotten since there are functions to calculate. One bit of trivia is that the 13th of the month is more likely to be a Friday than any other day of the week.

Each business day everything had to be printed out.

I did a payoff calculation for each loan and printed it one the open balances report. That made me quite a hero.

Interest was calculated as add-on. If a loan was made for $1,000 at 6% for three years, the total interest would be $180. The total payback would be $1,180, or $32.78 per month for 35 months and a final payment of $31.98.

If the loan was paid off early there was a complex calculation rather than pro-rating. All completely proper. The actual principal balance declined monthly though not straight line. The formula was called Rule of 78.

The name came from the sum of the numbers from 1 to 12 which was 78. N squared plus N divided by 2. N was the number months in the loan. For a 12 month loan it became 144 +12 which was 156, divided by two which was 78. In a 12 month loan 12/78 of the total interest was the amount earned in the first month. 11/78 in the second month and so on. Today it is all done with APR, annual percentage rate and daily calculations to 5 decimals of a percent.

What would be called 6% add-on is actually 11.08% APR. The computer could easily do the payoff calculations.

After moving to programming, going home did not work. I found some roommates at Georgia Tech and we got an apartment in Atlanta.

We had some free time on Thursday morning and that is when we would do our worrying.

I get a job with the FAA.
I worked at the Atlanta airport for the Federal Aviation Agency, the FAA, now Federal Aviation Administration, as a computer programmer/operator.

It was just me at night though I came in just before the day shift left.

One day shortly after I was hired by the FAA, I stopped by the water cooler in an alcove off the hallway. At the back of the alcove was a large bulletin board. My boss was looking at it.

He called me over and showed me the open jobs listings that were frequently updated.

He told me what I could do if I found a job I liked. He said he would help me with the paperwork.

With a smile he added,

"Unless I have found another job before you and have left."

I could move around the computer room and would have all the machines running at once including the collator in the middle of the room.

I could do all the work on my schedule in about an hour and a half. Each job had a number and a description so it was clear what to do and was clear if it had been done or not. I got into a little trouble for moving ahead and doing the day shift work.

For most of my shift, work all done, I studied or chatted with the guard.

I find a faster way to sequence punched cards.
I got a monetary award from the FAA for a faster way to sort cards. It involved not using the sorters. Card sorters could only sort one column at a time. If there were non-numeric characters it got more complicated and took more passes.

So if there were many columns to sort, and if there were alphanumeric columns, it took a long time.

What I did was split up the cards into two groups and fed them into the collator merging the cards, first with a different color card between each card.

As they came out, I kept feeding them back in.

The idea was that each pass would get larger and larger groups of in sequence cards.

If there were 1,024 cards in exact reverse order and requiring all eighty columns to be sorted it could be done in just 12 passes counting the pass to merge in the blank different color card.

I have always been fascinated by compound interest and by multiples of two.

I love the old story of working for a penny a day to start, then doubling every day. Here is what would happen.

The pay for just the 30th day would be over $5 million dollars. The total pay for the first month would be around $25 million.

Day 1: $.01, Day 2: $.02, Day 3: $.04, Day 4: $.08, Day 5: $.16, Day 6: $.32, Day 7: $.64,

Day 8: $1.28, Day 9: $2.56, Day 10: $5.12, Day 11: $10.24, Day 12: $20.48, Day 13: $40.96, Day 14: $81.92,

Day 15: $163.84, Day 16: $327.68, Day 17: $655.36, Day 18: $1,310.72, Day 19: $2,621.44, Day 20: $5,242.88, Day 21: $10,485.76,

Day 22: $20,971.52, Day 23: $41,943.04, Day 24: $83,886.08, Day 25: $167,772.16, Day 26: $335,544.32, Day 27: $671,088.64, Day 28: $1,342,177.28,

Day 29: $2,684,354.56, Day 30: $5,368,709.12. If there was a day 31 that month, the pay that day would be $10,737,418.24.

I got another monetary award for what made no sense.

I made another suggestion that also gave me a monetary award but it made no sense to do the idea as it was approved.

When something had to be repaired a facilities outage form had to be completed and signed with multiple signatures. It was the same form and same number of signatures if a light bulb burned out in a closet or if terrorists blew up the whole airport.

The data from the form was punched into cards.

All kinds of regional reports were made that no one ever read. Two duplicate sets of cards were then made. We kept our set of cards, ten cases per month. We sent the two other sets of cards, 20 cases per month, to Washington so my counterparts there could sort them all together for the nation and make national reports that no one ever read.

The piles of source documents, cards, and reports consumed a lot of space.

I suggested that the source documents be microfilmed and the paper be destroyed to save space. Washington thought it was a great idea.

GSA added the requirement that after microfilming and before destroying the originals, that two photocopies of each document be made.

I was on my way to learning how things work in the government.

I get a job at The U.S. Rubber Company.
I took wholesale orders for Keds shoes at The U.S. Rubber Company, now Uniroyal.

There was a man whose job was to destroy returned shoes with a hatchet.

I asked him why they could not be given away to the needy even if they had to be sent to darkest Africa.

He told me that if they did that the shoes would never get to the poor, would end up in discount stores, and would take away from sales of new items.

I was even faster learning about how things work not just in government but everywhere.

I get a job with a big thinker.
I worked for David Schwartz, author of *The Magic of Thinking Big* and other books, at his business, the National Association of Women's and Children's Apparel Salesmen, NAWCAS. The hours were flexible, fit my school time, and was close to the school. I used a service bureau and automated membership data by having it punched into cards, sorted, and tabulated on a computer.

I sell advertising for the Clayton County Journal.
I sold advertising for the Clayton County Journal. When I took advertising orders into the office, I would pass by the house that was the plantation house Tara in the movie *Gone with the Wind*.

Some advertising was sold on a due bill basis.

Advertising was traded for hotel accommodations and restaurant meals of equal retail value.

Withy the approval of the publisher, I got a weekend at Ida Cason Callaway Gardens, a golf resort though I did not golf.

Newspaper ad sales jobs were high turnover jobs. No relationship existed between the salesman and the client.

A new salesman would go back to the same places as his predecessor, who might have called at some of the places only days earlier.

The pitch was:

"Would you like to buy advertising? You don't? OK. Bye."

I spend time at the Varsity.
While at Georgia Tech, I did spend plenty of time at the Varsity. The Varsity is known as the world's largest drive-in. Great food. Chili dogs. Fresh fries. Apple pies made fresh. There was beer but it was not advertised, not on the menu, and not visible.

For many years the car-hops reigned. They were all black men that were great servers. Many were college graduates that made better money at the Varsity than anywhere else. Like the experience of Jews, blacks had a tough time getting jobs. Jews simply started their own business.

The black carhops were in their own business. They were respectable independent businessmen. The Varsity carhops each had a number. One would put a big card on your windshield to show that you were theirs. Often they did this just as you drove in. They then rode on your back fender.

The carhops got a discount on the food when they bought it and collected at menu price that was on a bill made up by the kitchen when they served it to your car. Plus they got tips.

The government said they had to punch a clock and be paid by the hour.

Overnight the carhop feature was gone. All the carhops quit. The Varsity could not find suitable replacements. The outside customers quit.

One carhop benefitted. Nipsey Russell went on to become a famous entertainer and was known as the poet laureate of television. Russell started at the Varsity in the 1940s after his WWII service. He had enlisted as a private, served as a medic, and came out as a lieutenant. He was in his mid-40s when he started his acting career after the Varsity. He died in 2005.

Other fine restaurants.
There was a real French restaurant in Atlanta as well as other, anything you want, places.

My favorite restaurant was Dales Cellar, downtown and really in a cellar accessible from the street. Steak dinners ranged at Dales from four dollars to seven dollars. The waiters were elderly black men that were true professionals. There are those that might view that statement as both racist and something of the old south.

I decide to start dressing well.
I dressed well for Dales Cellar, a requirement for getting in the door, and for work at the bank.

When I first decided I would start dressing well, I splurged and bought a suit for $60 at the finest men's store in town, an upgrade from a typical $19 for a men's suit at the chain store Robert Hall. That $60 would be $475 in 2017 dollars.

One night at the bank two of the janitors, both men, were talking. One was elderly, the other a young man. I don't know how much they made but I would guess somewhat less than I was making. The older man was educating the younger man on how to buy shoes.

"Take $75 and go down and buy two pair of really good shoes. They will last longer and if you buy two you can switch them and they will both last longer."

There was another reason for dressing well. A man in Georgia was legally required to be wearing a coat and tie in order to be served a drink. The legislative intent was to keep Blacks and Indians from drinking as they would not be likely to own a coat and tie.

1960s Pink Pussycat is not the same as the later strip club Pink Pussycat.
There were places like The Pink Pussycat nightclub in the black section of the

city. There was no place like The Pink Pussycat. It was the best nightclub and always had well-known black singers and bands.

The music was Motown with songs like *Tramp,* and *Sittin' by the Dock of the Bay.*

There was a long elevated stage in the middle of the room surrounded by a bar with bolted down bar stools. There were tables filling the rest of the room.

Outside there was a black, uniformed, Atlanta policeman, perhaps off duty. At the door he checked IDs, dress, and other factors. He could and would refuse admittance for whatever reason, though only to blacks, even though it was a black-owned club with black people being the majority of the customers and all of the employees.

As a white man, I would be greeted with a smile, could enter without a coat and tie, did not have to show ID even when I was clearly underage, and the door would be held open for me and my date, if I had one.

"Have a good time, sir!"

I was not comfortable with how it worked. I tell this only as a record of the times.

The Pink Pussycat was a great night out, at a reasonable price, and I was completely safe. I had no fears about my car, my wallet, or my personal safety. I don't think there was any violence or crime anywhere around the place.

How the laws about drinking and gambling were skirted.
At VFWs and American Legions, the only requirement to come in and buy liquor was to be white and be able to reach up and put money on the counter.

No worry about the sheriff. He was in the other room gambling though gambling was illegal in Georgia.

Nevertheless, every January 1, *The Atlanta Journal and Constitution,* covered all of the front page and as far back in the paper as needed with a detailed list of all in the state that had bought a federal gambling stamp for the coming year.

Under Georgia law, possession of a federal gambling stamp was not prima facie evidence of gambling.

The list was a small print, run together, directory of the VFW and American Legion posts in the state.

My first new car.
I bought a new Ford Falcon from Beaudry Ford, the only Ford dealer in Atlanta. The salesman was my father's cousin.

I had two choices in my price range at that dealership, of vehicles in stock.

One choice was a four door with an eight cylinder engine. The other choice was a two door with a six cylinder engine. That is the one I bought.

No money down. $75 a month for 36 months, a typical term for that time. The only option on either car was an AM radio.

I was disappointed by some Christian elders.
There was one event that really got me to thinking on my own.

I was involved in a minor crash at a stop sign intersection, my fault for pulling out too far.

The insurance adjustor was my Sunday school teacher. The body shop manager was my Sunday school superintendent.

One day I went to the body shop to check the progress on my car repairs. A worker was using body putty to fill in the dent on my fender. The damage appraisal showed that a new fender would be used, paid for by the insurance company.

The worker told me that they did this body putty filler all the time. I asked the body shop manager, my Sunday school superintendent. He told me the same. I asked the adjustor, my Sunday school teacher. He told me the same.

I take my first road trip alone.
I made a trip by myself to the Florida Keys in my Ford Falcon.

I went all the way to Key West. A goal was to find an old Key West dump. I had done some research and believed I could find it. And I did find it near a beach area. I dug up a lot of bottles of all kinds.

On that trip I also went over to Fort Myers, thence to Sanibel and Captiva Islands. I camped out on the Sanibel beach on the Fort Myers side. I had heard about all of the things that crawled up on the beach at night. It was true. Some had legs. Some did not. I could not identify any of the creatures.

There was not much development on the islands, or anywhere around that part of Florida.

To show how development advanced, years later I was trying to locate an associate named Bob Jones that I knew had retired to Naples, Florida.

I called information, no internet, and was asked by the operator for the address. I told her that it was a new number and that I did not know the address. It seems that there were about 30 listings with the name Bob Jones. More if Robert Jones was added.

"Do you know just the new ones?" I asked.

"That IS just the new ones" she replied.

Peace Corps.
I was in the Peace Corps at a training center near Albany NY. All of those in our group were to become chicken experts so that we could teach people how to raise chickens. Yet one man of Italian descent from New York City had never seen a live chicken.

One night in the rain we were dropped off in groups of five in various towns.

We did not know the names of the towns, we had no money, we could not tell anyone we were with the Peace Corps, nor why we were in their town. We did have official ID in the event of a problem with the law.

We were to spend a week in that town and gather intelligence for a written report. We had an outline of data to gather. One example was to report the names of the elected officials. Another was to list the names of the real leaders in the town, naturally not those that were elected.

It was cold, dark, wet, and late at night when we were dropped off in our town. Everything was closed except for a bar. We found out that just outside of town was a private golf club where there was a party. We went there and the place was all locked up.

Our man that had never seen a chicken had seen plenty of locks. He opened the door faster than I could do it with a key. We slept on the floor. No theft or damage. We left early and no one could tell we had been there.

The rest of the week we were mostly not together. We did pickup labor to make some money to buy food. We slept wherever we could get a place.

While I can understand what was going on, there was nothing illegal or unethical about data collection, it was not something that I wanted to do. I was there to make a difference not to spy. I met some great folks.

I went back to Atlanta.

La Cuerpo de Paz.
Shortly afterwards, I did a project with La Cuerpo de Paz, Peace Corps, in Panama. In the transportation of agricultural and other products, bribery was an essential element. The solution was that you pay the bribes.

Volunteer activities in the 1960s.
I was active in the civil rights movement with Martin Luther King Jr. in the Southern Christian Leadership Conference, SCLC, and then in the Atlanta Workshop in Nonviolence (WIN), a part of the SCLC. I did tutoring in the Techwood Housing Project in Atlanta.

I coached young men wanting to legally avoid the draft as well as military people wanting to get out or to otherwise avoid going to Vietnam.

The most interesting way of legally avoiding the draft was to register for the draft and get into Draft Board #100 in Washington D.C. No one has ever been drafted from Draft Board #100.

It appeared to be designed for the sons of Members of Congress and the Senate as well as anyone else that had political connections or had the special knowledge required.

The way it worked was that the young man had be out of the country when he turned 18, then register at a U.S. Consulate. A short visit to Canada was a good place to do it. A hotel address would suffice.

Who can fault someone with wanting to obey the law requiring registration?

It was then true that these young men had not asked for any of the many deferments, including being or pretending to be homosexual, that the law allowed.

Then neither of their parents, as elected officials or otherwise in the public eye, could be faulted for having a draft dodger son.

Many of these young men became elected officials, including several, both Democrats and Republicans, that became President.

There were many thousands that either left the country or failed to register.

On January 21, 1977, one day after his inauguration, President Jimmy Carter issued a blanket pardon for the draft dodgers as they were called. Deserters were not included.

A military man getting out of going to Vietnam was fairly easy. Draftees had two year terms.

Once on duty he could file to go to Officers Candidate School. Then about a month or six weeks later he could apply for discharge as a conscientious objector. By the time the two items were sorted out, the two years was up.

What did I do for my own situation? I had a 2S student deferment.

By the time I was reclassified as 1A, a draft lottery had been set up. My number was so high that it was highly unlikely that I would be drafted.

I face a possible draft reclassification.
I was called for a physical exam that was the first step in draft reclassification.

There was a questionnaire with a list of organizations. Next to each one was a checkbox, yes or no.

Had I ever been a member or given money was the question. I could not tell a lie.

I had to answer yes to the Socialist Workers Party.

I had gone to the Space Expo put on by the USSR in New York City. It was a big event and many people went. Outside there were tables and various Communist and Socialist groups were set up. While waiting for my parents to pick me up at a prearranged time, I looked around the booths and paid five cents for a booklet that seemed of interest.

After turning in my paper at the draft physical location in Atlanta, I was pulled aside and questioned. Then I was told to come back in the afternoon.

When I went back I was sent to a room with two FBI agents and a stenographer. I was told that I had a right to a lawyer. I declined. There was a questioning about the five cents and about the booklet. Was it more than five cents? Was it more than one book? Did I still have the book?

Finally there was a written statement with the meeting transcript. I signed it on every page.

Then I was told that I would still be able to be drafted because buying the book at a legal venue in the United States was not illegal.

They felt that I was not to the level of being subversive.

Girlfriends.
In high school, I did not have much time for girlfriends.

I had goals of education and preparation for career work.

I had current school and a part-time job, sometimes several at once. That continued on through college.

The evenings were for family dinner together, Bible reading, and homework.

In my senior year at Ayer High School in Ayer Massachusetts, I had one date. We went just to a movie. I don't know why I did not call her back though I saw her frequently.

My male schoolmates viewed her as being someone that would make someone a good wife. I never heard that said about any other girl.

Ironically none of these guys ever dated her as far as I know. She did have many simultaneous visitors, mostly male, to her old fashioned front porch where she held court. She was not much for going other places.

The whole first summer after graduation I only had one date. It was with an Armenian girl. We went to the Varsity and then to the Fox Theatre to see *How the West Was Won*. She was quiet.

When she did talk she was quite pleasant. Her parents were nice folks and I enjoyed meeting them. I never called her back after that first date.

My first year in college, I dated an Orthodox Jewish girl for a while.

I had met her at the Atlanta library. She was one of twin sisters and lived in the wealthy northeast part of Atlanta. The family had a butler that opened the door. When I came over to pick her up for a date, the butler would show me to the library where I waited and would offer me a drink.

One time, the girl commented about the three gears on the steering column:

"Why did you pay extra to get a car with a shift?"

The only extra on my 1963 Ford Falcon was the cheapest radio. That girl was from the world of automatic transmissions and air conditioning that was a rarity for most people of that time. Her older brother had an Alfa Romeo which of course had a shift. I guess she equated my Ford Falcon to the Italian sports car.

Atlanta, from the end of the Civil War, had a large Jewish population who had originally come in as carpetbaggers. Someone had once said:

"Atlanta is owned by the Jews, worked in by the whites, and enjoyed by the blacks."

I get married.
I had a brief marriage to a girl almost two years older than me who I met at Headland High in my graduating class.

I was moving into social activism and ladder climbing, she into a settled life of the status quo.

I was ready for children, she was not.

I don't fault her and I don't think she faulted me. Sometimes a couple think they know each other and they don't. It was sad nonetheless.

Someone once said that: "Women marry men thinking they will change and they don't. Men marry women thinking they will not change and they do."

I upgrade my ride to a Jaguar.
At the suggestion of Mills B Lane, I bought a black Jaguar sedan. I got it from a dealer in Atlanta. Four speed with a Laycock de Normanville overdrive. It was a four door. A great sounding car. I wanted a Rolls Royce like Lane had. A new Rolls at that time went for $14,000.

After I was seen with the Jaguar, one of the top civil rights people that I knew, told me that he could get me a Porsche or anything I wanted in any color and options at a really good price. He was a fine preacher and a great rabble rouser I must admit, yet was well known from the press to be alleged to be connected with an organized car theft ring. I found that to be believable.

He owned a fine restaurant, and lived in an upper class white neighborhood.

He died some time back.

My parents move out of my life.
I did not keep up with my parents after they moved to Gallup, New Mexico except for a few weekend visits when I had business in California.

I was building my own adult life and had moved to Connecticut.

They took my Ford Falcon with them. It was about 20 years later before I found that my Falcon reached its end on a train track in Gallup, New Mexico after changing hands several times. No one was injured from what I have heard.

They went from Gallup to Charleston, South Carolina and from there to Arvada, Colorado.

I know that later they went to Winter Haven, Florida, bought a new house in Golden, Colorado, and went somewhere in Georgia before coming back to Denver, Colorado.

Exact order and dates I don't know.

At the time my father died, my parents lived in Georgia.

After my father's death my mother made several moves between Georgia and Colorado.

A sermon as related by Guy Howard, "walkin' preacher of the Ozarks."
He took his text from the 11th chapter of John, the command at the tomb of Lazarus, when he said, "Take ye away the stone."

The minister spoke softly but his voice was vibrant with sincerity.

"Jesus always had a reason for everything He did," the sermon began.

"He had a very great lesson to teach these people for as you know, as I know, that Jesus could have cried 'Lazarus come forth,' before the stone was rolled away from the grave and the stone would have rolled itself away, as the dead was resurrected.

Since Jesus did not do it that way, he must have had a reason. He had a reason.

Let us think this morning of that reason. The sinner is as dead spiritually as Lazarus was physically.

"When the sinner recognizes he is lost, then by God's grace rolls away the stone of his stubborn refusal, the Holy Spirit will guide to the blood of Christ, that washes away all sin.

If you are a sinner this morning, will you respond to the invitation of the gentle loving Jesus?

Jesus said. 'Him that cometh to me I will in no wise cast out.'"

My added comment:

Contrary to what seems to be popular belief, our relationship with Christ does not require joining an organization or paying the costs of operating a building and hiring professionals.

Our faith is that we believe in Jesus and His promises. Watch a small child. The child knows that all is taken care of by parents, particularly the mother. In line at places like the post office, that child will cling to her as protection from all the strangers.

It is amusing that there are so many that believe that the God of Genesis chapter 1 mapped out a hierarchial church where at a set time on Sunday we assemble in one place facing a stage for 45 to 60 minutes in order to validate Jesus' finished work on the cross and assure ourselves eternity in heaven.

In some denominations an attendee has to fill out a card every Sunday before taking communion. There is a computer data base for a continual record.

A works salvation if there ever was one.

CHAPTER 5: FORMAL CAREER START

"Find your passion in life and figure out a way to make money" - Anonymous

How I became a department manager and really started my career.
I found out about an opening with Litton Industries Credit Corporation, LICC, in Atlanta quite close to the Georgia Tech campus.

The position was the manager of accounts receivable.

The position was open because the department manager and staff had all quit suddenly with no notice. The regional manager had no clue what to do next.

I interviewed and got the idea that it might be a long process as the regional manager did not know exactly what qualifications would be needed. There was no job description. Whatever he was thinking did not apply to me. I had no knowledge of the accounts receivable function.

Nothing I had ever done was even remotely similar. The bank work did not seem to be relevant. I had done things in the past related to transactions that became accounts receivable but nothing in overview, management, or efficient record-keeping. Bookkeeping at that time was done manually. There was no backup of anything. A fire could easily destroy all of the records.

The interview ended and I felt that I was out of the running. I left disappointed. I really wanted that job because I could learn something and make a difference. I had an idea.

Sitting in my car, I hand wrote a list of reasons why I felt my experience at McDonalds several years earlier qualified me for the job at LICC.

I remembered that at McDonalds I was so ignorant of the function of management that I had been surprised that in the restaurant there was an office with a desk and that there was a manager.

I included:

- Showing up.
- Sticking with the task.
- Doing what had to be done without waiting on direction.
- Neatness.
- Timeliness.
- Accuracy with money.

- Safety of all things tangible and intangible.

I went back. The regional manager was out to lunch so I gave my list to his secretary. I went home. After he got back he called me.

"I read your note. I see no reason to interview anyone else. When can you start?"

"How about right now?" I replied. "The job needs to be done and there is no one there to do it."

I went in and became familiar with what was there.

I was too dumb to know that there were so many important things to do that had nothing to do with the job. I did ask the secretary to get me the employment forms when she could and I would fill them out when I had time.

A year or so later, I got a letter from the Litton corporate human resources department telling me that my normal retirement date would be such and such month and day about 42 years in the future. I sent the letter back with a notation asking them to send me the forms needed so I could start reviewing them. I asked when they needed to get them all back.

I hired three clerks in the next few days after I started work. They, like me, had no specific experience with accounts receivable anywhere. They did have good attitudes.

I would not have been hired if there was a human resources department. In looking back I can see that if a human resources department had been involved I would not have been hired.

If I had been offered the job, right now to start would not have worked. It would have had to be on some Monday in the future. To a human resources department, no one starts on any other day than Monday. For that matter, in a company with a human resources department, no one returns to work from home sickness or a hospital stay except on a Monday. Sickness and injuries can happen any day. Being able to return to work is still on a Monday. On that start to work Monday, the morning would be consumed with filling out paperwork and getting new hire orientation.

Within one month of my starting we had an accounts receivable department fully staffed and with work up to date. Had there been a human resources department, my job would not have a new hire within just one month. There would be advertising, of resumes, interviews, and decision making.

At some time in the future the position would have been filled by someone with a degree, with a job history in that industry, with a job history that had no gaps of time, someone with more age, with someone that would only do what they were told. Over many years I have learned that often, if not always, a person is only hired if they are not a threat to anyone else. Hiring the clerks would have taken several more months.

Good managers try to avoid human resources departments. So do applicants. I later learned that many of the jobs advertised in Sunday papers do not exist; the ads tested the waters for applicants and expected salaries. Prospects are today selected from a file of digitized resumes. Use of keywords in a resume has become a job skill.

Three elements of a good hire.
I don't know who first said this, maybe it was me, that there are three elements of a good hire:

- Can this person do the job?
- Will this person do the job?
- Will this person fit in?

I start business travel.
The overall plan was to centralize the accounts receivable from the regional offices into New York City with an automated process. I was a go-getter and it was felt that I was the man for the job. Travel was frequent after I got the clerks trained and things running smoothly.

I remember my first trip to New York for a meeting. I did not know much about business travel on an expense account. I had a room at a Holiday Inn in midtown. I went to a Howard Johnson's in Times Square. My entire dinner, a drink, appetizer, salad, entree, dessert, coffee, and the check all arrived at once. Payment was due in cash when the food was delivered. Credit cards were not accepted.

Travel increased further when I was transferred to New York. I had trips to Atlanta as well as to other places around the country. I planned my own travel needs as well as travel details.

Air travel was so easy.
For travel by air I would just go to the airport and start by looking on the board for the time of the next flight to wherever I was going. Let's say that flight was on American. Delta might not have a flight as soon as American so the line for tickets at Delta was short. From Delta I would buy a ticket on the American

flight. I would pay Delta with a company-issued credit card from Pan Am. One way was no problem. Advance reservations not needed. There was always a nice hot meal on the flight. There was no security check. Just go straight to the gate.

Another way to fly would be to see the handmade signs in the windows of airline ticket agencies at Rockefeller Center in New York City. Big discounts on flights leaving today, in some cases as quickly as one could get to the airport. The airlines wanted to fill as many seats as they could. There were enough people looking for last minute deals that the window signs posted as long as possible were a good marketing tactic.

How Litton Industries worked as a conglomerate.
Litton Industries would buy private family-owned companies and pay with new stock issues.

The sellers would have the advantage of publicly traded stock. Much better than taking back a promissory note or keeping the company that they may have inherited. We consultants would generate cash quickly from the acquired company. We would go to the accounts receivable department.

"What do you mean letting customers take longer than 30 days to pay?"

We would go to the accounts payable department.

"What do you mean paying bills in less than 90 days?

Standard terms were 1% 10 days net 30 days. In school, the teaching was that discounts should be taken. That forfeited 1% bought 20 days of credit. Annualized that was 18 percent interest. Note I said school. Waiting to 90 days to pay made the interest rate a little over 4%. Better still was to wait 90 days and still take the discount.

I marry Cheri.
There is much to be said about my wife Cheri. She has been the light of my life. She is the same to me today as the day we met.

We had not known each other long before we decided to get married.

Cheri and I were married at the courthouse in a little town. She did not want anything formal and I guess neither did I. We had met through a mutual friend. The day I met her I knew we would get married.

No, things have not been perfect. We have not been together on everything yet

Cheri has always been there for me in good times or bad. She has supported what I have wanted to do. I have been able to trust her in every way.

It at least used to be true that couples might have "our" song. For us it might have been only me as I was not much for visible romance.

The song was *Make it With You* by David Gates, group leader of the band Bread, released in 1970 on their second album. An abridgment of the lyrics is:

"Hey have you ever tried, really reaching out for the other side? I may be climbing on rainbows but baby here goes. Dreams they're for those who sleep, life is for us to keep, And if you're wond'ring what this song is leading to I want to make it with you. I really think that we can make it girl. No, you don't know me well. In ev'ry little thing only time will tell, If you believe the things that I do. And we'll see it through. Life can be short or long, Love can be right or wrong, And if I choose the one I'd like to help me through, I'd like to make it with you."

Cheri and I made no conscious decision to have a large family though I am extremely grateful nonetheless for all of the children. I cannot imagine it any other way.

Each child has developed in their own way, not as carbon copies of Cheri and I. We made opportunities for them as best we could. We did not try to make things equal at all times though no one became a favorite.

The children have all done well in a variety of avenues though they have by no means stopped.

The grandchildren too are coming along.

I am proud of all of them.

I have associates my age that have done well financially, much better than me. I could have done the same but might not have ended up with the same wife or as many children or grandchildren.

I am conscious of having had to give up on many things as the family took priority. Sometimes, maybe many times, it may have not seemed like it.

I had to travel in my work. I enjoyed it but also regretted it.

I can think of so many things I would do differently. Less travel would be one.

Again, I say that I am well aware of what Cheri has given up for me during our marriage. She has been my God-ordained helpmeet.

Our first home as a married couple.
We lived in a small, modern, two story apartment building just off Peachtree Street in Atlanta, Georgia. When I first showed it to Cheri she said "I'm proud 'a yuh" and gave me a kiss. Made my day.

Shade trees all around. Great air conditioning and building maintenance. We lived on the first floor. There was a nearby A&P grocery store. A small movie theatre was at the corner. That theater showed quality foreign films often in another language and with English subtitles. *Umbrellas of Cherbourg* was one of the movies we saw there. There were other stores, all close by. I could walk to work.

The death of Martin Luther King Jr.
On April 4, 1968, at 8:05 PM Atlanta time, Dr Martin Luther King Jr passed away. I don't recall how we found out. We were out walking with our first child.

We move to a house.
We rented a house in the regal Virginia Highlands area of downtown Atlanta.

Why we moved I don't recall. The apartment and its location was much better. I guess I just thought we would want a house. I had to drive to work and we had to drive for groceries and everything else.

Many years later, I showed the house to one of our daughters. It is still a good quiet upscale neighborhood.

An ambitious young man selling newspapers.
On the way home from work I would buy an afternoon newspaper from a certain young man who had some form of mental disability. He was a worker and had a great attitude.

One day he told me that he had a new policy. He wanted my money before he would hand me a paper. He told me why he went to that procedure.

Previously he would hand the paper to the driver. He would note the amount of payment and hand the change to the driver. Then he would take the dollar or whatever.

Earlier that day just at the point where a driver was to hand over his money the light turned green. The man said:

"You stooge. You lose." and drove off without giving the money.

I admired the young man's ability to realize a dangerous procedure and to quickly find a way to deal with it for the future. He did not seem bitter nor did he seem to dwell on his loss.

We liked western movies.
One of the things that Cheri and I liked to do in Atlanta was to go to the drive-in theatre to see western movies. We did this frequently as this one theatre only showed westerns. Maybe we were getting set up for Wyoming.

Lester Maddox becomes governor of Georgia.
Lester Maddox became governor of Georgia in 1967. He was the last of the fist-shaking segregationist governors. He ran as a Democrat against Howard "Bo" Calloway, the Republican. There was a write-in for a prior Democrat governor. No one got a majority in the general election. The legislature, pretty much all Democrat, elected Maddox even though he had the lowest popular vote of the three candidates.

Maddox was somewhat of a paradox.

He was opposed to integration. His view was that the races should be separate but equal.

Maddox filled more appointed state jobs with blacks than any prior governor.

At The Pickrick restaurant that he closed in 1964 rather than allow blacks as customers in the dining room, Maddox had a reputation for a place with the best pay and the best working conditions, and which had an all black staff. He had many employees of 20 or more years longevity.

Maddox was the first governor to live in the new Governor's mansion though he had nothing to do with building it. That was all done in prior years. Maddox got a lot of mileage out of saying that he was the only resident of northeast Atlanta with a black neighbor. When the state bought the land there was a provision that an elderly black man who lived in a shack on the property be allowed to live out his life there and to have a small job to support himself. He did yard work.

Maddox was totally opposed to alcohol. Yet he fought hard and succeeded at getting a new Budweiser brewery in Georgia. When challenged on what appeared to be hypocrisy he said that he was not against those putting beer in the bottle but only those that took it out.

I-95 was built in many small pieces in Georgia. It was a pain for travelers to move back and forth between interstate and two lane highways. There were two factors in play.

1. *The Atlanta Journal* published chains of ownership of land that was taken for the interstate. Various political and business biggies would own the land for short periods of time and then sell it to someone else at a profit. Eventually it had been milked for as much as possible and the last owner made his profit selling to the state.

2. There was quite a business running speed traps to catch out of staters heading through to Florida. Under Georgia law which the legislature would not change, any area where there was a certain density of population, the residents could set up a speed limit, have people in unmarked cars stop speeders, and take them right away to a magistrate's home for a trial even late at night. They would be fined and had to pay right then in cash. The fine was split three ways between the patrolman, the magistrate, and the state. A typical speed limit was 15 miles per hour, down from 55 or 60, on what appeared to be a piece of highway in the boondocks. At the most notorious sites Maddox had signs put up warning of a speed trap. The signs were cut down so Maddox had state police guard the signs.

Jim Rohn.

While still in Atlanta we found out about a motivational course given by Jim Rohn. At the beginning of the class we were given a card and were asked to answer some questions. We kept the cards for own use. One question was:

"How much income would you like to have in five years?"

I wrote down $10,000 a year which seemed to be impossible when I was just making $6,000.

Five years later I was making $15,000!

I get a job offer in New York City.

I was offered a promotion and a job transfer to New York City, still with Litton. Completion of the Industrial Management program at Georgia Tech was not to be. There would be no degree.

In the move to a job in New York City at 850 Third Avenue I moved from a non-exempt job to an exempt job. My base pay went from a $120 a week to a $140. My overall gross pay dropped since I could not get overtime pay.

I was not really prepared for the increased cost of living.

I continue to dress well.
For the corporate consultant image, I bought good suits, usually from Barney's in New York, because I liked the modern styles. I also bought from Ed Mitchell in Westport because I liked the conservative styles.

First National City Bank.
I opened a checking account at First National City Bank at 399 Park Avenue.

I get a Diners Club card.
As a young man on the way up, I got the requisite Diners Club card.

All my subsequent renewal cards from Diners Club have shown that I have been a member since 1969.

I have never missed a payment, payments being the full balance that is due each month.

I have wondered if at some point I will simply not be able to get a renewal. Someone might notice the member since date on the card.

I have a large credit limit.

Amounts spent are much smaller than they once were yet do get paid each month.

We go to New York to look for housing.
Cheri and I took a trip to New York to look for housing. We were looking in Connecticut as I knew that I would be moving to a new office location in the near future in Stamford when the new building at 600 Summer Street was built. Anyway some of the townhouses in New York were selling for as much as a $100,000! Today they are all in the millions and tens of millions. We had a room at the Americana in New York arranged by the office, because I did have work to do in the city while we were on this trip. We had a rental car.

I called about an apartment in Connecticut in our price range. So that the lady could get a time from her husband to show it I gave her the phone number and room number at the Americana. The lady said :

"If you are staying at the Americana Hotel you would not like this apartment. It is strictly working class."

She would not show it to us. Little did she know that I was on salary, worked long hours with no overtime, and made less per week than the so-called working class.

In Darien, Connecticut, I asked a real estate agent where to live in Darien if you made less than $30,000 a year. She said probably nowhere. While we never had the pleasure of living in Darien, it became a destination for work and leisure.

I rented computer time at a bank in Darien for my job with Litton Industries. Like in New York City, I did not operate the computer but submitted jobs and waited for results. I would keypunch changes if there were only a few cards. For anything more I would leave coding sheets for the regular keypunch operators.

The rental was $100 an hour for the IBM 360. There was a timing system that would detail when our jobs were running even if just a few minutes at a time. I was often there all night. The night security guard at the bank was quite amusing.

He had an old beat up car and was afraid it would be stolen. He parked it on the sidewalk near the door. To get in the building people had to walk around the car and go through a narrow path between his car and the door. He left his gun in his car as he was afraid he might fall asleep and someone would take his gun and shoot him.

We get a place to live in Bridgeport, Connecticut.
We rented a nice first floor of a large two family house in a good location in Bridgeport, a house with a wide, wrap-around porch. Bridgeport was an all-American type town. Like so many cities it has changed.

There was a supermarket grocery store only two blocks away. That store became one of the first to be open 24/7.

In 2019 in Wyoming, we live close to a supermarket that has cut out 24/7. It is closed from midnight to 5:00 AM.

In Bridgeport, it was a nice walk from our home to the beach. We would pass Petes Subs, near the University of Bridgeport campus, that was the first store of the Subway chain.

We found that the annual Fourth of July parade passed right by our house. We viewed from our porch.

I remember buying a balloon for our first child at the parade and talking with the vendor. He was an American that lived in his beach home in Mexico in the winters. In the summers he sold balloons. That was his only job. He said it was great money, all cash, and there was no income tax.

To get to work, I walked to the bus stop, took the bus to the train station, then the 6:16 AM train out of Bridgeport to New York City. I would catch some more sleep on the train. I would walk from Grand Central to my office at 850 Third Avenue.

I would have a breakfast on the way at one of the many small restaurants, all with counters, a few stools, and open fronts in good weather. 55 cents was the price for eggs, bacon, toast, and coffee. That would be just under $4.00 in 2017. If I needed a haircut there were plenty of barbers along the way. All opened early.

Going home there was time for a gin and tonic in the bar car. The plastic cups used were quite large and had plenty of ice. One thing that I did frequently was to pick up some chuck steak and the small frozen cinnamon rolls that we still get today, on the way home from the train station. I would fire up a small charcoal grill and we would have a nice cheap dinner.

We had been going to a laundromat. We decided to buy a washing machine and borrowed money to do so. With each load Cheri would put a quarter in a jar. This continued until we had paid back the loan. We would buy really old refrigerators. Then we upgraded to a small new Italian-made refrigerator.

Cheri and I had favorite restaurants in Connecticut.

- **The Red Coach Grill.**
  The Red Coach Grill was an upscale part of the Howard Johnson chain. It was on the north side of the Post Road in Darien. The menu was diverse and service was designed for leisurely meals.

  Unlike most of the Howard Johnson chain, the Red Coach Grills had bar service and a full list of bottled wines. Cocktails, appetizers, wine, dessert and then coffee were standard features. I don't know when the after dinner coffee went away. One day it was gone. The entrees at the Red Coach Grill included prime rib, lobster, and fresh fish.

  Eventually Red Coach Grills were was taken over by El Torito, a chain of Mexican restaurants. Then El Torito went away.

- **Chucks Steak House.**
Across the Post Road in Darien from the Red Coach Grill and a block or so south was Chucks Steak House. Chucks did not take reservations and usually there was a line. The steaks were great and the outside was charred. There was a salad bar. The french dressing was out of this world. Life after Chucks has been a search for the french dressing. I have never found it. The bread was excellent.

My favorite drink at Chucks was a dry Beefeaters martini up with a twist. How a martini can be different from bar to bar has always baffled me. Chucks knew how to make a good one.

There was a Chuck, Charles "Chuck" Rolles. He graduated from the Cornell Hotel and Restaurant School in 1956, moved to Hawaii, and started his chain of steakhouses in 1959. After opening the second one in Waikiki, he began opening locations in the continental United States.

- **The Red Barn.**
Another restaurant in the area was The Red Barn in Westport. How a restaurant can have so many fresh items always available has been another mystery. The Greek diners in the Northeast from Pennsylvania and New Jersey on up are at the top of that list. The Red Barn had many types of seafood, Italian food, steaks, and desserts. Cheri liked the creme brûlée.

On one night we planned to go to The Red Barn, I called for a reservation and was told we would not need one. No reason given. When we got there I think we were the only guests there. I soon was to find out why. I ordered a drink.

"It's Good Friday and state law prohibits the sale of alcohol."

"Is that why the place is empty?" I asked.

With a smile the waiter said:

"Yes sir."

We did have a nice dinner anyway.

- **The restaurant on the island.**
There was an island in Bridgeport connected to the mainland by a small short bridge. I cannot find it on a map though I think I could find it by car if I went to it now. We would go out there to a really neat

- **The dining car on the train.**
  A few times, Cheri met me at Grand Central Station and we would go home on a train with a dining car. There was just enough time for a leisurely meal at a table with a white cloth tablecloth and fresh flowers. Dining cars on Amtrak today are good but not like they used to be. In the near future I can see trains in the United States with no dining cars. I can also see no long distance trains at all.

A trip to East Orange, New Jersey.
Sometimes going to work meant going somewhere else.

One snowy morning, I needed to go to Sweda Cash Register, one of the Litton Industries companies, in East Orange, New Jersey.

As usual I walked to the bus stop near our home in Bridgeport. I took the bus to the train station, then the train to Grand Central Station. From Grand Central by taxi to Penn Station, a train to Newark, then a bus to Orange. I walked from Orange to East Orange. I stood in the building doorway for about an hour until the first employee arrived who opened the door.

"Sorry for the weather delay getting here this morning" he said.

I mainly develop software.
Overall, I was mainly developing software.

There was no regular nine to five day. I had freelancers doing coding.

A common meeting place was in the quiet southwest corner of Grand Central Station.

All of us would be in the station twice a day so it was a good place to meet.

The room was solely furnished with old wooden, high back benches. You might call them oversized.

A few years ago when I was walking through Grand Central Station, I noted that the same area now has a food court and is not so quiet.

I would give out programming specs I had written and pick up completed code sheets.

I would pass out checks and pick up time sheets for the next check.

I would then get the code punched into cards at a keypunch service bureau.

I would test and debug.

Often that meant really late nights. Often I would stay in town overnight as the trains had stopped.

My favorite restaurant in New York was The Office Pub, so named for the call home to the wife:

"Honey I'll be late at The Office tonight."

I usually just had time for a quick meat and potatoes dinner at a reasonable price and then back to work across the street at American Broadcasting Company headquarters where I rented computer time.

Working 24 hours straight was not unusual. My longest stretch was 54 hours. A lot of time was doing nothing while waiting for jobs in the queue. I would take naps sitting upright in a chair until the computer operator would wake me.. Work completion time was unknown as the number of bugs was unknown. I would keypunch my own coding fixes.

The anthora coffee cup was ubiquitous.
I would order out for soggy hamburgers and coffee. The waxed paper coffee cups used by all of the delis were called by the name anthora, a play on the Greek word amphora. The anthora had a Greek design and all were blue. One size only. Often I would have the hamburger and coffee multiple times in an evening. After I thought that the anthora was long gone, one of our daughters found me a porcelain souvenir anthora and some of the real ones, made from waxed paper. When one of our our grandsons was quite small he was in a thrift store in a cart. He spotted another one.

"Grandpa has one of those."

His mother, our daughter, bought it. I then had two anthora. I have continued to be careful not to break them. I have not used them in the microwave. I only pour direct from the pot.

Helmut.
My boss, Helmut, had come to the United States from Czechoslovakia when he was in his forties.

His experience was in being a drafted paratrooper in World War II in the Hermann Goering Division, then selling milking machines to collective farms. When he moved to the United States, Helmut would weld fire escapes during the day while studying accounting at Columbia University at night.

When I had come up for my first work visit to New York City from Atlanta I went in to work at 9:00 AM. 5:00 PM did not end the day.

Around 9:00 PM Helmut said:

"Dave, I'm hungry. Let's go have some dinner."

Around 4:00 AM he suggested we go get some sleep. We both had rooms at a nearby hotel.

We met for breakfast at 7:00 AM, three hours later. I have always enjoyed working like that.

One time Helmut took me to his home on Long Island for the night and to meet his wife and young son.

We both were taking a trip to California the next day.

From the driveway there were some steps up to the house. Helmut stopped halfway up and turned to me.

"Dave," he said. "On this tree right here we hang all of our work; no talking about it in the house. We pick it up in the morning when we leave. Then we can talk business."

Helmut's wife sewed zippers into dresses.

This was when manufacturing was still in the United States.

If the son was sick or had a school holiday, she stayed home with him.

Her Jewish boss would load up his Cadillac with dresses and bring them to her to sew zippers at home.

When Helmut and I got to San Francisco, I rented a Mustang. Off we went down the 101 to Palo Alto. At one point there was a sign for San Jose that was further south from our destination. Helmut pronounced it with the J as a J instead of as an H. After I corrected him he said,

"Well, will people here call me Jelmut?

Back east we were used to people wanting to go to the west coast for surfing and other good times. The east coast was obsolete.

At a restaurant in Palo Alto that night the waitress asked where we were from. When we replied New York, she said:

"I've always wanted to go there. I've heard the east coast is the place to be."

For a while Cheri and I had no car nor we did need one.

We had easy access to the train and we could walk where we wanted to go in town.

Trips to New York City when we had no car.
I remember when Cheri and I went to New York City to see *Hello Dolly*, starring Pearl Bailey and Louis Armstrong.

Another time we saw Lloyd Bridges in *Cactus Flower*. Bridges had on a large bulky diver's watch that he wore in his TV show *Sea Hunt*. Wiki does not mention him in *Cactus Flower* but the Internet Broadway Database does.

One New York City trip that we'll never forget.
On our first child's first birthday we were in New York City watching a movie. I was holding our baby daughter. Her eyes rolled back. I jumped up and went to the lobby. There was no 911.

Somehow a police car was flagged down and took us to St. Vincent's Hospital where they were waiting for us.

She was cooled down in some ice water.

She had a febrile convulsion which we learned was quite common at her age. She never had another one. The doctor told us to keep her cool.

On the train ride back I stood holding her in between the cars where it was cooler. It was safe as it was designed for passengers to walk through.

Trips to Port Jefferson, Long Island, New York when we had no car.
A favorite trip was the Bridgeport to Port Jefferson Ferry.

That was always a great family trip.

I have fond memories of the early times of our marriage and our first two children on those trips.

We could walk from our house to the ferry landing.

The ferry was like an ocean liner that might be seen on Marx Brothers and other movies. Multi-decks. Wooden folding deck chairs. There was good food and drink.

On the other side we stayed in a motel near the harbor or maybe go back home the same day.

Even when we had a car we never took it as there was enough to do in Port Jefferson.

We buy our first Volkswagen beetle.
One day we bought a black 1962 Volkswagen beetle.

When buying a Volkswagen not just any one would do. The pre-1967 Volkswagen beetles had their own personality. A buyer had to get one that fit.

There was a book called *How to Buy a Volkswagen.*

While I saw no need, it was recommended that one take a lotus position by the car and to meditate.

This 1962 Volkswagen beetle felt exactly right just from walking around, though when I first saw it at a distance. I already knew.

Volkswagen had its biggest profit year in 1966.

In 1967, the electric system was changed from 6 volts to 12 volts. At 12 volts a Volkswagen no longer seemed to run right.

The seats had the headrests, automatic transmissions were added, as was air conditioning.

There was still no good heat. The heat was simply a pipe over the exhaust with no fan. Turning on the heat was done by turning a valve that opened the pipe.

The Volkswagen engine was air cooled, the reason that the heater did not work well. Good car heaters need hot water and a fan.

Many Volkswagens had no gas gauge. When the car ran out of gas, the driver could reach under the front of the driver seat near the floor and open the reserve tank that contained a gallon of gas.

A good side effect of the Volkswagen was that a new engine could be bought cheaply and installed quickly.

Many repairs required that the engine be removed.

I remember the charge for taking out the engine and putting it back was $19. Jump starting a Volkswagen was simple.

One cold winter night when my battery was dead, I opened both doors. I gave a small push. The wind was from behind and it got the car moving fast enough to start.

We have had four Volkswagens, two beetles and two buses.

I prepared tax returns.
I did personal tax returns during the season. There was no software. Since I did the returns at the taxpayers' homes I had to handwrite copies because no one had a home copier. Often there would be neighbors present and I would do several returns in one session while a social time was taking place. No one was concerned about privacy and all sat at the dining room table. I learned a lot about the people.

I have always told people that I do returns as accurately as I can. No cheating or false information. I may ask them questions if I see something that might be missing or I also tell them that I may know deductions that they don't. I'll tell them and do whatever is needed to assure them that it is legal. I have always said to them that anything I say I would say if there was an IRS agent sitting there with us.

The man in the living room playing with the children.
A young family in Bridgeport had just moved in from a long distance away in another state. There were still unpacked boxes. I noticed that there was a man playing with the children and they all seemed to know each other well.

'Don't feel I'm being nosy but may I ask who that is with the children?"

"He's a life long friend of ours. He has trouble keeping a job so he lives with us," the wife replied. "He is our sitter while we are at work and when we go places alone.

"Do you support him?, " I asked. The answer was a yes.

"Then why don't you deduct him as a dependent?"

I asked a few more things and then determined that he qualified as a dependent.

I showed them what it looked like after I entered him to the right place on the tax return.

They were quite pleased.

The Italian immigrants.
The Italian immigrants were really great and hospitable people. Always there was coffee with a shot of anisette, and anisette toast, a type of cookie.

There is a joke where the question is:

"How do you take an Italian census?"

"Count the basement windows and multiple by 5."

This joke was partly true, as are all jokes.

The Italian people had nice homes yet often there was no furniture in the main part of the house.

Several generations actually lived in the basement.

All those in the household who had a job would give their pay to the grandmother who would pay off the house as quickly as possible.

After the house loan was paid off, they would buy furniture though might still not move upstairs. Often the living room and dining room would be roped off and would be view only. The plastic was never removed from the lamp shades and the couches and chairs.

The Italian immigrants would have multiple savings accounts and would send money home to Italy. They drove old beat up cars and wore old clothes. None of them had good pay. Their spoken English was poor, the written worse. It took me a while to be able to read their deduction notes. "Giorch" was always a fairly large amount. That was the church offering.

I remember one older Italian man in Bridgeport that lived alone. His wife had died; the children were grown and gone. He had been laid off from his career machine shop job. He did not expect to get another job because of his age and because manufacturing jobs were going overseas. He was sad because with just his unemployment check he could only put aside $100 a week into savings. I hardly earned much more than that.

The Americans.
So I might do the tax returns for an immigrant family. Then I would go next door to a typical American family.

High income. Deep in debt. No savings. House full of stuff they had bought on impulse.

One American exception.
I did a tax return one year for a bartender. He and his wife were a nice couple.

They had an immaculate, well-ordered, late 1940s house. They were typical Americans yet spent most of their time in their basement family room.

After the tax return was completed he showed me his retirement fund.

He had over many years, from his tips, completely filled a metal milk can with the 90% silver coins, dimes, quarters, half dollars and silver dollars. None had a date after 1964. He told me to see if I could pick up the milk can. I could not make it budge the slightest. He felt it was quite safe. He had started another can that was not quite half full. He was not adding to that one because only 40% silver coins were in circulation.

I did not go back to them after that. I did not want to be the one that had to deal with the tax return when he cashed in the coins in the milk cans at much more than face value. I suspected he would not be reporting anything.

The Florida retirees.
I had numerous tax return clients that retired and moved to Florida.

They asked me if I could continue to do their tax returns. I told all of them that they should get a new preparer in Florida.

I did not want to be the one to tell them about the capital gains tax that might be owing on the sale of their homes.

I suspect they may not have mentioned it to a new preparer in Florida.

Rob and Mary.
I had several what I call big tax return clients as I had work year round.

One was Rob. Rob and his wife Mary were the ultimate pragmatists. I have often wondered why all were not like them. They knew the way to do everything.

Rob had a simple business. Business computer equipment was usually from IBM and was rented rather than purchased though IBM had no problem with selling equipment.

Plain and simple, Rob could offer a prospect rental of the same machine, with the same serial number, with the same phone number for service, the same quality of service, and exactly the same contract in every respect with only two changes. One, the monthly rental was about half of what they paid IBM. Two, the check would be written to his business instead of IBM.

Rob would buy their equipment from IBM. The prospect could validate authenticity by calling their IBM rep. Rob's business grew and grew as time passed. He never lost a customer.

The problem was that most prospects would say no to the offer. There was still the truism that no one has ever been fired for buying IBM. I guess it applied to who got the equipment rent checks.

Rob never kept an accounts receivable file. He had great faith in the systems of his customers. He told me that their systems would not allow them to not pay.

He would not cheat on taxes and a thorough field audit found no problems. Except one.

The auditor wanted to disallow one bad debt deduction. Rob was most upset because he felt he had followed all the rules for bad debts.

I asked the auditor to excuse us while we went into another room to talk. I explained to Rob that the auditor was rated on how much tax and penalty he collected. He had been there all day and was worried about going back empty handed. Rob understood. We went back.

I told the auditor that we were in agreement that the bad debt was taken too soon and asked if he saw any problem in taking the deduction for the following year that I was even then preparing. He said that it would be no problem.

The auditor wrote up a form. Rob signed it and gave the auditor a check for the added tax, interest, and penalty. The total was a not a large amount Everyone was happy.

I become aware that there is rapid change occurring.
During the time from when we moved north in the late 1960s, there was a radical change just in Bridgeport. It was like there was a sudden shut down in manufacturing. The support shops went away. The factories shut down.

Many people moved away. Florida was a common destination. Housing was small and cheap. The people had a lot of house equity and there were buyers that were commuters and buyers that worked in the corporate headquarters that moved into Fairfield County.

GE built an office campus in Fairfield, Connecticut in 1974, right off the Merritt Parkway.

In 2016 GE sold that facility to Sacred Heart University and began the move to Fort Point in Boston into an old candy factory built by NECCO. Two buildings and a large lot that after remodeling and some new construction will become the new headquarters. 800 people will be working there.

We move to Trumbull, Connecticut.
Our first son was born in Bridgeport. I felt that we needed a bigger place. We had a car. I was working in Fairfield, Connecticut. We moved to Trumbull, Connecticut. Trumbull was just north of Bridgeport across the Merritt Parkway.

I have regretted not learning more about Bridgeport while we were there. I knew about P. T. Barnum, who was mayor, and of the graves of Charles Sherwood Stratton, stage name General Tom Thumb, and Lavinia Warren, his wife. I knew of Elias Howe and the sewing machine. I did not know the quaint streets and old neighborhoods.

We rented a house in Trumbull, built in 1736, for $175 a month, up from the $125 a month for our apartment in Bridgeport.

There was a huge almost walk-in fireplace in the kitchen with a dutch oven in the back. The bathroom, a later addition of course, was built in a hallway. To get to the attic required going through the bathroom that was on the second floor.

The house is still there though now has a modern front porch made with plastic railings and there is new siding. I hate to think of what has been done inside. There were not many windows because at the time of construction taxes were assessed on the number of windows. The roof covered both the second floor and the attic that was basically unfinished living space with high headroom.

Trumbull was a transition for us. Georgia was over, as was New York City, and Bridgeport.

In Trumbull, I remember a warm New Year's Day when both Cheri and I weeded out all of our old papers and other material and bagged it up for discard. There was so much we had to have someone come in to take it all away. It was at that point that we really became soul mates.

At the end of 2018 we did more dropping of things we had felt we had to keep.

A Christmas trip to Colorado.
When we lived in Trumbull, Connecticut we made a visit to my parents at Christmas in Colorado. Cheri, our oldest son and daughter, and me. My parents lived on 64th which was at that time the northern end of Denver. Beyond where they lived was all prairie. Today it is all city.

In Denver we bought a used Volkswagen bus and turned in our airline tickets. It was a cold ride home. Our heat was a portable kerosene catalytic heater. The Volkswagen heater was worthless in that space and at 14 below zero. Near North Platte, Nebraska, the points broke in the engine distributor. I hitched a ride into town and found that there were two types, for hot air and cold air engines. What? I had never heard of such. After we got going again we stopped for the night in Grand Island, Nebraska. The hot shower sure felt good.

We sold the Volkswagen bus after we got back home.

We bought land in New Hampshire.
We bought 14 acres of land in New Hampshire for $2,000.

Later it was determined to be 22 acres. It had 1800 feet of road frontage.

The land was not accessible in winter because of the snow but we could drive past. When weather was warm we would camp, or, more frequently, just visit.

That land was my frontier. It would be possible to live there though would have hardships involving an outhouse. Even a garden would be difficult due to the thick tree growth. It was several miles to a town that only had one small store.

None of our land would pass a percolation test for a septic system. We knew that when we bought it. New Hampshire is quite strict and became stricter as the years passed.

With two of or our sons, I built a camp building heated with a wood stove made from a small oil drum. We had electricity. The power company put in poles to connect us to their existing system that stopped a mile or so from our land. The wire from the last pole at the road were strung from trees, an acceptable practice at the time. My electrician mounted the switch box on a tree.

New Hampshire passed a law that on a state highway that no more than three driveways could be put into a piece of land as it existed on deeds in 1970. That applied to us and we knew that when we bought the land. Further a driveway permit was required. We did get a driveway permit though it was some time later that we built a driveway.

We did sell timber, mostly oak. No pine trees. Clear cutting was not permitted. An intent to cut had to be filed with the town. A consulting forester had to decide what to cut. The total board feet planned to be cut had to be reported to the town. The timber cutters had to later report the actual board feet cut and where it went. The owner had to report to the town the board feet to be kept for firewood. A tax was charged for that.

Property taxes were going up and it did not seem to be good to keep it or to give it to family members. Most of the land was in a current use category to minimize tax. Even at that the tax was more than on our house in Wyoming. Land value increase even due to inflation was never enough to offset tax increases. Even at that any decision we made was possibly wrong.

We sold the land in 2005, after we moved west, as part of a project for bobcat migration. Cheri had said that she wanted a new bathroom floor when we sold the land. She got it!

Living off the grid was not a term that I knew at the time. Even today I'm not sure what it means. Maybe everybody has a different definition.

Sometimes living off the grid seems to mean getting electricity in a different way than from a power pole. Other times it seems to mean doing modern things but in harder ways. There are all kinds of things to buy. There are even small sawmills so that you can cut your own boards after you cut down the trees. There are ways you can spend little or no money in exchange for spending a lot of time. One of the best of these is taking apart old pallets, saving the nails, and then building a cabin. If doing this one it is best not to divide the cost of a building from Home Depot by the number of hours you spent with the pallets building a house that leaks when it rains.

Horace Kephart, author of *Our Southern Highlanders*, a book about the people of Appalachia, and author of *Camping and Woodcraft*, was a librarian in St Louis. He succumbed to what he later called nervous exhaustion and concluded that urban life was a major contributor to his problems.

He lived off the grid in western North Carolina in a nicely built, though not luxurious, cabin, so far as cabins go. It had been built by a mining company. He got permission to live in it. So that meant no long drawn-out building process. He had no mortgage, no taxes, no insurance, and no utility bills. Nice independence off the grid. Yet he stayed less than three years. Why we might ask?

He went to Bryson City, North Carolina, a town that at that time, around 1910, had only 612 people, yet less than 60 miles in each direction to substantial, even at that time, cities.

Did he find a balance between extreme off the grid and extreme on the grid?

I'm reminded of the man that was told by his doctor that he had six months to live.

"Doc, what should I do?" he asked.

"Marry a Jewish woman and move to Montana."

"Will that make me live longer?"

"No but it will seem like it."

I have had a man back east ask me if we had any supermarkets. I have had numerous people as close as Ft Collins, Colorado tell me that Wyoming was too far out for them to visit.

In Chugwater, Wyoming one can get a free lot in town with water and sewer hookup by building a house or moving in a trailer and staying there two years.

The last I heard only one taker so far.

Only 45 minutes down I-25 to the state capital city.

Not exactly wilderness living.

The problem is that commuting cost to Cheyenne would be $60 to $80 per day, $300 to $400 per work week, not counting the time.

Wheatland workers would certainly see no advantage to Chugwater.

An old quote summarizes the overview:

"In America a man born and raised in the country works to get enough money to move to the city so that he can work and get enough money to move to the country."

I have read plenty of books about people in modern times living off the grid. Lumping them all together, I would describe them as books about people that wanted to live like people of earlier times.

The Good Life, by Helen and Scott Nearing published in 1954, is a 60 year story, beginning in 1932, of what they called self-sufficient living. While they did what they did out of necessity after being drummed out of academia at Columbia University for their socialist views, they lived their philosophy quite successfully, starting with a written constitution for their farm.

Guests were welcome at any time for as long as they wanted to stay though after three days they would be given work to do. When their town in Vermont wanted to buy part of their farm for a town park, the Nearings priced it at what they had paid per acre many years earlier. Their philosophy was that it was the town that had made the value increase and not them so the town owned the profit. They did not keep animals as they would become the servants of the animals. Consequently they did not eat meat or eggs.

The Nearings later relocated to Brookeville, Maine to get away from the growth of their area of Vermont. Scott, approaching the age 100, simply decided one day that he had lived long enough. He quit eating, while continuing what he was doing. Helen died in a car crash several years later.

We Took To The Woods, by Louise Dickinson Rich, published in 1942, is a story of continuous life off the grid, in the northwest corner of Maine, not just a temporary adventure.

A very general book on the subject is *Small is Beautiful, Economics as if People Mattered,* by E.F. Schumacher, published in 1973.

The Schumacher Center for a New Economics in Great Barrington, Massachusetts has the mission: To **envision** a just and sustainable global economy; **apply** the concepts locally; then **share** the results for broad replication. We believe that:

- a fair and sustainable economy is possible and that citizens working for the common interest can build systems to achieve it.
- our natural commons are best held by the regional community.
- money issue can be democratized.
- ownership should be more diversified and that labor should have a part in the ownership structure.

We favor the face-to-face relationships fostered in local economies. We deliberately focus transformative systems and the principles that guide them.

Mary Lasswell.
Some of the most practical books I have read on what I think is a good definition of living off the grid were works of fiction that could have been true stories. These were the works of Mary Lasswell. Those stories, situated primarily in San Diego and National City, California, involve the lifestyle techniques of three elderly ladies, Mrs Rasmussen, Miss Tinkham, and Mrs Feeley.

The three ladies with no monetary assets nor much income lived in San Diego and through many innovative techniques survived many problems. Their attitudes led them to solutions.

Their break-even point was to have a few loaves of day old bread and a case of cold beer.

They gave of their time and other resources to help others in their social class or higher that were in need.

The ladies knew how to find what they needed free or at very low cost.

Old Timer was a member of the household and functioned as a handyman and chauffeur. He never spoke.

Some proof of the practicality is that at the request of some members of the military during WWII, Lasswell wrote *Mrs Rasmussen's Book of One Arm Cookery* in 1946. It was to be the recipes use for favorite meals of the fictional ladies. An update was done in 1970. Same title with the addition of *"with Second Helpings."*

The books involving the three ladies, illustrated by George Price of *The New Yorker,* are:

- *Suds in Your Eye* 1942
- *High Time* 1944
- *One on the House* 1949
- *Wait for the Wagon* 1951
- *Tooner Schooner* 1953
- *Let's Go for Broke* 1962

Lasswell wrote seven other books on a variety of topics and stories not related to the three ladies.

The lady that thought that cutting trees should be a crime.
On a day that the loggers were working, I was doing some trimming along the road at our place in New Hampshire.

The driveway inspector was coming to see if a driveway could go in at the spot we had picked.

While waiting, I was making sure that the sight line on the wide curve was acceptable.

A lady stopped and asked if I was the owner.

She said that I should be in jail.

"That may well be true but could you tell me why you think I should be in jail?" I asked.

"For allowing trees to be cut," she replied.

Then she drove off.

I did not get a chance to ask her if she would like the idea of plastic toilet paper.

I work in Stamford, Connecticut.
I was working in Stamford. Summer street had been all residential with big homes. They were bulldozed down for office buildings.

I remember watching one three story house being taken down. A raccoon came out of an attic window and jumped all the way down. Unhurt, it took off running.

My favorite lunch place in Stamford was The Wedge Inn on the side street directly in back of the Dairy Queen on Summer Street. It is still there and I go again whenever I can. The chili dogs are not as good as I remember them to be but are still ok.

I had asked if I could get the chili recipe. I had gotten no reply. I learned later that someone had bought that recipe for $250,000. Maybe the seller could no longer use that recipe and then made up something close.

We buy a boat.
We bought a boat, a wooden 26 foot Pennant fixed keel sloop, that we initially moored in a slip at the Bridgeport Yacht Club where it was when we bought it.

I have always liked wood boats and am one that believes, as someone once said:

"If God had meant for us to have fiberglass boats he would have made fiberglass trees."

My mother sent me a plaque with an old saying that has plenty of truth:

"A boat is a hole in the water, surrounded by wood, into which one pours money."

The slip cost at the Bridgeport Yacht Club was high so we moved the boat to Black Rock Harbor to a boatyard and marina owned by John and Marge, an elderly couple that lived in a house right on the shore.

Parking was in their driveway or out on the street. Their back yard was on the water. They had a dock for loading and unloading. All boats were moored in the harbor. There was a rowboat to get the bigger boat or to take the bigger boat back out. We had our own dinghy.

The Black Rock Harbor light on Fayerweather Island marks the eastern entrance to the harbor. A light has been there since 1808. Seaside Park runs along the northeastern shore of Black Rock Harbor.

Having the boat was fun but a lot of work. Twice a season we would beach the boat at high tide at Seaside Park, across the harbor, scrape and paint one side.

The next day have the boat turned around and do the other side. Even with antifouling paint a lot of stuff grows on the bottom of a boat.

Sailboats have more underwater surface and get slowed down by the plant growth.

We cruised on Long Island Sound, often across to Port Jefferson, New York.

Sometimes we would sleep in the boat. Other times at a motel in town near the waterfront.

On one occasion, we hit some rather bad weather in crossing.

We were blown quite close to the Stratford Shoals, in the exact middle of the Sound. At low tide the rocks are exposed. There is a lighthouse.

Cheri and the two children, were sleeping in the cabin. I was not concerned. I knew the boat. And I knew the Lord.

The boat did not have reefing so there was too much sail.

Just in case I had to take down the sails, I started the outboard engine and left it idling. Even with a long shaft, the propeller was mostly out of the water.

I was of course glad to get past the jetties and into the harbor at Port Jefferson. That night we stayed on the boat as it was quite late when we reached the town dock.

I did not look to upgrade the boat, the usual path of ownership.

That was one of the many times that I had to make a decision involving family as we were targeting buying a house.

As time passed I grew and got to where there were no regrets.

When I think of our family, I know that even a slight deviation would have resulted in something totally different.

I am quite certain that the Lord's will was achieved in our family with our children, their spouses, and our grandchildren. Still there was much that I did not understand.

The man that quit his job to rebuild a sailboat.
There was a man at that marina that was rebuilding an old sailboat.

At the time I knew him the boat was in the water and he was doing interior cabin and on deck work.

He told me that he had been a mining equipment salesman until he got the boat.

When he realized how much time would be needed for the boat he knew it had to be the job or the boat.

His wife was agreeable that she would hold a job and he would work on the boat for as long as it took.

He carved all of his fittings, made sand mold and had the parts cast in a local shop. Then he would carefully finish the parts. He made his own icebox.

Rebuilding was a slow process especially as he was willing to chat with me and with others. Finally he finished the boat.

He took it out for one short trip. Then he lost interest and put it up for sale.

I met him again several years later in Maine. He had taken to repairing sets of antique china. Initially he charged $25 per hour, then he went to $50, then to $75. With each rate increase he lost potential business. Since he still had more work than he could do he had made a smart move.

Boats are often unused.
Pleasure boats do not get used all that much.

No matter where you go the marinas seem to have boats that never go out even on good weekend days. I have seen stats that the average boat only goes out maybe ten times in the season.

At the public marina in Port Jefferson there were many of the old Chris Craft type wooden boats. Those boats never went out. They were backed into a slip and there they sat. All had large after decks and the owners would sit, watch the passersby, and chat with folks in neighboring boats. The boats were like summer cottages.

A trip to Jamaica.
We took a trip to Jamaica with our, at that time, two children. The man at immigration said that there was a problem with the children as they had no identification. I got the impression that some cash would solve the problem but did not want to do that. Just then, such a surprise, up came my friend Val Turnbull, one of the top government officials. The problem went away. Val had a government Land Rover and a driver. So our transportation problem from Kingston to Port Antonio in Portland Parish on the north side of the island, was also solved.

CHAPTER 6: McKESSON LABORATORIES

"At some time in the life cycle of virtually every organization, its ability to succeed in spite of itself runs out." - Brien's First Law

Jobs were easy to get.
The job market in the 1970s was like a dream. Jobs were so easy to get. It was possible to interview today, get an offer tomorrow at 10% more pay and start right away. Head hunters would call and say that they were looking for someone for a certain position and wanted to know if I knew anyone that was looking. Of course they meant "Are you looking for another job?"

How I became a COBOL computer programmer in manufacturing.
I wanted to move into COBOL programming and into manufacturing. Even with a good job market, making two big changes at once was not easy. I figured a way to make it happen. I decided to apply for a job where the interviewer would know less about COBOL and manufacturing than me. For sure it would have to be a job where I would not have to go through the personnel, now human resources, department.

The hiring manager knew less than I did about COBOL.
At McKesson Laboratories, the hiring manager was a vice president. Further, he was not just a resident of Greenwich, not just a resident of Old Greenwich, but a resident of Riverside. He was a great guy. I really enjoyed working with him even though he and I were too busy to meet often. He was not a young man but he was open to new ideas of which I had plenty. I vowed to be like him when I got older. Little did I know what he had planned for me as soon as I came on board. While I did not tell him that I did not know COBOL, he did not tell me that there was no one on staff that did.

I get a job at McKesson Laboratories.
At the interview, I was told that McKesson Laboratories wanted to install an IBM software package called COPICS and customize it for their manufacturing and inventory needs. It would be a first in the industry.

Little did he or I know that I would do another industry first involving a sacred process involving master formulas.

To become employed I had to go through some formalities involving tests, a current business fad. I did well on all of the tests except for sales aptitude. The personnel manager told me not to worry. He said that he had given the tests to the salesmen and that none of them had passed.

Health insurance and life insurance.
There was a requirement of the health insurance carrier for a physical examination. I was told that there was no rush and that everyone passed.

Because there was a news article about me joining the company, the next day I got a call from a life insurance salesman from whom I bought a policy. The insurance man that called on me was a proponent of whole life insurance. I bought insurance though it was term insurance. I sold him on selling me that. He was a young man just starting out that had only been trained in whole life. I increased my insurance to $1,000,000 as my needs increased and later lowered it. My plan still had me covered for $100,000 until almost age 73. After that age, life insurance would be too costly to be of any value.

I had two appointments for a physical exam the same week in Fairfield, Connecticut. One exam for the health insurance, another for the life insurance.

Both doctors were about the same age. Both doctors in the interview phase asked me if I drank alcohol.

One doctor told me that I had a certain makeup such that I should never drink alcohol. The other doctor told me I had a certain make-up such that it would be good if I had one or two drinks a day. Later I will show how this was one thing that led me to not believe that God works today through doctors.

I start work at McKesson Laboratories.
My first day on the job at McKesson Laboratories I learned four things:

1. The IBM 360 had just been installed and no one knew what to do next. While it did have a compatibility mode for transition, it would run exactly like a 1401, it would be a costly substitute.

2. COPICS only existed in sales brochures. There was no software.

3. No one in the company knew COBOL.

4. My boss wanted me to benchmark some existing programs by rewriting them in COBOL. These were programs that were standalone, using punched card input.

All work at the company was done on an IBM 1401, a computer that I knew well. I did not panic. I just knew that I was going to have to deliver sooner rather than later. I knew several programming languages. I knew that if I could make a program read a card, rearrange the fields, and then print them out that I would already know most of a language. A friend showed me how to do just that with COBOL. I quickly rewrote the first autocoder program on my to do list into COBOL and it ran. I had reached my goal. I had become a COBOL programmer, albeit novice, in a manufacturing environment though I did not yet know anything about manufacturing. McKesson Laboratories had the 2314 disk system with its 360 computer. This disk allowed locating keyed data without the use of the processor. What really helped was when I found that IBM did have a bill of material processor program that linked record metadata using the processor and then accessed the records without using the processor. I had the raw material to build a system in what might be called 3-D as opposed to the 2-D of the 1401. I completed the initial comprehensive system ahead of time and under budget.

The first automation of pharmaceutical master formulas.
I did the first automation of master formulas. At first the Food and Drug Administration, the FDA, said no on doing it in real production. No one else had automated the process so there was no need for us to do so. Clearly I would have to do something other than use logic. I thought of an old parody of MacBeth:

"Double bubble, toil and trouble
Punch the cards and sort them double
Data isn't verified?
Courage don't be terrified.
Make the printout twice as long
They'll accept it right or wrong
Round the big computer go
Every second costs us dough."

My master formula system demo looked good. I had bought a special design manila colored card stock continuous form for the master formulas and for the batch tickets. The FDA inspector from Washington arrived to see how it would all work. Of special interest was how we would keep from printing out a wrong formula.

With a little bit of logic, I was able to explain to the inspector a bill of material and how the master formulas were just that, a bill of material. Procedures for mixing the ingredients were also a part and were built into the bill of material.

In the past the master formula had been hand-typed. Then there would be ten people, starting with the three doctors in the lab itself that would hand sign directly on the master formula document.

Each time a batch was made there would be a typed copy of the master formula, a batch ticket, with a number and date, that was only checked by the typist. It was not difficult to show that the existing process was much more prone to error than the computer system.

We went to the computer control desk. I had already loaded the fanfold continuous, 8 1/2 x 14, forms in the big IBM 1403 printer. One push of a button at the control desk and the printer, sounding like a diesel engine started spewing out forms. After it stopped I took out the forms, stripped off the side margins with the sprocket holes and separated the forms. We went to a table and the inspector could match up the formula with the batch ticket and the old style typed paper. The inspector liked the solid feel and the neat computer type. He had no clue as to whether or not the ingredients were right. The process worked, I answered his questions, and he gave approval to use computer printed master formulas and batch tickets. He did not ask to take any samples as he did know that it was company confidential.

I did not tell the FDA inspector what caused the most errors, a human nature condition that had nothing to do with hand typing or computer printing. There would have been nothing he could have done and it was a problem at all manufacturers. Every day there would be new and changed master formulas. The first signer might just sign without reading. After all he was a busy man and there were nine signers of integrity after him that would all check the formula. Each of the following signers had the same attitude. Number two through ten had further assurance because the prior signers would have read the formula and there was no need to second guess those distinguished and well-educated signers. The next signers would also read the formula. It was possible that none of the 10 would check anything.

A part of the computer process, key punching, had a checkpoint that did not exist in hand-typing. Key punching had a second process called key verifying. The verifying machine looked like a key punch. What it did was read the card and make a notch where the keys entered did not match. The card of course had to be redone. That was our real sign off process. I was quite certain that the two high school graduates would have given the computer the exact formula as given to them.

I had become not only an expert COBOL programmer, I had become an expert in manufacturing. I had some specific credibility after the redesign of the master formula/batch tickets under the bill of material concept and software.

Schmoozing can make a difference.
When the FDA inspector arrived to see my master formula system, we first talked about his trip and of the beauty of Fairfield as well as the beauty of all of southern Connecticut. His journey had been pleasing so far. I told him that I

was sure he would like lunch at a French restaurant, the Cafe de la Plage, a cozy place that had been on the Long Island Sound beach in Westport since 1957. He did like it. This was in the day of the three martini lunches. That restaurant became Positano's in 2001 and later moved to downtown Westport. The building, at 117 years old, was torn down in 2017. The land sold for $4 1/2 million to become a McMansion.

I get a promotion.
I became assistant data processing manager. This was to me a better job than to be the data processing manager because I did not have to deal with the day to day supervision of the department staff nor monitor the monthly schedule of work to be done. The data processing manager, Lenny, was approaching retirement and did not want to be involved with the IBM 360 and COPICS any more than necessary.

Lenny.
Lenny had an interesting story.

He had six grown sons. Five of them had at least a bachelors degree, several had masters.

The remaining son, I don't know where he fit in age ranking, had dropped out of high school. His main business was pumping septic tanks. Because he stayed right in his town where he grew up he eventually met the people he had not already known. He had knowledge of everything that went on. He bought pieces of land before real estate agents knew that they were for sale. He bought cars, trucks, and farm equipment. Of course he sold at much higher prices than he bought. Then there is a lot of money in pumping septic tanks, especially in towns with no sewer system. He became quite well to do.

All of his brothers were often short of cash. He gave all of them part-time jobs at one time or another on the side of whatever else they did.

The lesson is that the real money is in performing the business activity and mission rather than holding a staff position.

I have noticed that college grads aim for staff positions.

Lenny was a great guy and we got along well. I learned much from him. He learned from me and from others. His favorite expression was:

"Is that so? I've never heard of any such thing."

Lenny always wanted to know more. At the same time, he had turned his job into an exact process.

His cubicle was always neat. He always knew exactly where anything was to be found. There was no stress and nothing ever got lost.

I save money on disk drives.
One of my first actions with my management title was to replace the IBM 2314 disk drives with ones made by Singer Friden. They were exact knockoffs even with the non-processor retrieval feature. The rental from IBM was $5,675 for each 7.5 MB removable disk, disk drive. We had three drives with a total capacity of 22.5 mb, not gigabyte. Megabyte. Total rent from IBM was a little over $17,000. Total rent from Singer Friden was $8,400 per month, less than half of IBMs price.

The IBM salesman tried to talk me out of making the switch. No result. Next step was for his boss to take my boss to lunch. My boss did not accept either that we should stick with IBM or that I was incompetent and was making the wrong choice.

IBM's only hope was to get me to leave McKesson Laboratories.

IBM wanted me out and I don't blame them.
I soon got a call from another IBM salesman about a job opening at another company.

I interviewed and was made an offer.

I got suspicious especially after talking with some friends. In short that company was fiercely loyal to IBM. Had I gone in and changed disk drive suppliers as I had at McKesson Laboratories, I would probably have been out of work.

I become purchasing manager.
Shortly after I became the assistant data processing manager the long-time purchasing manager retired. The prior purchasing manager and I had spent a lot of time working together. He handled the materials. I controlled the data and the metadata of the materials. I suggested to those above and around me that I add that job to mine and I could then save time by talking to myself.

His office, that became mine, was the original office of George Musica, alias George Dietrich, the brother of Philip Mariano Fausto Musica, an Italian swindler, alias Dr F Donald Coster. As Coster he acquired McKesson and Robbins and sold plenty of product that had a high alcohol content. He later got involved in crude drugs borrowing against fake inventory. *Magnificent*

Masquerade is the book that was written about this major scandal.

I shake things up.
There was a sign in the reception area that salesmen would be seen on Tuesday and Thursday with an appointment. My first official act was to take down the sign. I told the buyers that it was their job to see salesmen whenever one came in even if we were having a department meeting. It was quite simple that these salesmen were travelers and only came to our door if they had something we might need. With appointments required we might get passed by or not know what they had to offer. I also set a policy that lunch meetings were fine so long as the buyers did not let the salesman pay. I told them that the company would cover the cost and they could choose where to go. I told them to buy the salesmen a good lunch.

I really shake things up.
I hired the first woman executive at McKesson Laboratories.

While wearing the hat of purchasing manager, I caused quite a stir by making the promotion. The lady I promoted had been working part-time doing filing while her children were in school and asked if she could go on full-time. She was expecting a filing job. I thought she would make a good buyer.

A few weeks earlier while she was still part-time, the cafeteria cash register had gone out. I told her to deal with it. She thought she could not do it as she knew nothing about cash registers. I told her it was no different than a home appliance. Call service. Find out what it would cost. Then either get it fixed or get a new one.

I told her that whatever she decided is what we would do. She and the cafeteria manager decided on a new one.

The funniest part was when I got a call from my boss wanting to know what she was doing in the cafeteria with the manager. She had not been there ten minutes and it was a long way from his office on the second floor. A woman out of her normal place was so odd that someone noticed and reported. When I told him what she was doing, he was silent, said ok, and hung up.

The men buyers did not mind having a woman as peer. My boss was not happy yet said that it was my department and it was up to me. The other women did not like it at all that a woman was moving up.

Most of the McKesson Laboratories employees had been there for a long time. I remember one woman that had started work when she was 15. 50 years later she retired. All of the time she had been there she had held the same job doing exactly the same work in the factory sitting on the same stool.

I meet the astronaut Frank Borman.
Frank Borman is best known as the Commander of Apollo 8 that circled the moon. After he retired from the space program he took a job with Eastern Airlines. He was McKesson's contact for setting up the flying part of junkets for doctors. He would stop in like any other salesman and we would work out the next order. Borman moved up quickly at Eastern airlines. In seven years he had advanced from CEO to Board Chairman.

Junkets for doctors.
Pharmaceuticals companies would give free trips to doctors and their spouses. They would have a flight from their home to a port where they would go on a private cruise. There would be seminars where the doctors could advance their education. They would learn about some new drug that would cure some or all of any ailments. The doctors would get free samples. I think think the whole trip concept is now illegal.

The woman closing out her deceased father's office supply business.
One day shortly after I came back from lunch, the general manager stopped by my office. He had taken a call from a woman whose father had died. She was selling out the inventory of his office supply business. The general manager had bought various items. He had not made a list of what he had bought. I would be able to see it all on the invoice.

Scams like this one have always been around. Just the technology changes.

Yellow pages bills.
The yellow pages scams may never go away. The yellow pages logo with the fingers doing the walking is in the public domain. Anybody can and does use it. The bills are quite clear that they are not bills but become one if someone signs it and sends it back. There is to be an ad in some printed or online directory. The bills say that they are not related to the yellow pages in a telephone directory. There must be good money in this scam as it never dies.

The salesman that wanted to make a sale that day.
A minicomputer salesman from a company that was new to me came in to sell a computer. He clearly did not know anything about computers. I think he believed that you simply plug it in and all will be well. I was curious and did ask questions.

He moved in for the close.

"I'll make it simple. Whatever I get as commission you get half."

I told him that I did not think we had any use for that computer and thanked him for his time.

I write a safety plan after OSHA was created.
As I was the unofficial guru of all knowledge at McKesson, I wrote the first formal safety plan after OSHA started. Inspections could take place at any time. That was a hazard itself. Many, if not most, of the early inspectors were affirmative action minorities that had a goal of citing for profit businesses for their many racist and price gouging evils under the guise of safety lapses. A signal system was devised so that the receptionist could give a warning. From the reception area there was a long flight of stairs to the rest of the building. This allowed some time for getting ready. In some areas, where there was no time to tidy up, work simply stopped and the workers in that area went to the cafeteria for coffee.

Matt.
Matt, while he was in the Navy, realized that while at sea he could not spend money. After leaving the Navy and going to work he became, what else, a cost accountant.

Matt owned a small store. After work he would go to the store. His wife ran it during the day. He ran it at night, every weekend and every holiday.

To him the prime advantage was that he was working all the time, seven days a week, morning until night, making money, and not able to spend any.

I knew Matt pretty well, though never asked him what that did to life with his wife and children.

The blind typist.
There was a typing pool at that had four typists. Executives would dictate on a dictaphone belt and take it to the pool. One of the typists, Annie, never made a typographic error. I was always glad when she got my work. She would say that she could not make a mistake because she was not able to correct it. Annie was blind from birth.

At the morning break she would lead the conversation in the typing pool about books and articles she had "read." The other typists, all sighted, never read much of anything.

At the afternoon break Annie would write letters, some by typing, some in braille. She was president of one organization and secretary of another.

Annie, lived alone, did her own shopping, and did the snow shoveling as the other two tenants in the three family house were too lazy.

Annie's favorite expression was "see you later." I would try to sneak up on her but it never worked. She knew who was behind her. She told me that blind people have abilities that sighted people do not have.

The general manager was the owner of the house that had been the home of Helen Keller, the accomplished blind person.

I set up what may have been the first payroll direct deposits.
I may have been the first to set up direct deposit for payroll and to have free checking accounts for employees. For sure it was the first for the State National Bank.

McKesson, like other employers, paid in cash weekly. Every employee, including the salaried executives were paid that way. The armored car would come up to the front door. Each person got their pay envelope. Each year it became more costly to pay by cash. We decided to pay by check instead of cash. The union balked and wanted each employee to have an hour off each week with pay to cash their checks. That would be even more costly. Imagine several hundred employees leaving in midday.

I worked out a plan with the State National Bank that on a certain day each week the bank would get a printout of net pay per employee.

They would give us the exact other data needed, date, account number, etc. for keypunching. They would not need any programming changes.

A few weeks later, I made it better by giving them cards already punched by our computer in the format they needed for theirs. In the days of punch cards, there were many systems where cards would be punched out even when there was mag tape and then disk storage.

I gave the bank a control sheet with the total dollars, the number of cards, and the printout. The bank would then deduct the total from the company account and make deposits.

Since very few employees had bank accounts, I worked out a deal where the bank would give free checking accounts to all the employees, including salesmen that lived in other states.

The controller thought that the out of state folks would not want a Connecticut bank account.

These employees had checks mailed to them. I told the controller that on payday each out of state employee could write a check to themselves from their free State National Bank account and deposit it in their local accounts. There were only a few people involved. They could call and find out their net amount or they could estimate and adjust when their pay stub arrived. No matter what, they were getting paid earlier.

The high speed tablet press causes inventory problems.
A big event occurred. A high speed tablet press was purchased and installed. All available space was used for fibre drums full of tablets. It was not long before even the hallways had the drums lined up. No one had considered that the packaging lines could not handle the output from a high speed tablet press.

An added boss when I became the purchasing manager.
When I became the purchasing manager, I added a third simultaneous boss, this time the Vice President of Manufacturing. He accepted new ideas even when it was something he did not like. He did not interfere with those under him. He was a chain smoker. Smoking was ok anywhere. For him and often for other smoking executives, the smoking was a way to gain time for thinking before asking questions or making a decision.

He was well organized and had a private secretary that was also well organized. He dictated vast numbers of internal letters on his dictaphone. Each letter only had one subject. If he had five things to ask or say, there were five typed memos, even when all to one person. He would keep one copy, Central files would get another copy. The copies were made with carbon paper and were not photocopies. He had a set time when he dictated letters and a set time when he would do phone follow ups.

There was one most rare event when he stopped by my office and gave me a verbal order to do something.

How I cornered the world market in ascorbic acid and rose hips.
Dr. Linus Pauling had announced that vitamin c would cure the common cold. I heard about it on the way home on my car radio. I told Cheri that I had to go back to work after dinner. I worked all night buying all of the ascorbic acid and rose hips that I could find all over the world. This work was all done on the phone. That was an accepted way of buying. The transactions were all honest and each party trusted the other. The seller would ship at the agreed price and the buyer would pay per terms. Early the next morning when my boss came in he stopped by my office on the way to his.

"Dave, I want you to stop everything you're doing and buy all the ascorbic acid and rose hips you can find."

I patiently listened as he told me about Linus Pauling.

When he was done, I pointed to my outbox full of handwritten purchase orders that were to be typed and mailed.

"I've been here all night," I replied.

"Good boy," he said.

He went to his office totally unfazed. He did not ask me how much I had bought, if I was done buying, or if I was going home soon. That was for me to know and to decide.

He and I both viewed that what I had done was par for the course. We all did our jobs. No applause needed.

Some time later, I found that I had bought more than we would need even though McKesson sold a lot of vitamin c, I had not worried as I knew that we could sell the excess at a profit, which we did.

Nine feet of water in the building.
One day there was a flood during a time of heavy rain. There was nine feet of water in the McKesson Laboratories building.

When I arrived at work the water damage had been done. It would be several days before the water went down but I was already thinking of how we would measure the loss of inventory.

What I knew would make a problem was that there were pre-printed boxes that were used for other items. Kraft labels were put over the pre-printing. I was quite certain we would find that the labels were off the boxes. I expected to find disintegrated boxes and product all over everywhere. I was right when I surmised that it would take machines to scoop up and shovel up the boxes and the product.

I decided that what we would have to do first is to inventory the good product since we would not be able to do that for the flood damaged product.

We would then make sure the computer inventory had all been posted up to date. We would subtract the physical inventory of good product from the computer inventory, cost the difference and make a report. Since this would take a while I made a separate computer file for flood damage. I made sure that the physical count of good product was done before any new shipment or production transactions were made. That was not difficult but I did have various people sign, date, and describe what they had done.

The inventory loss was not covered by insurance. It seems that rain damage was not covered but overflow of rivers and streams due to rain was covered. There was no overflow but the lawyers felt they had a case to sue the state because I-95, constructed some 12 years earlier had in effect created a river during heavy rain that flowed onto roads underneath bridges.

I spent quite a bit of time in court during the trial giving testimony about how I had determined the loss.

In cross examination by the state's attorney I had to describe many details about computers and how I knew that the computer gave the right answer. I had to describe how disk drive platters are constructed and how the data stayed on it. The goal of course was to discredit my work. McKesson Laboratories won the lawsuit.

The beginning of the end of McKesson Laboratories.

My job at McKesson Laboratories was my first experience with manufacturing. It was a good one because McKesson Laboratories was the quintessential long time factory.

There were lifetime careers for blue collar workers with no advancement.

A bell would ring for breaks and lunch. Everyone, from the general manager on down, would observe these times. The same was true for the annual summer shutdown with the exception of those that had maintenance and rehab work scheduled for the shutdown time.

The general manager was just as much a part of the daily and hourly routine as a machine operator. My department and the buyers were not. We could be absent for lunch with salesmen.

McKesson Laboratories packaged under its own name and did some packaging for big name brands like Squibb, for commodity items that by the USP, *United States Pharmacopeia,* had to be made exactly the same.

Every year there were discussions about dropping products such as mineral oil because they did not make a profit. Every year it had to be explained that these products were a big part of the business and, while there was not much profit, did make a hefty contribution to absorbing overhead. There were no high profit products that could fill the gap. Drop mineral oil and close the factory.

McKesson Laboratories began to see that the future did not look so good.

It began doing acquisitions.

Adele Simpson.
The manufacturing and marketing rights to Adele Simpson's Fashion Fragrances Ltd line of collage products was the first. The idea was to move McKesson Laboratories products into new markets.

Adele Simpson was an American fashion designer with a successful career that spanned nearly five decades, as well as having been a child performer in vaudeville who danced in productions with Milton Berle and other entertainers.

I did not want to be a part of the acquisitions arena. And certainly not the Adele Simpson products. McKesson Laboratories had no expertise in that type product.

I did get involved with the physical inventory of what was bought and I learned some new things. My contact was with Adele's husband Wesley Simpson. He was a retired textiles executive. He was impressed with my knowledge of textiles that I had gained from Georgia Tech and from a general interest in history including the Ten Hour Movement in the New England mills.

Wesley had a chauffeured Volkswagen. His driver wore a uniform and cap and Wesley rode in the back seat. It was good that he was a small man.

We went to this old warehouse in Newark, New Jersey. The multi-storied building had individual locked cage like sections for each cosmetics brand. Security guards accompanied a crew of Puerto Ricans, that did the packaging, to different cages based on orders from stores. Perfume and other fragrances were in dirty, corroded, 55 gallon drums. It did not take long to do a full physical inventory.

The product itself was the cheapest part of the product package that sold for $100 an ounce. Bottle caps and sometimes the boxes were of much higher value.

The Adele Simpson line was a low volume, money losing venture. From its outset, McKesson Laboratories was a manufacturer of items that were sold in independent drug stores primarily in small town and rural areas. The pharmacy industry was growing with the development of chain drug stores. Selling high retail price fragrances to department stores did not work out.

The end comes for McKesson Laboratories.
When the end came, I was already off to greener pastures.

After a few other similar deals, and with attempts to sell long time products in grocery stores, while independent drug stores were going out of business, McKesson simply shut down one day.

The McKesson Laboratories factory building on Kings Highway is gone and became the site of a Home Depot.

The decline of American manufacturing.
The demise of McKesson Laboratories was part of an overall systemic problem. The decline of American manufacturing occurred in an accelerated way during my career.

Some say that it was because of cheaper labor in other countries.

What happened was that real value was coming from marketing.

Products had become commodities. There was a practical use, they were the same from brand to brand, there were fewer brands, and everything was made to last.

William Wrigley was somewhat of a radical with the idea of making something that people would buy on a regular basis. Chewing gum was cheap but over a year's time each customer would spend a lot of money on chewing gum.

The story about USP 5 grain, 325 mg aspirin can teach much. USP 5 grain aspirin always has to have exactly the same ingredients and combined the same way. The tablets have to be compressed with exactly the same pressure and be exactly the same size.

I don't know about today but in the past the ads were correct while giving the impression that Bayer was somehow different. The FDA was always in court with Bayer. So that a cease and desist order could be issued, there was a long process of writing, in legalese, exactly what Bayer was required to stop.

The cease and desist order occurred just as the offending ad campaign was winding down. With a new ad campaign the court actions started again.

The Bayer lawyers and the FDA lawyers became lifelong friends.

One thing that the FDA could not stop was Bayer's higher prices.

Even without the ads, Bayer may well have done well because most people with pain believed that the higher price was for a product that was better and more effective.

They did not know that the USP on Bayer and on the one fifth the price supermarket brand meant that there was no difference.

One oil company had an idea. It advertised that their gasoline with platformate would do all kinds of wonderful things for you.

It was finally forced to stop the ads because all gasoline had platformate and consequently all gasoline would do the same wonderful things.

W. Edward Deming.
The story of W. Edward Deming, an American farm boy, is a part of what happened to American manufacturing.

Deming was born in Iowa and lived there until he was six. His parents moved to Cody, Wyoming. From there they moved to nearby Powell, Wyoming where his sister was the first white child to be born in that Indian village. The family lived in a tarpaper shack.

Deming went on to graduate from the University of Wyoming, the University of Colorado at Boulder, and Yale. Deming had an idea for manufacturing.

The American steel industry and automobile industry was not interested. Deming went to Japan and Japan was interested. Soon Japan ruled the world in steel, automobiles, and everything else. Eventually, the American companies took an interest. It was then too late.

Quotes from W. Edwards Deming:
"It is not necessary to change. Survival is not mandatory."

"If you can't describe what you are doing as a process, you don't know what you're doing."

"It is not enough to do your best; you must know what to do, and then do your best."

"Profit in business comes from repeat customers, customers that boast about your project or service, and that bring friends with them."

"You should not ask questions without knowledge."

"Lack of knowledge... that is the problem."

"Competition should not be for a share of the market but to expand the market."

"Everyone is a customer for somebody or a supplier to somebody."

Penguin Jokes Part 2
Why do penguins carry fish in their beaks? Because they haven't any pockets.

What do you get if you cross a penguin with an alligator? I don't know but you better not try to fix its bow tie.

What is black and white and goes round and round? A penguin in a revolving door.

What does a magician penguin say? "Pick a cod, any cod…"

Yesterday I had coffee with a penguin. He said he would rather have had a fish.

I saw an Emperor penguin wearing a toga. It was Julius Freezer.

A penguin walks into a bar. He asks the bartender, "Have you seen my brother?" The bartender asks, "Well, what does he look like?

Why can't penguins fly? They don't have enough money for a plane ticket.

What did the polar bear say to the penguin? "Welcome to the zoo." Penguins don't normally live close to polar bears.

What is black and white and red all over? A penguin with a sunburn.

CHAPTER 7: HOW I DIVERSIFIED

"Life is the art of drawing sufficient conclusions from insufficient premises." - Samuel Butler.

My first business as an adult.
While I was working with big corporations, I had an interesting business on the side. I would use keypunch and computer service bureaus and sell the results. I would write programs for special purposes. One project I had was to take bowling scores and produce an annual book for bowling associations with names and scores.

The non-profit executive director that asked for a discount.
I did a project for a large, well-known non-profit. I had quoted the price and I did the job.

When I delivered the agreed results and expected to be paid, the executive director asked me how much I would discount the bill. He said that they were a charity and they asked their suppliers for discounts. I asked him to set the discount. He did not know how he could do it.

I said I would discount by the same percentage that he gave back of his salary. He smiled and called for a check for the full amount of the contract.

That man was a character. We went out to lunch one time. His secretary helped him put on his overcoat. At the restaurant he wanted me to hang my overcoat over his. He said that his coat was expensive and he didn't want it to be stolen as it might be if it was visible.

He had a new Cadillac, when Cadillac were still bug and showy. I noticed it was registered in Illinois. I knew that he had been on the job in Connecticut for at least a few years, before that model was on the market.

The non-profit fallacy.
Everyone wants their donations to go to non-profits. There is a fallacy there. The employees are not non-profits. They want to make as much as they can. There are no stockholders so there is no one to hold the board in check. The profits that would have gone to stockholders go to the execs. Studies have shown that the rate of return for nonprofits is almost identical to that of for-profits.

Many nonprofits select directors that only care to have a line for their resume. They will not read the reports nor will they question anything or rock the boat in any fashion.

I knew of one quasi-government organization with 54 directors. For the board meetings, the main concern of the executive director was to provide a good cocktail hour and dinner.

I turn down a vice president job offer.
Quaker Oats bought Marx Toys. I was offered the position of Vice President of Data Processing. I declined and am glad that I did. Quaker made negative profit on Marx Toys. After a few years Quaker Oats sold what was left of the company.

We look to buy a house.
Cheri and I began looking to buy a house. Due to the increasing numbers of two earner households, real estate prices were skyrocketing. I figured that somehow we should make the move while we could still do it on just my paycheck.

At Short Beach in Stratford, Connecticut we found an antique beach house for a great price. The problem was that it was on land rented from the town. The beach community and a number of houses had been there for a long time. The town was planning on building a park. All the houses would have to be moved or torn down eventually. We decided it was too much of a risk to move a house then or later when the town made its move. It turned out that the park construction was delayed for many years though it eventually did take place. We found a nice place in Milford, Connecticut but the inspections showed some problems. We did later find what we wanted.

We move to Sandy Hook, Connecticut.
We moved from Trumbull, Connecticut to Sandy Hook, Connecticut, a section of Newtown to our first owned home that cost us $32,400. We did have the common homeowners fear that one or more of the septic system, the well, or the furnace would fail.

Though Newtown, Connecticut had only 14,000 population, it had four post offices. There was Newtown, Sandy Hook, Hawleyville and Botsford. Earlier, there were at least two more, Dodgingtown and Hattertown. These were some of the earliest post offices in the United States.

We sell the boat.
After we moved to Sandy Hook, we sold the boat.

We learned the truth of a certain saying::

"The two best days in a boater's life are the day he gets the boat and the day he gets rid of it."

Our interests turned to gardening and general rural life.

We try rural life.
We had goats, sheep, and chickens. Several times in bad weather someone would stop at the door to let us know that our sheep had gotten out. I had to explain that sheep like to stay out in all kinds of weather. They have thick fur. Even an outer shell of frozen fur does not bother them. The animal do-gooders were a reminder that with the completion of I-84 that commuters would move in from greater distances.

The doctor that was to show me how to live a long life.
I went to a local doctor for a check-up. She told me that with regular visits she could teach me and help me to have a long life. She herself was maybe early 40s. There was no subsequent visits because she suddenly fell over dead one day.

The temporary plate scam.
It was not hard to see that all of the big trucks that were from a certain Connecticut contractor had paper temporary plates.

It took a reporter to publicize this and to point out that none of that company's trucks ever got regular plates. It had something to do with avoiding excise taxes. With hundreds of trucks it made for some big savings.

None of the registry people had ever gotten suspicious, even as the temporary plates were renewed over and over for the same trucks. That construction company was noted for big campaign contributions. That could have had something to do with it.

The dirt scam.
While not illegal, unethical, or immoral there was another practice that was profitable for the construction company though bad for the taxpayers.

At the same time that I-84 was under construction, Newtown was building a high school next to the new interstate.

Site preparation required the literal removal of a mountain. Because of the proximity and the short road travel it was quite obvious that the trucks with the temporary plates taking dirt from the school site were dumping it on the interstate site.

Again a reporter found that the construction company was paid to remove the dirt which was then sold to the state for the highway.

Both projects involved state and federal funds.

We meet Warren and Judy.
We bought firewood from Gary. I later bought a pickup truck from him.

I met his sister Judy and her husband Warren.

The couple later moved to a small town close to the Canadian border where they had a photography studio and published a local newspaper.

There were a number of interesting folks in that area.

There is one that I remember well, a lady that had come from Switzerland. She was in America yet thought that the culture was the same as it had been years earlier in Switzerland.

She had a vision of changing the town.

She contemplated a dance hall so that young people could come down from the mountains into the village every night to dance.

I went to their town mostly in the winter and early Spring during tax season.

One time Warren and Judy kept our children while Cheri and I went to Montreal.

They later later moved south.

The first time I visited them down south, I did not know the exact location of their street. I asked at a convenience store just off the interstate.

Prior to giving me the precise directions the Arab clerk looked out the window.

"Where's your truck?" he asked.

I realized that I fit the stereotype of a truck driver because I was wearing a cowboy hat. Maybe both of us had erroneous ideas about each other.

I've always liked this riddle involving hats:

"Why do cowboys wear baseball caps? So no one will think they are truck drivers."

Warren died of the effects of agent orange from when he did military service in Vietnam. Judy remains as an active Christian.

A ferry pilot.
I knew a man that was what is known as a ferry pilot. He delivered airplanes from the factory all over the world and would take them back and forth for maintenance.

By himself he could fly a single engine airplane across the Pacific with electronics and inflatable plastic fuel bags filling the cabin. Returning he would get two seats on a commercial jet, one for himself and another for the bag of electronics. He said that if he checked the bag the electronics would be stolen.

He would carry cash in different currencies to pay off air traffic controllers that had the authority to keep him on the ground for a long time.

As Rodney Dangerfield pointed out in the movie *Back to School*, bribery in various forms is universal.

I can honestly say that I never took a bribe or gave one, even to a maitre d' to get a good table.

Weekend trips.
Weekend trips when we were living in Connecticut were of great time and money value.

We could go anywhere in New England and if desired be home that night.

Even if we made it a two day trip we rarely spent more than $50 including gas yet we lived well.

One time a motel proprietor in New Hampshire wanted to see our marriage license. There we were with two children. Who carries a marriage license? We were allowed to stay though with doubts about our morality, legality, and the status of our children.

New England fairs.
From mid-summer to mid-fall, on weekends we went to fairs. New England has plenty of old-time fairs. There is a directory for each state that categorizes fairs by size. We generally went to what are called major fairs though we did not go to the really major fairs such as the Big "E" in Springfield, Massachusetts. In

one way of viewing it, the major fairs we attended should be called small fairs. The fairs are in flat fields where permanent buildings have been for a very long time.

There was no parking fee and often no admission. We went for the exhibits, the food, and the nostalgic ambiance. If midways were a part we did not go on any rides. The season ends with the Fryeburg Fair in Maine where it might be cool as winter was coming on. If I had to pick one fair as the best, I would pick the Skowhegan Fair in Maine. All the others were a very close second.

Flea markets and auctions.
On our weekend trips we would also go to flea markets, yard sales, and auctions. We bought antiques that we liked and that were functional. Oak was our favorite. At an auction in Stafford Springs, Connecticut, we bought a round oak table. We actually got it into our Volkswagen.

I find memberships are the cheapest way for large families.
We bought a membership in Mystic Aquarium, in Mystic, Connecticut on the day that the aquarium opened. Later we upgraded to a charter lifetime membership. As the family grew we found that memberships could pay for themselves on the first visit. Mystic became a favored place to go.

Survivalism in Mystic, Connecticut.
We were in the gift shop at Mystic Aquarium in the summertime. During a thunderstorm the power went out. There was plenty of light as there was a lot of glass.

The gift shop was run by four young ladies that looked to be college students or maybe college grads. For sure they were from upstanding white New England families possibly of Mayflower descent. Their parents might have been Ivy Leaguers.

I wanted to buy three items that totaled about a $130. Since the power was out it seemed to the young ladies that me and the other customers could just come back the next day. As this was a tourist site the odds of us being in town the next day would be low. Even if we were in town we might decide not to buy anything there but go elsewhere as there were plenty of tourist traps all around. These young ladies saw no connection between the gross margin on sales and their paychecks.

Most of the would be customers left. We did not.

The young ladies said they would work out the sale. They were smiling until I brought out my membership card that entitled me to 10%. They located a calculator. Then they had a discussion on adding up the prices of the three items and taking a discount or taking the discount on each item and then adding up the total. After some time, that problem was solved.

Then came the real challenge. There was 5% sales tax. They searched high and low for a sales tax chart. They found one but it only went up to $100. I won't fault them for not knowing how to take the tax on $100 and add that to the tax on $17 since they normally had the register do that work. I showed them how they could take the calculator and multiply the total sale amount after the discount by 1.05. They were amazed that the answer was the amount to be paid.

I was asked if I worked for the state sales tax department.

Mystic Pizza.
In Mystic, we would often have lunch at Mystic Pizza that was made famous by the Julia Roberts movie.

How we started the new year.
Every year for many years, we celebrated New Year's Eve in Boothbay Harbor, Maine. A great time of the year with few or no tourists. The weather is relatively warm right at the end of the year.

En route we would stop in Freeport, Maine for a visit to L.L. Bean and to other factory stores.

It is true that there is no lock on the front door at L.L. Bean. It has never closed.

McDonalds in Freeport is located in what appears to be a colonial style house. It was built as a McDonald's in compliance with the local building code.

In each trip to Boothbay Harbor we would go through Wiscasset, Maine. We witnessed the continuing natural deterioration of two abandoned freight schooners, the Hesper, and the Luther Little. Both visible from U.S. 1. Both now gone.

At the quaint little town of Bath was the Bath Iron Works, where surface ships are built for the U.S. Navy. Submarines are built at Groton, Connecticut.

In Boothbay Harbor, we stayed at the Tugboat Inn that was built from an old tugboat brought ashore. The restaurant is in the boat. The motel part is attached at the stern and goes out into the water. For New Year's Eve, we would go early to Montsweag Farm in Woolwich on Route 1 for dinner. Great ambiance and baked stuffed lobsters. There was a popular local breakfast place close to the hotel in Boothbay Harbor. We would have a meal or two at the Tugboat. Going to the beach is never good in Maine as the water never gets warm except in the very southern area near New Hampshire. Even there, not the greatest.

There was a small garage type building on a small lot right downtown in Boothbay Harbor, not on a beach but close to the harbor and with good Maine waterfront town ambiance. It was for sale for several consecutive years. The price was cheap. I have often wished that I had bought it and had remodeled it to a cottage.

The emotional draw of Maine real estate and the fallacy.
Real estate in Maine had a certain stigma. We looked at residential property from time to time as did many other tourists and dreamed of Maine as being the same year round. We all ignored the sayings such as:

"Maine has two seasons, Winter and the Fourth of July."

In good weather, quite limited in Maine, the New Yorkers would buy a house, at a price quite cheap by New York standards.

After watching different properties, including an octagonal new construction house on several acres, that started at $65,000 and never went up despite time and multiple owners, I began to realize what was happening.

Only later would they realize how far Maine is from New York, easily a 10 hour drive if not more, and that moving to Maine full time would create new problems including long trips to New York to see family.

These Maine houses had two year turnovers.

Most sellers were motivated sellers hoping to at least break even in one sense by selling at the price they paid.

There were still real estate agent commissions to pay.

The houses not for sale, houses not in the continual turnover, were owned by native Mainers going nowhere soon, who had no need or desire to sell.

The Old Mill.
I first went to The Old Mill restaurant in Westminster, Massachusetts when I was in high school living in Ayer. It is on Route 2A near the Route 2 junction. The site inspired the song *By the Old Mill Stream*. There was always plenty of

stale bread for feeding the ducks. Duck was available on the menu. I always asked our waitress if the duck was fresh. Never did any waitress make the connection to the ducks outside. Many times as adults we have dined at The Old Mill and taken our children.

We become Unitarians.
We were members of a Unitarian church. The church building was a y modern design with plenty of glass. It was built on a small hill on a wooded lot. There were no pews. All folding chairs. That was so that the sanctuary could quickly be reconfigured for whatever function was desired. To Unitarians, the trinity has been humorously said to be the Fatherhood of God, the Brotherhood of Man, and the Neighborhood of Boston. As a liberal church, anything could and did happen.

I don't recall the details but the Sunday school teachers went out on strike, though there was no union and the teachers were volunteers. There was some liberal issue with local church implications that required some type of action.

Cheri and I ran the youth group at the Unitarian church. It met on Sunday nights.

Once the minister was to be away for the weekend. He asked me if I would do the sermon on Sunday. I preached with an evangelistic theme.

There were a number of celebrity types, as well as eccentrics, that were members. Writers, artists, actors, and other professionals. Paul Newman and Joanne Woodward for example. Their house with the famed treehouse was nearby. Norman Cousins, famed for laughing his way to health was another member. The writer of a top current TV series of that time was one more. First name John. I don't recall the surname.

The couple with the pool and the ground cover.
There was one couple that became our good friends.. The husband told us that they had a swimming pool and that we could use it any time subject to three rules:

>1. We should not call to say that we were coming.

>2. We should not be offended if we come and they do not come out to greet us or to be with us.

>3. We could come over whether they were there or not. He told us that there had been many good impromptu parties at their pool that they

missed. He said that the showers and changing rooms in the basement were always open.

They had a problem. They wanted a larger dining room table so as to have more folks for dinner. The interior decorator said that they would need to enlarge the dining room. They called an architect who said that they would need to enlarge the living room as it would be too small for the added guests. The cost was staggering but was ok. A new problem arose. They had quite a growth of ground cover that would have to be displaced. They spent a lot of time finding a home for all of the plants.

The single mother with the farm.
There was a lady, divorced, who always spoke of her farm that was her only occupation. One day we went home with her for lunch. She had a large expensive home, too big for she and her two small children. There was a small weed filled garden and two chickens in an enclosed pen. There were no cows but she was obviously milking a well-heeled ex-husband.

Edward Rowe Snow.
I knew Edward Rowe Snow, the historian-writer. He invited me to join with him and a small group to commemorate the Boston Tea Party on Rowes Wharf. He had inherited a small quantity of the original tea and would be serving it. It tasted like tea that had been thrown in the harbor 200 years earlier!

Navy Commander Grace Murray Hopper.
I met Navy Commander Grace Murray Hopper in an elevator. She had given me much inspiration. Her ultimate retirement was when she fell down in 1992, while still working, and did not get up. That is my goal. None of this sitting around in a rocking chair at the old folks home.

Hopper's work in finding a way to have computer programs written in near English that would run on any computer, led to the founding of **COBOL**, **CO**mmon **B**usiness-**O**riented **L**anguage.

She described herself as the second programmer on the first computer. In 1943 she enlisted in the Navy Reserve. When WWII ended she asked to go on active duty, at the age of 38. The Navy said no because she was too old. In 1966 she retired from the Navy Reserve with the rank of Commander. Years later, she was asked to go on active duty, did so, and retired again in 1971. In 1972, the Navy asked her to go on active duty at the Pentagon. She has said that it became conditional on her being able to go home to Vermont every weekend at Navy expense. In 1985 she was promoted to Admiral. She retired again in 1986. She was almost 80 years old. She then went to work as a senior consultant for Digital Equipment Corporation until her death at the age of 85.

The U.S.S. Hopper, one of the Arleigh Burke destroyers, was named after her. On November 22, 2016 she was posthumously awarded the Presidential Medal of Freedom by President Barack Obama.

Ed.
We had a visit one day in Sandy Hook, Connecticut from some friends Ed and Eleanor. They were headed to Florida. Ed had an interesting occupation.

He determined feasibility of big projects. He wrote a book about the colonization of space. He had calculated the costs and the process.

Ed did tell me one time that when government was ready to do something they would make it feasible. Up until that point anything could be called not feasible.

Two days later we got a call from Eleanor. Ed had died suddenly. That type thing happening to someone close is a real wake-up call.

It lets us know that we need to make sure of our priorities.

I maintain a to do list for Cheri should something sudden happen to me. That is something every head of household should do.

Data Processing Management Association Southern Connecticut.
I was president of the Southern Connecticut chapter of the Data Processing Management Association, DPMA. I was the only president in office for two terms. That was because there was a change in the fiscal year ending and all officers stayed in place an added six months.

The Certificate in Data Processing, CDP, recognized people with experience that could pass an all day exam. I was one of the first recipients. I passed the exam the first time I took it.

During my time with DPMA, a national by-law was changed, Women were allowed to become members and of course become officers and directors.

The board met monthly at homes of directors. As just men we would have beer during our meetings. Women liked downing hard liquor shots. The men decided they were tired of beer and joined the women.

I moved the meetings to a regular location at a hotel/restaurant meeting room in Stratford, Connecticut just off the Merritt Parkway. I banned drinking alcohol during meetings. I moved the meetings along with a fixed agenda. After the meetings any of the board that liked went to the bar for a social time.

I had battles in advancing the mission of the DPMA.

One man on the board that had accepted the responsibility for doing certain things was falling behind. I found that he had taken on some job on the side of his regular job. His excuse was most dramatic:

"Dave, doing this means MONEY in my POCKET." The emphasis was his. Everyone has to decide what percentage of their time goes for "money in my pocket. "

The remarkable Marty.
Marty was a data processing manager and a member of my chapter. He had lost his job during a recession at that time. He was replaced with someone at a much lower salary and with much less capability. Marty searched for a job and was having no luck. He and I were close enough that I knew of his job-hunting efforts. Out of desperation he took the job of last resort. He became a car salesman.

Very rapidly, Marty became the top salesman and kept doing better and better. He did this by doing things that car salesmen don't do. He did things the way detail-oriented data processing people do things. He practiced science, science being simply organized knowledge. He kept a stock of blank IBM cards. It was always easy to tell data processing people, including me. When a note was to be made, out of the suit jacket came a blank IBM card. On the back of IBM cards, Marty recorded the date, name, address, and phone number of every person that was thinking of buying a car. He did the same for everyone that bought a car.

In the cases of those that bought a car he recorded when their last payment would be due. With his records he could call people that were in the market for a car and he could call people 36 months later, when their car was paid off, when it was time to trade in for a new car.

Marty did not have time to sit in the showroom. He worked off of appointments. He would even take a new car to a prospect's home for a test drive and to make the sale. When Marty left one dealership and went to another, there was a large ad in the newspaper with the headline "Marty is now at _____ dealership. The ad had a large picture of Marty.

Joe Girard was in the Guinness Book of World Records as the world's greatest salesman. He was not a sales manager or a dealership owner. He was simply a salesman. In his book *How to Sell Anything to Anybody*, Girard tells of the things that he did to make sales, all ethical and aboveboard. He did not give any account of anyone, even other salesmen at his dealership, that did any of the things that he did..

The Japanese businessman's comment.
Our DPMA chapter hosted a group of Japanese businessmen to tour several businesses in southern Connecticut. We went to the Schick factory in Milford, Connecticut.. A Schick representative told the story of what Schick had done. He was very proud of the new state of the art factory with all the automatic equipment. As we were walking around, the leader of the Japanese group asked me,

"You call that production?"

I knew firsthand that American manufacturing was on its way out.

I become a systems analyst.
At a government contractor, I developed a cost accounting system. I designed the system for reports to be in a logical order. I was overruled and told to print reports in a random unsorted order because we had to have reports for the cost plus contracts but were not required to present results in any order.

Executives, including me, took turns entertaining the government auditor who was on permanent assignment to our office. Whoever had him on any given day could do whatever he wanted just so it kept the auditor from doing his job. The auditor liked the stock market so I talked stocks with him all day.

One of the rules of that time was that no job could make over a certain percent profit, I don't recall the number. One of the uses of reports was to make sure the costs stayed as high as possible. If costs were not not high enough exempt employees would be charged directly to jobs.

Jobs could have a profit limit but the company overall could have any level of profit.

This company built behemoths for the military. There was a jeep and trailer that could go in water and swamps. The problem was that the pump switches would short out before the pumps would run.

There was a napalm tank that worked fine on a paved lot in upstate New York. In the field the tanks got stuck and could not be reloaded or refueled. I heard they were all abandoned.

The CEO came and went in a really long chauffeured limousine.

Part of my time was with the subsidiary robot manufacturer.

As soon as I finished my initial hiring commitments I left.

I get a data processing management offer.
I was offered a job as head of data processing at an old line manufacturer.

Everything looked good. Cheri and I liked the area and the job would be great.

We found a Better Homes and Gardens type house in a small town on the water.

I went to the local bank to see about a mortgage. The loan officer was already aware of my existence and asked if I was to be the new data processing manager at the factory. I told him no and I left.

A paternalistic employer I did not need.

Cheri was disappointed but she understood. We went home.

A sad point in growing up is when you have to start making one of two or more mutually exclusive choices. Not choosing is choosing.

With many children I have had to be the bearer of this news many times.

Jean Paul Sartre wrote a book on that subject. *Condemned to Freedom* was the title.

A great deal of effort is done by mankind in all walks of life and business to eliminate freedom by choice and not just by force.

When man is thrown into the world he becomes responsible for everything that he does.

Some say that Sartre spoke that way because he was an atheist and viewed that we are all alone.

As a Christian I see it somewhat the same way. God has a plan for each of us but we can refuse and can choose to do nothing or choose a way that is not in God's plan.

Many times I have wondered what would have happened if I had made different choices than what I actually made.

This old line manufacturer thing was one of them. There have been many others. I can see so much good for us that could have come from that move.

The job itself would have been great. I know we would have lost much that I could not yet see.

During the interview and house-hunting phase we stayed at the Mattapoisett Inn in Mattapoisett, Massachusetts, and got a good taste of the area. New Bedford, Fairhaven, Mattapoisett, Marion, Wareham, and on up to Cape Cod.

Have I had many regrets? Many for sure. Frank Sinatra sang that

"Regrets? I've had a few. But then again too few to mention."

There are two kinds of regrets.

1. Of what was done that should not have been done.

2. Of not taking a different choice than the one taken, albeit a good choice, that was taken when there were other good alternatives. This is the one that bugs us all. What if we had gone a different path? Would we then regret not taking the choice that we did take? I can look now at my children and grandchildren and know that with just slightly different decisions the family would not have ended up the same as it did. I believe that the Lord is involved in every choice and decision that we make, good or bad, and that His will becomes true. This belief is an element of the faith life.

"And we know that all things work together for good to them that love God, to them who are the called according to his purpose." Romans 8:28 KJV

I become a teacher and an adjunct professor.
I taught a class in data processing at a high school.

I was also a counselor with Junior Achievement. Young people would learn business by starting their own stock company.

I was an adjunct professor at a private college. I resigned after an accusation of racial discrimination by one student.

I had announced in advance that there would not be any makeups for the final exam. That was acceptable and common practice. All the students were there except for the one black student. The exam time was 5:00 PM.

She made a complaint that I gave her an F because she was black.

Her evidence was simply that none of the other students, all white, got an F.

Grades for each class were posted on the office doors.

At a meeting with her, me, and the Dean I asked her why she did not come to the exam.

She said her car would not start. Yet, the next morning it had started.

I determined that she lived about a mile from the school.

Buses ran regular routes on that street. She said she did not know how to ride the bus. Same with taxis.

She had no friend that could drive her.

Walking the one mile on a sidewalk on a very safe street was not acceptable though she seemed physically fit.

She had no excuse for not working something out even though she had all day to do so.

To avoid escalation I was ordered to give my one black student a final exam makeup. I gave her the same exam that others took at a time convenient for her. No added pay.

The sad thing is that today that the victim mentality has gone way beyond what it was at that time. Many folks, white and black, do not realize that they are in bondage with that attitude.

CHAPTER 8: DICTAPHONE

"Every organization has an allotted number of positions to fill with misfits." - Anonymous.

I become a programmer analyst at Dictaphone.
I went to Dictaphone initially at the Norwalk, Connecticut computer center. It functioned as a staff department that in effect was like its own business with one customer.

I transfer to the Bridgeport factory.
I went to the Bridgeport factory as Director of Systems Development. I was in the third floor ivory tower on mahogany row with the two top division execs and a shared secretary. If there had been a published organization chart I would probably have been in a staff position of the president of the Dictaphone Division, 99% of the of the entire company operation.

The programmer that saved me some time.
The programmers and system analysts in Bridgeport reported to me. As a good manager I met with each of them one on one when I started work there. One of the programmers came in, shook my hand, and sat down.

"Can I call you Dave?" he asked.

"Of course, that's my name."

"Dave, I can save you some time."

I waited eagerly for what he had for me.

"I've been here a long time. I know exactly what you are going to say. I have seen men in your position come. I've seen them go. I see you come. I'll see you go. I do my job and I do what I'm told to do. I don't work nights. I don't work weekends. I come in about 10 or 15 minutes late every day. I may stay until five. I may leave 30 minutes early. I don't get stressed. You may want to fire me. I won't take it personally. Likewise I hope you don't take it personally when you find out that you can't fire me. I get a raise every year no matter what. It's not that I have someone protecting me."

"At this company, someone that doesn't rock the boat is what to be. You go getters are the ones that don't make it. One good thing you should like is that you will see that I am not out to get your job. I don't want it or the pay."

The cheerful lady.
While I was staff, I did make line decisions. In one case I halted production of a new product because of a problem that had been discovered that would have resulted in defective products. At the point in the flow where the problem was first spotted there was this really exuberant, always cheerful woman. I always admired her attitude. I did not have to say anything but I did.

"I'm sorry we have to do this. I know you've put in a lot of work on assembly so far."

With a smile she burst my balloon.

"That's ok. As long as I get paid, I don't care."

I was the go to guy.
At Dictaphone, as I had been at other places, I was the go to guy for quick and creative solutions to any problem. One time the U. S. Marines had an urgent need for a certain part for an obsolete product. No parts were available. The problem was turned over to me.

"We must have one of those in the museum. If we have one, take the part out of that machine and test it. If it works ship it no charge," was my reply.

Despite the urgency, the Marines returned it as there was no purchase order. In working out the purchase order, the Marines could not accept a free product. The sales department wanted to know what they should do. They needed a price. I made a quick guess.

"Charge them $10."

A purchase order came in and the item was shipped, accepted, and billed. Case closed? Not quite. The Marines never paid so I told the accounts receivable department to write it off as a bad debt.

The timekeeping system that was not because of the union.
At Dictaphone, one of my projects was to automate the timekeeping function. There were three timekeepers that would be displaced. Finally we were ready to implement the project where employees would use a card and would key in a job number and push a button for either start or stop. The time was automatically entered from the internal clock. Data would be uploaded to the computer. It was expected that this would be a sensitive issue with the union because it meant timekeeper layoffs. The division president led the supervisors and managers orientation. Just as he got started, one of the sweepers, who was there because he was the Union Local president, interrupted. He, perhaps the

lowest ranking employee in the company, called the division president, the highest ranking employee, by his first name, in the presence of all the supervisors and managers. He said "there is no way in hell this system will be used here." He walked out of the meeting. He was right. There was a grievance and a strike threat. We in management spent most of our time in union grievance meetings.

One of the timekeepers had other duties at the factory.
One of the three timekeepers to be eliminated wore fine clothes and shoes. His watches were the best and he had diamond rings. Every afternoon at three when the factory let out I could look out the window of my office and see this man delivering cigarettes, liquor, TVs, and other costly items from his Cadillac. He was also a bookie, a functionary for illegal gambling at every factory.

My turn to order the liquor for the annual management-labor ball game.
It came my time to buy the liquor for the annual management-labor softball game and picnic. My boss smiled as he told me. He wished me luck. I sent a bid request to one of the factory workers, a union member of course, who owned a liquor store, and who always provided the beer and liquor. I also sent a bid request to two other liquor stores. The employee barged into my office, threw down the bid request, and demanded to know what was happening. I told him we would take the lowest bidder. He left without taking the bid request. He filed a grievance and it went to arbitration. It was determined that supplying the beer and liquor, at whatever his price, had become his job and could not be taken away. I was not faulted for handling it the way I did even though it failed. It became a point of amusement for all of us. None of the other managers, including the division president, had ever had the guts to try getting bids.

The other Jean Tierney.
There was one secretary for the three of us on mahogany row, an old battle ax, yet nice and professionally well qualified, named Jean Tierney. With all male execs there was a protocol for coffee where a secretary had to get the coffee. Here was a case where I did not have the guts to try anything different. Jean kept making a fuss that I wanted three sugars and cream. She challenged me to try black coffee for two days and said I would never go back if I did that. I took the challenge. She was right. From that point it has always been black coffee for me.

Acquisitions.
I was involved with acquisitions as I had been so involved with Litton Industries corporate consulting.

GrayArc.
GrayArc did what was called crash-printing. It made multi-part forms with

carbon paper. Crash-printed bills of lading was the main product.

The presses would print the customer's name, address, and phone number and the impact would make the impression from carbon paper onto the following pages.

GrayArc operated as a mail order company.
A company might order from a direct mail ad and send a check with order.

GrayArc would send a formal invoice marked paid. The customer might pay that. GrayArc would send a credit invoice marked as such and with a different color. The customer might pay that.

I made the discovery that a GrayArc employee had set up a separate bank account in the company name for these overpayments.

If a customer asked for a refund the employee would write a check for the refund from that bank account. Those transactions were not on the company records. From time to time he would withdraw in cash from the account. When we fired him there was quite a bit in the account.

The industrial help company.
Another acquisition was an industrial help company in Canada. I made several trips to Canada. I learned plenty about that industry. What is most important to know is that the industrial help business requires a lot of cash. Employees must be paid weekly. Invoices are sent to customers weekly, after the employee has worked. So there was another week plus a few days to bill and mail. The invoice is not paid until at least 30 days after receipt of invoice, often longer. Cash flow is a reason that many companies use an industrial help company. I learned something else about business.

Some people get paid daily, some weekly, some bi-weekly, some monthly. There are some that get paid annually. The highest pay goes to those that can wait several years. The lowest pay goes to those that get paid daily. Frequency of pay is not the same as rate of pay. Billing by the day can be quite high for consultants and other specialists yet they do not get a daily check of course.

I consider moving me and my family to Canada.
I did not have much time for sightseeing but liked what I saw in the old part of the city. During the Vietnam war I had contemplated going to Canada. So while I had the opportunity I pursued the idea of looking for a job and moving. In retrospect, I made a mistake in not involving Cheri enough in this idea. It started looking like there would be long daily hour, seven day work weeks.

I should have stopped looking right then.

Job interview process.
Interviews for computer professionals were often done on weekends, in both the U.S. and in Canada. I had such weekend interviews a number of times. The interviews were done by headhunters that were the real employer as so much was done by contractors. During the week, interview scheduling was totally unpredictable for systems developers. Since I had made the decision to accept the transfer to New York City without involving my wife, a decision to move to another country should be no different.

How husbands got new jobs.
At that time husbands would plan and develop their careers separate from their family. I saw that happen when I was growing up. I remember my father leaving one morning around 7:30 AM as usual. Before noon he made a call and told my mother to call a moving company. After leaving home, an opportunity in another state had presented itself and he had accepted it. He had even sold the house in that four hours before he called home. While I can be criticized for saying this, I believe that God prepares men for all events. Being able to sell the house quickly is one of those events. It was also not the first time that this quick house sale had happened with my father.

The seller of the industrial help company.
The seller of the industrial help company was a married couple in late middle age, no children left at home, that lived in an English-speaking suburb. They told me I could stay at their home and use their address while doing job search. They were winding down and unloading as much as possible. I was instrumental in making the company sale go through. I did a few things at the industrial help company on my personal trips. If I had time on a Saturday, I could talk with the staff about transition problems. I could tweak a program I had developed for them on a programmable calculator. I did have a Canadian work visa, not quite the same as a green card in the U.S., yet one that allowed short term work. I also had gotten a Canadian social insurance card right after leaving the Peace Corps. It would have allowed me to get started if I found a job and did allow me to look for work. That impressed the potential employers.

The Fall party.
In the Fall the couple had an outdoor party for clients and ex-clients. The party arrangements were quite simple. It was all outdoors in the backyard. There was an inflatable rubber boat with ice, beer, and soft drinks. There was a round metal wash tub over a fire with boiling water and corn. That was it. I met one most interesting character at that party. He was an itinerant operator of swiss style screw machines. He had been working while in school and had experience with the swiss style screw machine, a machine for making small parts. He

wanted to travel. Blueprints are language independent and there were always jobs available worldwide. The pay was way above average everywhere. There was no learning curve so he could be productive immediately. He could arrive in a city, immediately get a job, and leave when he was ready for another place.

When the winter came I lost all interest in moving to Canada. The snow was unbearable. In the city as soon as snow approached all vehicles had to be removed from the streets. Towing would occur before the first flakes fell. Snow was not just plowed. It was removed and melted or dumped into the river. Even the sidewalks were cleared. Snow plowing was organized like a military operation. There were zones with zone commanders. Each piece of equipment was scheduled for doing its part. There was no waiting for the snow to stop. Removal began very early in a storm.

In retrospect it was a different work culture in Canada than I knew in the United States. It was also a different culture in so many other ways. I did not care for the food in restaurants except for the chain barbecue restaurants that were all chicken. I began to see that leaving the United States would not work for my family.

Brother André.
The most visible building in Montreal is on Mount Royal. Built at the top of the mountain is St. Joseph's Oratory. It is a big concrete building, quite unlike most Roman Catholic churches. St Joseph's Oratory is an outgrowth of the healing ministry of Brother André, André Bessette, C.S.C., now Saint André of Montreal since his canonization, a lay brother of the Congregation of Holy Cross (no "the"). Many thousands of miraculous healings have been attributed to his prayers and anointing with oil. At St Joseph's there are piles of crutches and wheelchairs. Brother Andre's story is most interesting. I have read it several times. I enjoyed visiting St Joseph's Oratory. I bought books in the gift shop.

The return on investment fad.
During my time in the big company world, there were at least two fad things that I saw happen, return on investment was adopted and accounting firms went into consulting.

Return on investment, ROI, sounds good. It is the net earnings divided by value of investment or capital employed, multiplied by 100. ROI can be calculated for a whole corporation. It can be calculated for one machine. It can be calculated for a product line. It does require that there be a way to know the value of the investment.

I have calculated ROI where there is a new machine that will cost a certain amount. While that will not make money it can save money which is the same thing. A $1 million machine is estimated to save $100,000 per year.

One manufacturing client of mine was famous for saying to his management staff:

"When you tell me about savings, I want to know their names."

So if the savings is people, you need to know not just salaries and wages but all related costs. You also need to know the depreciation on the new machine, energy usage, insurance, etc. If all that is included in the example above, then the return on investment is ten percent.

It is also true that as investment amount goes up the ROI goes down. As the investment amount goes down the ROI goes up. Here the problems begin. If you sell an asset and lease it back, the investment goes down and expenses go up. The ROI may go up or it may go down. It is quite likely that the ROI will go up. Is sale and leaseback what you really want to do? It often was a poor move to sell an asset but the game had to be played.

Accounting firms go into consulting.
The treasurer of one of my clients was directed to have a consultant study the telephone system for the company. Hiring the long-term CPA firm was the safest thing he could do, safest for his job of course. The cost of the study was $50,000, done by the same people that did the audit. The study report was quite lengthy. The results can be summarized quite simply:

- Get a new switchboard while the old one still works. At the time switchboards were already on the way out.

- Remove all unused telephone extensions in the factory.

- Get an 800 number for incoming and outgoing long distance calls.

How I made an investment and cut costs.
In the early days automation was mainly used to replace people.

I set out to automate a stand-alone spare parts inventory division at Dictaphone.

I met with the salesman from a reputable computer company. I knew him already from the Data Processing Management Association.

"How many girls do you have in the office now managing the inventory?"

"Nine," I replied. "OK, so you'll need nine terminals, maybe ten."

"Three" I said. "What will the other six girls do?" he asked.

"Look for a new job" I replied. "Otherwise we don't need a computer."

I meet Cal.
Shortly before leaving Dictaphone, I met Cal, a salesman that called. Since his product was an oddity he was sent to me.

Cal had a product that was a dedicated computer with a small tv as monitor. The purpose was to calculate Economic Order Quantity, EOQ. The formula involved a square root and was not easily done. His machine had big square buttons to go to an input field for each of the three variables, demand, order cost, and carrying cost. Use them to set up an EOQ formula:

- Demand: The demand, in units, for the product for a specific time period usually annual.

- Ordering cost: Ordering cost per purchase order.

- Carrying cost: Carrying costs for one unit. Assume the unit is in stock for the time period used for demand.

Note that the ordering cost is calculated per order. The carrying costs are calculated per unit. The formula for economic order quantity: Economic order quantity = square root of (two x demand x ordering costs) ÷ carrying costs.

CHAPTER 9: I GO OUT ON MY OWN

"Charge for value added and not for your costs incurred." - David Newton Sneed.

How I became a business owner.
The merger of Dictaphone, input word processing, and Wang Laboratories, output word processing, was not to be though the stockholders of both companies would have benefitted. The two boards could not agree on the name of the new company.

I decided it was time to fulfill my dream of being on my own.

Shortly after I left, my boss at Dictaphone, with whom I had stayed in contact, noted how happy I was to be out of the corporate world. He resigned as the division president and moved his family to Orleans, Cape Cod to the Community of Jesus. It was not a cult but was a neighborhood of like-minded Christians of a variety of denominations, mostly Episcopalian.

Each family owned their own home though did have a sign on their lawn with a biblical name and the connection with the Community of Jesus. My old boss took a job in a hardware store selling wood stoves.

I visited a few times and was impressed with what I learned about the community. The residents bought an old garbage truck and took turns collecting garbage and making dump runs. I met Peter Marshall Jr, son of the well known author and U.S. Senate chaplain. Peter Jr and David Manuel, had co-authored a book, *"The Light and the Glory."*

The Mad Duck.
I took our oldest son on one of those visits to the Community of Jesus. We also attended an event at Yarmouth Port on the north-side of Cape Cod, next to Barnstable, sponsored by John DeBrine of Songtime Radio. Songtime was a long-time favorite car radio program of mine. We ate at a place in Barnstable called The Mad Duck that was owned by a man named Raymond Chaplin from Florida. We stayed at a motel nearby.

My business.
My business was two fold. I was developing customized minicomputer software for small, owner-operated business. Since they needed continuous forms, invoices and checks, I also designed and sold forms. I had no experience with minicomputers. For that matter, no one else had that experience.

At that time the computers had no ability to index data. It's one thing to enter data. It's another to find it and get it out. There has to be a way to take a data key, such as customer number, and using just the data key find the record on the disk drive. At its simplest the key plus some fixed number can locate the sector. In practice there must be a way to find locations where the key can be alphanumeric or a combination. Data needs to be reorganized over time and the locations can and do change.

I started my own business. As differentiation I wanted to find a way to simulate tacit information with explicit code. There was a need in regard to customers and inventory as well as for business philosophy. As just one example, I wanted to dispel the fallacy of :

"I can write it off."

I did not know much about owning a business. I ended up taking on too much business. I had one employee.

I could not find others with the same drive that could learn coding and keep up a schedule at the same time.

One man wanted to work with me but required $23,000 a year, no weekends, no late nights, paid vacation, paid medical insurance, and some other benefits. I suggested he take over the business and I would work for him.

I tried having an office over a deli in Sandy Hook, sharing with the man that had designed the computer language that I was using. Next step for an office was to remodel the garage. A nice job was done by an Italian contractor. Ahead of schedule and at the price quoted. The neighbor had asked him what he and his men were doing. He had told them that "we make-a some-a repairs."

Some years later as I moved into other things one of our associates took over that business. She needed a job and I wanted to avoid any conflict of interest in new ventures and new business relationships. The future was limited in what we had initially set out to do. No more custom-written software for mini-computers in small business. I had no formal business plan when I started out and little capital.

What I did have was confidence that I could do anything if I worked hard enough.

I decided not to develop computer hardware.
I got some initial publicity in the Danbury News-Times. I had been doing some work in exploring whether or not I wanted to go into making hardware. That effort started at Dictaphone when it could be seen that the future would not be

in mainframe computers. I had looked at how I could piece together components. I had known that in the early days of cars that some car companies simply bought parts, even sub-assemblies such as engines, from one place and frames from another. They might have a body design and would job that out. I could see computers going the same way.

Radio Shack introduced the TRS-80, also known as the Trash 80. Data storage was on an audio tape drive. The package cost was $599 that was equivalent to about $2,600 in 2017. 10,000 units sold the first month. I considered the possibility of writing software for the TRS-80 but I could see that there was going to be a market problem. I could see that level of expectation was going to rise rapidly. A business might buy a computer to do a certain thing. Small business had no knowledge of what automation of their processes meant. As time passed they would want more things, obvious things. They believed that they always had wanted those things. Rising level of expectation became my nemesis.

The doctor that wanted a good payroll computer program.
Radio Shack had come out with a simple payroll program for the TRS-80 computer that cost $10, delivered on audio tape. One day I got a call from a doctor. He had bought the Radio Shack payroll program and found that it did not do everything he wanted. He did not understand software but he understood payroll. Everyone understands payroll. He wanted a new program written from scratch. He would be willing to pay $50, even $60 if need be.

"Doctor, can I ask you a question?"

"Sure" he said.

"How much do you charge for an office visit?"

"Usually $65 if it is not too complex a problem."

"Doctor, how do you think I, as a professional, could find out what you want a program to do, then write it and deliver it for less than you charge for an office visit?"

"How much would it cost?"

"Maybe $4,000 if you don't keep asking for more features. I wouldn't do it now even for that because I do not have time."

There was a huge disconnect. I had enough experience with COBOL and I knew how long it would take. Payroll programs end up costing much more than

$4,000. Remember that this was 1976.

The doctor that wanted to further his education.
One of my associates at DPMA had to have some fairly simple surgery. At one doctor's visit before the surgery the doctor found that he was in the computer business. He asked my associate for the name of a good book he could read so he could set up a computer system on his own. He told me that he was amused and put out at the same time by the doctor's request. He asked the good doctor if he could tell him the name of a good book so he could do the surgery himself.

I selected the Wang 2200.
I went into marketing the Wang 2200.

From the Dictaphone project I already knew all I needed to know. Actually marketing was not the right word. Order taking might be it. An even better word might be cashing checks that were thrust into my face.

A Wang 2200 package sold for $17,000 in 1976, $72,000 in 2017 dollars.

It had 16K of memory, a hard-wired operating system, two 0.25 megabyte floppy disks, one monitor, and a printer. Just the computer, no software. A maintenance contract was extra.

Wang could not make computers fast enough. Level of expectation rose before the software was all written. Xerox, in their Diablo Division, came out with a removable hard drive. The fixed platter was 1.25 megabytes. The removable platter was 1.25 megabytes. Total storage was 2.5 megabytes. This unit cost an added $10,800, $40,500 in 2017 dollars. Maintenance was $180 per month, $608 in 2017 dollars. Xerox could not make them fast enough. It was a wild time.

At that same time a new Mercedes Benz sedan with a diesel engine sold for $10,400. I know because I bought one.

A computer with no provable benefit cost almost as much as two brand new Mercedes Benz cars.

I get really busy.
Very rapidly I became swamped with business. I would work late, maybe skip dinner, maybe get in a hamburger, then sleep for a few hours or drive to my next call and be working when the staff came in to work. That was the nature of coding and it still occurs today. All of the apps, websites, and order processing requires coding and debugging. If anything it was easier years ago when we used the one for one languages where we had to code multiplication and division and we had to code rounding. One programmer command for

each computer instruction. Tedious but fun.

I was the first third party reseller for Wang Laboratories. It was totally informal as Wang had not thought too far ahead and thought that computers could be marketed the same way as calculators. They thought that small business owners could be handled the same way as engineers in large companies. When I made my first sale, two Wang salesmen that I did not know got a commission without any involvement in the sale.

I had keys to two Wang service facilities. I could get repair parts on weekend and late at night. That was a help to service in the early days of Wang and computers.

My sales were all turnkey where I also wrote the software. At first, I did not have a Wang computer of my own so the customers allowed their new computers to be delivered to me.

Later I was able to transfer the software into an Advanced Revelation database on a PC when PCs became became better and cheaper than a Wang computer.

I used what I call heuristic design. I bypassed formal system specs.

My experience from big companies was that the real purpose of system specs was to protect the data processing department. Users did not know what they wanted but a system had to be produced. System specs took time and were ultimately worthless. As things progressed the level of expectation would rise.

With small business I took the position that I was the expert and would do whatever it took to make the result be what they wanted.

To help for the future I developed reusable code. Not the same as reusable modules.

As I started working with small businesses I might do a write-up of what the end results would be. Often it was all verbal. I would try to understand their business, code what I thought would work, make a basic functionality, and then upgrade it as needed. I designed and coded many small business systems in BASIC and in Advanced Revelation, both character based languages.

Key to all of this was operating on a project basis that has allowed me the ability to have many overlapping positions.

I am a proponent of defining many jobs in that format and know how to make it work.

Another son is born.
We named one son after the man that sailed alone around the world in a small sailboat. What made it helpful to explain to those that did not know of that sailor is that either the next month or the following month after our son was born the *Reader's Digest* had an article about the sailor.

Many years later, I found a replica of his boat in South Carolina and had contemplated buying it and sailing to England. Many so-called replicas of the boat have been made and later been made available for sale. Unfortunately most of them are nowhere close to being a replica.

Our son finds the wheel to the boat.
When that son was maybe eight years old he went with me to a Rotary club meeting at a yacht club. While I was talking with some folks prior to the meeting our young son came over and pulled on me to come see something. The wheel from the boat that went around the world was in the lobby, a donation from the man that made the trip.

We almost lost our new son.
His birth was fine.

However he soon began to lose weight and he threw up a lot. The doctor did not seem to know what to do. We realized that he was not going to live much longer if something was not done.

I did some research at the library. No internet at that time.

It seemed to me that he might have what is known as pyloric stenosis, a condition where a stomach valve has not opened. It was a fairly common condition primarily in first born males, though he was not the first.

The doctor was offended when I asked him about this.

I consulted another doctor that wanted to do immediate surgery, a simple procedure that only took a few minutes.

This new doctor was not a doctor at that hospital.

After some argument, full details I do not recall except that I told the hospital that the lawsuit I would file in the event of our son's death would be heavily publicized, that doctor was permitted to operate. Problem solved and only a small scar after a 20 minute procedure.

A trip to Cairo, Egypt.
I was in Cairo, Egypt. The streets are very crowded. Suddenly a man was in my face nose to nose as Egyptians do. He had grabbed the lapel of my sport coat, the one that had my Rotary pin.

"I see you are a Rotarian."

He smiled at me.

"Would you come as my guest tonight at my club in Heliopolis?"

Heliopolis is a connecting suburb. I went and it was great except the meeting was mostly in Arabic. There was some English. I was introduced, banners were exchanged, and I got a make-up card.

I visit Commodore Computer.
Around the time that one of our children was due, I made a 24 hour trip to California to meet with Jack Tramiel of Commodore Computer regarding taking over parts and service and locating that in New England. An associate that ran a computer store went with me. He had never travelled much and I upset him somewhat when he became concerned about details.

I rent a car in San Francisco.
I had intentionally not reserved a rental car before we left home. We had a stopover in Chicago where I called and asked for the cheapest car they had. When we arrived in San Francisco we found that they had no cheap cars available. They would give us a Thunderbird for the same price.

The birth of a daughter.
We did not know exactly when the baby would be born. Cheri and I worked out details for in case the baby came while I was away. A neighbor had an ambulance at home and could quickly take Cheri to the hospital. As it happened I was in San Francisco when our next daughter was born. I got a late evening call before my flight for home left. Because of the time difference I knew the birth details about her the day before she was born!

Jack Tramiel.
Jack Tramiel was an interesting character. He had lived in the Auschwitz camp in Nazi Germany when he was a small child.

He had come to the United States and had opened a typewriter repair shop.

He had started Commodore Computer.

Later he sold that when he bought Atari from Warner. Warner could not make a profit. Jack and his sons came in and quickly turned things around.

Their first official act was to fire everyone in customer service. It was a costly bureaucracy. The new customer service model was vastly different.

There were two Atari products, let's call them Model 1 and Model 2. If either model went bad it was either in warranty or not in warranty. If a Model 1 came back the owner would get a new one at no cost if it was in warranty, could pay a certain price and get a new one if it was not in warranty, or for a certain price upgrade to a new Model 2.

If a Model 2 came back the owner would get a new one at no cost if it was in warranty, or could pay a certain price and get a new one if it was not in warranty.

The manufacturing cost was so low that it was not worth the time to repair. All returns were junked.

No one in service had recognized that it might be more economical to throw it away.

At the Commodore office, the secretary told us to make our presentation as rapidly as possible as Jack could rapidly absorb what was said.

She told us that he might be opening his mail while we talked and not to get upset.

We had our meeting with Jack and with Chuck who was the brains behind the Commodore computer.

The idea did not work out.

Dinner in Sausalito.
We were scheduled to take the red-eye flight that left San Francisco about midnight. I had wanted to go to a certain restaurant in Sausalito. We went into the lobby and the place was packed. There would be a long wait. My associate was downcast. We went out to the parking lot where there was a pay phone. I called the restaurant and asked for a table for two.

"When would you like your table?"

"How about five minutes from now?"

"Your table will be ready."

We walked back in past the crowd, were shown to our table, and had a great meal. I know that there can be mixed reaction to these and other types of action.

One thing I had learned from Jim Rohn back in Atlanta was that there were natural laws, laws other than legislation by government. He had said that laws are how things work. He said that our success was based on knowing the laws and knowing how to apply the laws.

How I got a classic framed print of George Washington.
We visited many bookstores and antique stores. At one new book store in Vermont, a new but quaint building of rustic pine lumber, there was a classic framed print of George Washington hanging on the wall, the print of the painting with the big white area near the bottom. The frame was simple oak. I think it was probably made as a school item. I asked the man at the register how much he wanted for George. He quickly answered that it was not for sale. Just as quickly he said:

"Wait a minute. Let me ask my partner."

He went in the back room and soon came out. He named a price that I thought was fair.

"We figure that we are in business to make sales, not to run a museum," he said.

That was a most succinct vision statement. I'm sure the store became a success.

I still have the print on the wall in our bedroom in Wyoming.

We collect certain books.
Cheri and I became collectors and avid readers of books by Joseph C Lincoln, E. Phillips Oppenheim, George Barr McCutcheon, and Horatio Alger. These authors were all early 20th Century. Oppenheim and McCutcheon were British, the others American.

The Joseph C. Lincoln novels had something unique.

On the very last text page, in parentheses, is usually a number.

That number is the edition. If there is no number it is a reprint from a publisher such as A.L. Burt.

At the end of 2018, with all duplicates gone forever, our inventory of these special author books is:

- 45 - E Philips Oppenheim

- 8 - George Barr McCutcheon

- 27 - Joseph C Lincoln

- 46 - Horatio Alger

- 16 - Elbert Hubbard with no relation to L Ron Hubbard and his books.

- 13 - Assorted other.

The New Tenant.
Cheri uncovered an E Phillips Oppenheim book from 1910 that I did not know we had. *The New Tenant.* Like other Oppenheim books, it includes a litany of woes of the very wealthy, woes that interfere with their occupation of spending. Already by page 5, Guy Davenant Thurwell of Thurwell Court, Northshire has a problem. He had decided to rent out a house on his property known as Falcon's Nest that was on a cliff overlooking the sea. The first applicant to rent the house was someone that he did not like. Thurwell would not rent to that man but did not wish to offend him. The second applicant is a stranger. Thurwell and his daughter were trying to make a decision. With regard to the stranger:

"How do I know that Brown isn't a retired tallow chandler or something of that sort?"

Oppenheim's characters rarely hold a job of any kind or otherwise make any of their own money. It is all inherited from many generations back. They look down on anyone that deigns to earn money even if they have become incredibly wealthy from doing so. They believe that their money, which continues to grow even though they spend it very lavishly, differentiates their physical and mental abilities and their character from everyone else. They have incredibly creative ways of spending money and never regret a spending decision. When they stop for a snack it always starts with at least one or two bottles of Heidsieck or other French champagne while they wait for the caviar. They can never be accused of racism as they look down equally on everyone not in their little group of the wealthy English. Nevertheless they are lovable people.

The room that was right out of a Joseph C. Lincoln novel.
My favorite hotel was in an old house. There were no water views and the hotel was not on the water. The room I always requested was right out of a Joseph C. Lincoln novel. It was a small room with a fireplace. There was one single bed and a study area near the window. I would have my work papers all set out for early morning and for the evening when I returned. I also had books that I was reading.

A most interesting character was in a Joseph C. Lincoln novel.
Joseph C. Lincoln novels had many interesting characters. To Cheri, and later to me, the most interesting was Jedaiah in the novel *Shavings*.

Jedaiah means "Jehovah knows."

Jedaiah, spelled that way, originally came from the Bible in I Chronicles 24:7.

Jedaiah Winslow, nickname Shavings, made toy wooden windmills.
"This something was a toy windmill fastened to a white picket fence and clattering cheerfully as its arms spun in the brisk, pleasant summer breeze. The little windmill was one of a dozen, all fastened to the top rail of that fence and all whirling. Behind the fence, on posts, were other and larger windmills; behind these, others larger still. Interspersed among the mills were little wooden sailors swinging paddles; weather vanes in the shapes of wooden whales, swordfish, ducks, crows, seagulls; circles of little wooden profile sailboats, made to chase each other 'round and 'round a central post. All of these were painted in gay colors, or in black and white, and all were in motion. The mills spun, the boats sailed 'round and 'round, the sailors did vigorous Indian club exercises with their paddles. The grass in the little yard and the tall hollyhocks in the beds at its sides swayed and bowed and nodded. Beyond, seen over the edge of the bluff and stretching to the horizon, the blue and white waves leaped and danced and sparkled. As a picture of movement and color and joyful bustle the scene was inspiring children, viewing it for the first time, almost invariably danced and waved their arms in sympathy. Summer visitors, loitering idly by, suddenly became fired with the desire to set about doing something, something energetic."

The downside of my business.
The business I was in required being present at the client site. That meant a certain amount of travel that could not easily be monetized. Looking back I hated the travel. It was not even reasonably manageable while we were living in New England though much of the time I was home every night or every other

night. Multiple clients demanded the same time. Once we moved to North Carolina the conflict was even more with family time and work time as I was gone for a week or two at a time. Travel did have some interesting times.

The lady that wanted to buy a Bible.
Often I would get off the New Jersey Turnpike onto U.S. 1 to stop at a certain small Christian book store. I didn't buy very much but it was a break and a chance to pick up some good teaching quick. One night a woman was there to buy a Bible as a wedding gift. The clerk asked if she wanted a Protestant Bible or a Catholic Bible. There was a pause to think of an answer to an unexpected question.

"It doesn't matter. They won't be reading it. I just want something big and white for their coffee table."

I buy a set of tires on the New Jersey Turnpike.
Early one morning while it was still dark I stopped for gas while heading north. Gas stations are right on the turnpike and self-service is not legally allowed in New Jersey After paying for the gas with my oil company credit card the attendant said he said that he noticed that I needed new tires.

"I'll have it checked when I get home," I replied.

"We have tires and we can replace them right now," he said. "You'll be back on the road within a half hour."

"I don't know how much that would cost on the Turnpike," I said.

He pulled up a sheet that had each size tire and the various elements leading up to a total. All of the amounts were required to be itemized. There was the tire price, several different taxes, installation charge, disposal fee, and valve stems. Then there was the final total. It was a reasonable price.

"You can pay with that same card you used for gas." he said.

"Show me why you say I need tires," I replied. We looked and I agreed.

"The bay is empty," he said pointing to the garage.

"We've got two guys to work on it together."

"Let's do it," I said.

I had occasion to tell the manager that I was amazed at the honest service.

"We only hire good guys," he said. "He's one of our best."

30 minutes later I was back on the road.

My timing belt breaks.
Another trip was not so good. Again on the New Jersey Turnpike. Again headed north. My timing belt broke. I was able to get off the highway in the breakdown lane. A highway patrol car stopped. The patrolman was courteous and sympathetic. He said he would call a tow truck. He gave me a printed form showing the established and permitted tow rates.

It was not long before a tow truck pulled up in front of me. The driver came back, determined where I needed to go and wanted payment that was much higher than what was on the form. I showed it to the driver and he said he didn't know anything about those rates. I told him that I would wait for another tow truck. The driver went back to his truck and I could see the microphone in his hand as he was calling somewhere on the radio.

Minutes later another patrol car arrived. This patrolman was not so courteous. I showed him the form with the rates. He said that it was the old rates. I showed him the effective date that was in the same month and year.

His response was that there was a two hour limit and that if I was there after that time I would be arrested.

I paid that most exorbitant fee in cash as was required and was towed to a garage. I asked for a receipt and the driver said he did not have a receipt book with him. He would not use a blank piece of paper.

The repair did not take long and the price was fair.

The question might be asked about carrying cash.

The use of credit cards that we have come to expect is fairly new. Not that long ago, many places would not take cards for many reasons. For one a phone call had to be made to an approval center that might be busy or not open. A tow truck driver had no way to make a call.

Even in 2017 there are many cash only places.

One is Peter Luger in New York City, perhaps the best steak house in the United States and long in business. It is suggested by restaurant reviews that customers bring wads of cash.

I meet Bob Clarke of Mad Magazine fame.
Dining alone at the bar at a restaurant in Mamaroneck, New York, I met Bob Clarke, also dining alone, who I recognized as the original artist for the *Mad Magazine Spy vs Spy* series.

He drew a picture of the two spies, black and white, and autographed it for one of our sons.

I learned that Bob Clarke was a native of Mamaroneck.

Other Rye area restaurants.
I have never been a fan of spinach except for the sole florentine at a restaurant at the train station in New Rochelle, New York.

Another area restaurant I liked was in a house built in 1792 that was originally the home of James Fenimore Cooper, the author of books such as *The Last of the Mohicans*. It was called the Fenimore Cooper House for many years. The ambiance was great though the outside looked like it was falling apart. Now it is La Piccola Casa Ristorante. I'd like to give it a try. It features simple Northern Italian dishes.

Playland at Rye, New York.
A favorite place to visit was Playland at Rye, New York. Playland is an old amusement park now owned by Westchester County. There are some unique rides such as the Steeplechase, a merry-go-round that children are not allowed to ride due to the speed. There are gigantic old oak trees and a big median on the sidewalks on the Midway. The place is quite spacious and most elegant. Some of the Tom Hanks movie *Big* was filmed there. In a section of the park-like area is the grave of the guinea pig named Skipper, that was a favorite pet of one of our sons. Skipper passed away while we were on a trip.

Traveling fears.
I had many fears while traveling.

I started work at a client early and finished late as much as I could. I did this to avoid down time where I could regret that I was not at home.

While I was away I feared that I would not be able to get home. While driving the 10 to 12 hours home, I feared problems that would keep me from crossing all of the waterways.

When we lived in North Carolina, I would often arrive back very early on Saturday mornings. There was the pervasive smell of wood fires. Land was constantly being cleared for farming. Bulldozers would make huge piles of trees. As daylight was just coming, I would pass country bars that catered to the black population. I could see people sleeping on pool tables and some on the floor and the ground outside. After getting home there was the need to soon leave again. Moving back north helped some due to the nature of what I was doing, but created new problems.

I remember one time of a daughter, at maybe age three, looking at me like I was a stranger. I did not know what to do. All of my time was consumed.

Around the same time, I can remember being at the beach with the kids. One other daughter, when she was about three years old, was into the *Little Mermaid*. I pointed out a round rock on the edge of the surf. I told her she could be like the Little Mermaid.

She stood on the rock and adopted all types of standing positions.

The man with the great idea.
Fred owned a printing business that he started after leaving the printing equipment company where he had been a salesman. At the time he went into business the computer companies around Boston were just getting their start and could not make product fast enough. The computers and peripheral products needed manuals. The normal printing process was too slow. Fred simply advertised a 24 hour turnaround. Overnight he was swamped with business. He had a simple idea. Black ink on white paper 8 ½ by 11, stapled, and no separate cover. As engineering changes occurred and product features were added, manuals became obsolete rapidly. Give Fred a new master set with a revision date on the front and within 24 hours new manuals were ready.

How I was able to beat Fred at his own game.
One time Fred needed to pick up a car in Rhode Island that he had loaned to a Navy officer. He asked me if I had any idea on how best to do it. I suggested that we go down in his airplane. I would drive the car back. That we did. The officer dropped off the car.

Fred and I went to a restaurant in an old building on Bellevue Avenue downtown that is part of The Tennis Hall of Fame. It was Fred's idea to go to that restaurant, ironically not mine. Fred always loved to create events that would leave others guessing. As soon as we went into the restaurant, I saw a possible chance to leave him guessing. I had been to that restaurant just the day before and had gained some knowledge.

In the small lobby of the restaurant there was an elderly lady, very small and thin, extremely well dressed. She really stood out. As Fred and I stood there waiting for the hostess, I addressed the lady by name. I asked her about her sister. Then I asked her what time her bus was coming.

The hostess was ready to lead us to our table.

I politely bid the lady a good day and a goodbye. Fred was curious about how I knew the lady yet said nothing. He knew there was something to explain.

I did not tell Fred that I had been to that restaurant the day before with a prospect. Before we left the prospect was using the pay phone. While he was on the phone, I was talking to the same elderly lady. She had asked my name and I had asked for hers. Every morning she would visit her sister. After leaving she would go to that restaurant. She would sit on a bench by the window to wait for the bus.

On this next day after I met her I wanted to control the conversation so that Fred would hear and to make sure the lady could not bring up the coincidence of two days in a row.

How I almost outran Fred's airplane with a car.
On the way back to the airport I got an idea for something that I could do.

It was a little over 100 miles to Fred's house. I wondered if I might be able to get to his house before he did. It would be great because Fred loved to talk about the advantages of an airplane. I let him out. I slowly drove away. I did not want him to guess at my plan.

As soon as I got out of his sight I really took off.

I would have a head start because he still had to get in his airplane, start it up, and go through the take off process. He would have to fly to the airport in his town, go through the landing and shutdown process, then drive home. I drove as fast as I could while avoiding a ticket.

I got to his house and his car was there so he had beaten me.

I went in the house. Fred was sitting in the living room with a beer. His wife got me one. Neither of us talked of our trip back.

Before I left his wife told me that Fred had come in just seconds before me and was upset that I had gotten back so quickly compared to his flying.

Fred only went to his office a few hours a week. He had some interesting ways to save time.

He would weekly sign the expense reports from his salesmen. He would take one at random. He would take one small item, maybe mileage on one local trip. He would question the item. Fred had no idea what was the right answer. He would then ok it and tell the salesman to be careful in the future. He would ok all the other expense reports without reading them.

I meet Paul.
I met Fred's brother Paul, who lived in Europe. Paul owned the only house in his sea front town with a swimming pool, not just indoors, but on the second floor.

Paul had been the head of the human resources department for a large firm in New York at its headquarters. He had quit and started his own business. He would find top executives for start-up firms. He would take his fee in founder's shares of stock and would only bill for cash for expenses, that included travel, to interview prospects, wherever they might be situated.

Paul had phone numbers in foreign cities that would ring in his office in Los Angeles. He told me of one experience. He got a call from a man that had called Paul's number in Ireland that rang in Los Angeles. During the conversation Paul realized that the man that had called was in the same building as his office. He did not let on to this fact. The man was looking for an executive in Ireland.

The sunken ship owner.
John was the owner of a sunken ship. He had bought it from the insurance company for something like $1,200. He had made dives to the site twice. He had done documentation and writing about the ship.

Our oldest son would play ball with John's young son and daughter. I remember one time hearing John's daughter say to him, with quite a British accent,

"That's not fai-uh. You're not givin' a lit-tle girl a chonce."

How the brick manufacturer got rich.
I met a man that was a brick manufacturer. I was curious about how to differentiate in that commodity market and make any money. He did it by meeting all the young lawyers he could, giving campaign donations when they ran for the legislature, and then later getting no bid contracts with the state.

I go fishing on Georges Bank.
One of our sons and I went as crew on a 10 day fishing trip to George's Bank,

the main fishing area about 150 miles offshore. We went in an 85 foot commercial fishing boat owned by Eric. When dragging for ground-fish, the primary technique, there was two hours for dragging, pull up the net, and repeat. This was a 24/7 process. After the trip I went to a fishermen's hotel, got a room, and slept well. I was done in. Our son stayed until every fish was off the boat. He even helped some with the unloading. Then he joined me at the hotel, just across from where the fish were unloaded.

The Perfect Storm.
We were living in New England at the time of what was known as the perfect storm in the book and subsequent movie *The Perfect Storm.*

I knew all of the real characters depicted. One of the fishermen that went down was one of the people I had known. The movie character of Edith of the Crow's Nest looked just like Edith.

The movie was partially a comedy for fishing families. The stories of the people were exactly true but the fishing boat and related events were very incorrect for Hollywood's purpose. The Andrea Gail was a 72 foot, 92 ton sword-fishing boat. The movie boat was 103 tons. There is a big difference but the movie crew needed more room for the cameras and lights. The movie boat left in the early morning with the sun shining. Offshore boats leave at midnight for the eight to ten hour steaming to George's Bank. The movie boat turned on the ice-maker as it left. Boats stop on the way out to fill the hold with fresh water ice. The boat ice makers make salt ice because it is freezing salt water as a supplement. The fresh water ice keeps the salt ice off of the fish because salt ice burns the fish. The mixture of ice and salt creates a eutectic frigorific mixture which can get as cold as zero degrees Fahrenheit.

There is an internet phenomenon called the salt and ice challenge. People put salt on their bodies, usually on the arm, then hold ice on it. There is a burning sensation and the idea is to see who can bear it the longest. What is happening is that there are second and third degree injuries that can leave permanent scars.

The movie boat arrived in the day time. The real boats arrive around 4:00 AM to 5:00 AM.

The movie boat docked where the movie Crow's Nest had been built.

The real Crow's Nest is not directly on the water. It is across the street, a few hundred feet from the water.

The real boats dock at the dealer where they will unload and sell the fish.

The crew, except for the skipper, might go home. They come back later to get their pay for the trip.

Perhaps the funniest scene was when the boats return, the families of the crew are at the dock waiting for the meeting after the 10 day separation. No, second funniest.

The funniest scene might have been the group that was singing a hymn and no one's mouth was moving.

One of our sons had a slush cart.
One of our sons had a slush cart and made some good money.

He kept the cart and his freezer in the hallway of a large old waterfront building where we had our office.

I took my children on business trips.
From the time I started in my own business, I took one or more of our children with me whenever I could which was most of the time. I would take them directly to client locations. Only one client ever objected but he was not serious enough to say that I had to quit bringing children.

For me a big plus of being self-employed was that I could spend more time with my children though not all of them at once. There were many fun times, fun for me, and fun for the child or children with me.

One time when one of our sons was with me I had planned to take him to Sesame Place in Langhorne, Pennsylvania. He had wanted to go. I did not tell him in advance. We were in the parking lot and I kept his attention while I talked about Sesame Place. I asked him if he still wanted to go. He did.

"How about right now? I asked.

He was quite surprised.

I did the same surprise thing to that son at Muir Woods, the redwood forest near San Francisco. When I said let's go right now we were standing right beside a large redwood.

I did the same for others of the family.

Muir Woods was to me like our backyard. We went so many times over so many years.

January 16, 2018 things changed at Muir Woods. A reservation system and offsite parking with a shuttle was instituted. No more just arriving and visiting.

The best opportunity time for one of our sons was when there was free airfare for each child accompanying a paying adult. In first grade he missed 54 days before his school principal complained. He said that he might have to hold him back. Now this was a boy that had read and given oral reviews of 98 books before he started kindergarten. If he had been out sick it would have been excused.

"So if he had been home watching TV it would be excused but when he travels around the country going to museums, art galleries, plays, and historical sites it is viewed as hurting his education?" was my question.

That son did get to see a revival of *My Fair Lady* with the real Rex Harrison. He saw the revival of *The King and I* with the real Yul Brynner. Both shows on Broadway of course. He saw a number of other current Broadway shows. He said that the plays always started with "noise."

We saw *Stage Door Canteen* in New Haven before it went to Broadway.

He got to feed sea lions off the wharf in Monterey until it became illegal to do so under the Marine Mammal Protection Act. It was most interesting that sea lions naturally know how to jump for the food, the same as they do in the shows. The skill is not taught by the trainers.

One time in Rhode Island when he was with me there was an injured seagull in the street. I stopped and moved the bird onto the lawn and off the street. He made the comment "You ARE a good man!"

He often came up with creative quips. I told him we were getting onto the New Jersey Turnpike. We had to go around this large cloverleaf circle. He said:

"This sure is a turnpike."

At another time he said "Dad, you know how the Bible says that Adam named all the animals? I know this isn't real but I'm just saying it. Did he name one Joey, and another one Tom, and another on Alice and so on?"

That was good thinking. He was referring to a very literal reading of Genesis 2:19 linked to our modern world anthropomorphizing of animals.

"And out of the ground the Lord God formed every beast of the field, and every fowl of the air; and brought them unto Adam to see what he would call them: and whatsoever Adam called every living creature, that was the name thereof."

One time at a restaurant he had a question:

"What are articles?"

When I told him they were stories in a newspaper or magazine, he seemed quite confused.

Then he pointed out a sign that said: "Not Responsible for Lost Articles."

The French Quarter restaurant in Fort Lauderdale.
I think at one time or another I took all of the children to the French Quarter restaurant on 8th Avenue just off Las Olas Boulevard in Fort Lauderdale, Florida. The restaurant is now gone as there was a large high rise complex built on the site and around it. Any new building just would not have had the same ambience. When one son went to the French Quarter, he wanted catsup. They did not have catsup. The kitchen put together something similar from what they had. The most memorable thing about the French Quarter was that no one ever asked:

"Is everything ok?"

There was never a need to ask because everything was always ok. The waiters were elderly men and service was outstanding.

I considered getting an airplane.
It was at this time that I developed an interest in having an airplane for my travel. I got training in a Beechcraft Bonanza, not the normal airplane for learning. The reason I was getting training, that was at no cost, was the expectation that I would buy a Bonanza. For the distances I planned to travel that airplane made more sense than one with lower power and performance. I remember one day of touch-and-gos at the Winston-Salem, North Carolina airport with one son in the back seat. There were several things that finally did away with the airplane idea.

1. Thunderstorms, that occur all the time somewhere, could be a frequent disrupter of a week's work and travel plan especially if there were to be multiple stops.

2. What would I do when I landed late at night at a small airport? How would I find and get to a place to sleep? My instructor, the salesman, would sometimes pick me up in Manteo to the east, rather than

Edenton to the west. That meant an hour's drive east for me, then an extra hour flying west to pass over Edenton, as well as his extra hour flying from Edenton to Manteo. Airplanes have a high cost per hour as they must amortize engine overhaul, propeller overhaul, and fuel as well as fixed costs.

3. How much extra flying time might I incur on a regular basis with similar inefficient flights?

Later I was to find that for distance less than 900 miles, driving was often superior to flying. Cheri and I flew to Kansas City. The flight was delayed. After we landed we realized how far it was yet to go to the city. We figured that by driving we could have gotten there faster.

Some of my clients over many years.

- **Speaking engagements.**
  Many years ago, at the age of 15, I did my first public speaking at the Optimist Club oratorical contest in Colonial Heights, Virginia where I came in third place in a field of three speakers. Don't laugh. I did the speech and I did get the third place trophy. The first line of the speech we all gave was:

  "The speed of the leader is the speed of the gang."

  Since then, I have done plenty of speaking engagements that included a Digital Equipment Corp conference, Women in Insurance, Lions club, Rotary club, and commercial fishing conferences. I did some idea presentations for nonprofits and churches. There was one session at the Massachusetts Institute of Technology, Sloan School of Management.

- **Fresh fish dealer.**
  The system was DOS-based. Cal had been the initial contact as the result of a news article about him and his EOQ machine. I sold the system by demonstrating that I could make the computer count to ten on the screen. I painted the picture of everything being built on that simple step.

  The company controller wanted assurance that the payroll would always get done and on time. They had been using ADP, the payroll service bureau. I made him that promise. Payroll always got out on time. For the whole 36 1/2 years of that system, payroll was never missed even by one day.

Years in advance we knew the end was coming for DOS. We talked about a variety of options. Neither me nor the client wanted to rewrite the system for Windows. Microsoft finally announced it would no longer support DOS in Windows XP or in any future Windows version.

While not the best choice a switch was made to QuickBooks. The man that had been supporting their network and other hardware, a former plumber, took over the software with my blessing. There were many crashes as I predicted but the system kept running. For the long run I do not know what will happen. There may be a good P2P, procure to pay, system to come along. All other functions could continue to run well on QuickBooks.

I found that all of my clients in all industries felt that the system I wrote for them was the ultimate way of doing things. They felt that all I had to do next time for someone else was make a copy, sell it as is, and I could make a fortune with no added work.

This was always difficult to overcome. It also made it even harder to collect the final payment as they wanted to modify the contract so that they would get a percentage of all my future work.

I finally quit using licensing agreements. I told my clients about source code and object code. I showed them that with Wang there was no source code as such. I then told them that Wang had the ability to create object code and it could run the same but that I never used that option.

I told them that they could resell it anywhere they wanted but that I would not be responsible for any modifications.

I liked Wang Basic and Advanced Revelation, both running on MS-DOS. I could get a call from a client about a problem. I could see what was in memory and/or tell them how to fix the problem. I could even tell them how to fix the data on the disk. There is no way under Windows and other newer systems that any of that could be done.

A lot was happening in the fish industry and not just computerization. Fish stocks were declining. Government was setting fishing restrictions. Consumer demand was increasing

Fresh fish dealers with everything the same as their competitors had to find ways to differentiate or they would fail. Most of them have failed.

I was at the home of the owner of one of these dealers for a Christmas party. This man was in his seventies and had more money than he could ever spend. A customer called and desperately needed more fish. I could not hear the customer side of the phone call so I didn't know the customer, or if he had a restaurant or a store. I knew the customer apologized because the man said:

"Don't be silly. Don't apologize. This is my business. You can call me anytime."

He left his party to meet the customer. Customer service, especially in the supply chain, has many forms and it is not all online.

I was living in Connecticut the day I got a call that there had been a fire at a client fish dealer's office building. I immediately loaded up another computer and headed out. When I arrived the place was still smoking.

Everything in the office was gone but the computer. I was able to get it out into the parking lot. It still had the plastic cover on it that I told them to use every night. There was a lot of smoke damage.

I cleaned it all up and plugged it in. It still worked and continued to do so for several more years. We had to wait until the next day for the safe to be brought out from where it had fallen into the basement. The diskettes were in the safe. They were all ok. I was able to give them reprints of outstanding accounts receivable, payable and other reports.

- **The high tech micromanager.**
  I had a fish processing client, literally a "mom and pop" business that was run differently from what might be called normal. The husband and wife owners were heavily tattooed bikers. He sat at a counter near the front door that had a glass front reception area. He had a broadcast microphone sitting on the counter. There were cameras in the production area and in front of the restrooms. He would call out workers by name for various infractions such as talking or staying too long in the restroom. Everyone loved him anyway.

- **The identical fish business.**
  There was another fish business that was just like my first fish dealer client, relatives also. The products, customers, and suppliers were exactly the same.

We all thought that it would be easy to set them up on the same system. It was even agreeable that we use not only the software but the data files.

The system did not work for them. Not even close. How could that be? Why could an invoice for the sale of cod fish from two companies to the same customer not be exactly the same? It was a problem.

And it was not just billing. It was payroll, accounts payable, inventory, and general ledger. There was such a difference that it would mean a total rewrite and years of work.

Other programmers had the same problems.

- **Mailing list broker.**
An interesting business renting mailing lists. Every broker has the same lists at the same prices. A broker has to be good at picking which lists a mailer should test. The owner of this business started in a house and later built an office building. He had a sign in his office that said

"My enemies I can handle; deliver me from my friends."

What I noticed that was unusual was that all 35 employees calculated their own tax withholdings rather than use the tax tables. This was because all of them had circumstances of income that the tables could not handle. Many people in that part of the country have variable income from a variety of sources. They are on top of their tax situation. Since their income may not be subject to withholding they have to make quarterly estimated payments.

- **Book distributor to corporate libraries.**
I would not have taken this job if I had any choice.

I had told another client that he would quickly outgrow the computer he wanted to buy. I told him that if he had a buyer for the computer when he upgraded I would do the software.

The owner of that business was crazy and looked it.. Open front shirt with hairy chest, plenty of gaudy jewelry around his neck and on his wrists. Diamond rings on both hands. We would go to lunch in his Alfa Romeo, him smoking marijuana, speeding, running red lights, driving down the middle of the streets. On the shelf under the dash was enough marijuana to get us both sent away for a long time.

I told the owner that we would be doing inventory control. He smiled.

"Are you gonna tell ME about inventory control? Come here."

He showed me a framed newspaper article about his previous warehouse burning down under suspicious circumstances. He said:

"This is what I call inventory control."

I told the bookkeeper, a rather plump middle aged Italian woman, that I was ready to start accounts payable. I asked for the unpaid bills.

"Okay honey" she said wryly.

She got out a box full of bills.

"I want just the unpaid bills," I said.

"Honey," she said. "That's what this is. He don't like to pay bills."

McGraw-Hill and other large publishers at that time did not have systems that could track outstanding bills by customer.

I arrived as usual through the back door into the shipping and receiving area. He always used plenty of colorful language that I will not quote.

"Let me show you something."

An invoice from a publisher was in his hand. There was a shipping charge of about $150. Then he showed me the postage meter cost on the box. It was maybe $25.

"They made two mistakes," he said. "The first was to way overcharge me for shipping. The second was not to have signature required. When they call me for payment, I'll ask them where are my books?"

- **Flexible packaging manufacturer.**
I wrote a system for a flexible packaging manufacturer on a programmable calculator with an audio tape for storage. This system could quote toothpaste boxes with nesting on the sheets and could do plastic thermoforming. It could decide which press to use. It could quote three prices:

1. lowest acceptable price.
2. expected price
3. highest target price.

This company is a public corporation. I would often go in on weekends when the office was closed. There was an old man who came in and emptied the trash cans. He and I had conversations about many things. I later found out that he was the founder, the board chairman, and a majority stockholder.

- **Investors accounting CPA.**
This was a complex system for a large family whose primary investments were in a company where they were heirs. Together, all or a few, would make other investments together. This system could make the proper divisions of dividends. There were a large number of special conditions that kept coming up. My CPA client owned a roller skating rink. He told me what a great business it was. All cash income and the same labor no matter how busy or not busy. I do not like any kind of dishonesty. I asked him how he knew his employees were not skimming. Somehow he had not considered that possibility.

He bought a pinball machine for his home. The seller would only sell him one for that use. It could not be used at the skating rink. He was told that if it was used at the business, it would end up at the bottom of the river with him attached to it. Need I add that New York is quite a place to do business?

- **Commercial printer.**
I developed a mission critical system that did all of the accounting plus job quotes and job costing for a commercial printer.

One day the controller called me. She had a question, thought she knew the answer but wanted to run it by me. She asked if the computer could add to one employee's year to date taxes and subtract from another's? My immediate answer was no. I then said let me try to guess whose year-to-date went up and whose year-to-date went down. I was right. The year-to-date of the bookkeeper and her boyfriend in the factory went up while the year-to-date for several of the factory workers went down. I could name a few because I knew that they would open their pay envelope, take the check, then throw away the envelope and the pay stub. It was caught because the total increases in year-to-date did not equal the total year-to-date decreases.

The husband of the controller was a lawyer in New York City. One day, he and I were talking about Geraldine Ferraro's husband, John Zaccaro, who pleaded guilty to false statements on a mortgage loan application. He did withdraw the application. He was fined $1,000 and had to do 500 hours of community service. I think the borrowers had inflated their income on a mortgage application. This New York lawyer told me Zaccaro was probably the only honest real estate man in New York City. His real crime was being Ferraro's husband. She was running for vice president of the United States. He told me that in New York City the ethics of real estate could be written on the head of a pin and there would still be room for the Lord's Prayer.

I became the interim controller when the controller retired and moved into the City. I was not interested in taking the job on a permanent basis. I just did it until they found someone good.

Because of declining cash, there was a need to set up a cash plan and to informally run it by the creditors so they would know that we might be slow but they would get paid.

I suggested to the owners that they engage a regular CPA to oversee the accounting. They agreed and began interviewing accountants.

As it happened they brought in a CPA that I knew quite well and for whom I had done some work. He and I did not see eye to eye on many things. For one, he was a Jaguar owner. I, a Mercedes. He was an active Jew, I an active Christian. Nonetheless, I respected him in every way. I was in a bit of a dilemma. I knew he had the ability to sell himself on getting the job. At the same time I knew that he was most meticulous and honest. I felt that he would not fit what this company wanted. With our time alone together that day, I told him why. I told him that I had mixed feelings about the ethics of telling him. I could see it both ways. I was quite frank that maybe he and I were not the best of friends but that we could both still act professionally. I felt he might be asked to compromise his ethics. It was my idea to have a CPA and so it was no threat to me who came in. I even saw the CPA as a way of getting out as the CPA might find a controller. He was appreciative of my candor.

- **Box manufacturer.**
  This company made boxes. It was owned by one man that had been a box salesman and started this business after he retired. I learned much from this man and he from me.

The project was a mission critical inventory and accounting system. There were several interesting events.

There had been some problems getting the accounts payable under control. On several occasions the weekly payment process was delayed. The owner of course had really gotten on my case. He said that he never liked to be late on payments. I did of course get the problems fixed. I worked in his very large office. Long after the accounts payable problem was fixed and I was off on other parts of my project I would often hear the owner on the phone with a supplier saying that he would make payment soon but that there was a computer problem. I would hear him say that the computer man was in right then working on it.

This company made setup boxes for one hardware manufacturer customer. Setup boxes are the two piece boxes made of thick cardboard that are used for certain types of metal hardware. The top fits over the bottom. The customer required that the boxes be shipped with the tops on the boxes. There was extra cost because there was a manual process to put on the tops. At the customer end there was the extra cost of removing the tops to insert product. That customer had a union. This is double extra cost was another reason for the decline of American manufacturing.

The owner did say that if he was doing it over he would start a different type of business. He said that there is too much bulk in the box business. I had my own comments.

The box business is simply printing on flat sheets and then die-cutting. Advertising products are made exactly the same way with exactly the same equipment. Boxes are priced on a lowest bidder basis. Advertising products are priced on a reliability basis for getting the job done quickly. With boxes there may be no long term relationships. With advertising products the vendor relationship is key.

A number of my children went with me to this place at different times.

- **Chemical distributor.**
This was a very simple business but became the hardest job I had. The owner kept coming up with more fine details. It looked to be a never ending project. I never was paid the full amount even though I went way beyond what I agreed to do.

- **Oil spill clean up systems and covers for valves and flanges.**
One thing I did for that company was to develop a worldwide database of booms and other oil spill cleanup equipment with the locations and contacts. Then when there was a spill and more equipment was needed deals could be arranged by both parties.

Fishing boat skippers kept a log of wrecks that they had encountered, usually based on where they had lost or damaged a net while dragging. I thought that I could use the same database idea with the boats. Did they like the idea? Not on your life. Their view was that they lost a net. The other boats could do the same. They never thought that they could benefit themselves by avoiding more net losses. There was a bit of irony. All of these skippers took two and a half percent off the top of their fish sales to be an offering to their Catholic church. On a $50,000 trip, that was $1,250. The boat settlement agent made the disbursements so this was a regular thing.

I produced a report showing that manufacturing of oil spill clean-up was a losing business while covers of valves and flanges was most profitable. The owner read the report and gave it back to me.

"Dave I know all this. I'm an old man and you know what part of this business I like the best. I'm the only stockholder so I can do what I want. Do me a favor. Please don't show this to Karen." Karen was his wife and she was the bookkeeper.

There were two kinds of valve and flange covers, indicating and non-indicating. The indicating ones could be inspected visually while walking. The non-indicating covers had to be untied, checked and then re-tied. The non-indicating ones were the biggest sellers because of union requirements to make more work, thus more pay, for union employees. It of course meant more cost which is why American manufacturing has gone away.

- **Multiple town school bus contractor.**
School districts, at least at that time, did not have their own buses.

When the owner took on a new town for school bus service he started building the budget with $100,000 annual salary for himself. That was back when a $100,000 was a lot of money. It was five times what I got as an executive with a Fortune 500 company.

The mission critical system was for the payroll. There was a flat rate per hour with bonuses for showing up and showing up on time five mornings in a row. A bonus for doing that in the afternoon. A third bonus for doing that in both morning and afternoons for the five days.

Meeting time was always at 5:00 AM with the son of the owner. Then I would go to work.

Almost every day I was there a mother would call in that the bus did not come. The standard reply question was

"Where are the other kids at the stop?"

There were none because they had left on the bus.

The owner, was a most interesting man. Most of my work was with his son though I did go often to the owner's house.

- **The specialty consultant.**
This company was quite successful in a tiny piece of specialized management consulting. I developed a cost accounting system. One thing is for sure. The owner liked everything to be first class including his computer system.

One night I was working late in the office. The office building was on a farm, very close to the owner's house. It had been built to look like a converted barn. I was not there all the time and wanted to finish one piece of the project. The owner came in holding a handgun.

"I saw the light and didn't know who was here," he said.

"Just me. And I'm leaving soon."

"Have you seen X? "We let him go and he has some of our stuff."

"No." I said.

I began to shut down what I was doing and get out for the night.

That owner was a highly successful businessman. He had started out selling vacuum cleaners door to door. How he got into consulting I don't know.

Property and Casualty company.
I was a subcontractor for a programming firm that developed a first report of injury system that was designed to capture data that could be

used for accident prevention.

My part was to develop the ideas and questions that would be a part of the programming. My contract ended on December 31.

Many people were off that day. Others gradually left. Finally it was just me.

I had some clean-up work to do including removing myself from systems. I had accesses to most of the company systems. I deleted my usernames and passwords. I boxed up material that would be shipped to various locations around the country. I had several keys.

I put the keys in an envelope in a place that had been designated.

When I was sure that all had been done, I turned out all the lights and left. The door locked behind me.

- **Large shoe distributor.**
This was a job I did not like.

I had to decipher and fix some legacy programs that were in a language I did not know very well. No one knew any of the language at all.

The systems were programmed in India. The local staff would document program bugs and would test work that had been done in India during our night time. They would then send instructions for the next night's work. The next morning more testing and searching for bugs.

- **Office desk drawer slide manufacturer.**
The owner, by age 55, had started and sold 50 companies, all very specialized.

I worked for him at a business where he manufactured office desk drawer slides.

There were three peculiarities:
  1. No employee or service provider could work at one time at more than one of his companies.
  2. The owner did not care to see the standard Balance sheets and P&L reports. He only wanted to see a graph of cash balances.
  3. At around $4 million in sales, big money at that time, he would sell the companies.

- **High class jeweler.**
  A most unique business with high priced products. It had a layaway plan. There were customers who would come in one day a week and pay maybe $10,000 all in cash. They did not want receipts. There was full trust in the jeweler.

  This was a simple accounts payable and payroll system or so I thought.

  All the employees had very long foreign names. This was in a day of fixed record lengths so I had to make a lot of change to accommodate the names. That of course mean changing reports and check formats.

  For accounts payable, once a week they would pay all outstanding bills no matter how much the total and no matter what the payment terms. The check forms they used cost $1.00 each. In 1978.

- **Plastics thermoformer.**
  This company made custom cocktail stirrers for bars and restaurants.

  It was also a supplier for a very large fast food chain.

  That customer added a large coffee to its menu. Right after that was rolled out, it realized that its existing stirrers would not work. No one had thought to order longer stirrers. There was a great deal of panic. A mold had to be made. Lead time about 90 days. When the mold was made there was then a long time to get enough long stirrers made to meet national demand.

  That customer required that all invoices from suppliers had to be sent electronically. It took a considerable amount of time for me to code the process that was used for one invoice a month.

  This plastics thermoformer was one of the first companies to do open book accounting. Each month a full financial report, including the owners and executives individual payroll was posted to the bulletin boards.

  Most of the factory employees were Cambodian immigrants. The company provided free classes in English as a second language.

- **Lamp manufacturer.**
  The company was founded in 1927 and dissolved in 1989. In my first meeting I could tell that they were not as competitive as they used to

be due to foreign manufacturers.

I told them some things that they could do using the computer system with better information. They were not interested. Yet they wanted a computer.

The owner was very elderly. His son was getting there himself.

I made a proposal for a computer and programming. About a week later the father and son wanted me to come to a meeting at their lawyer's office. There I was presented with a most onerous contract with the same date as my proposal. They had the right to cancel for any reason. I would be obligated to repay them everything they had paid to me and to the computer manufacturer. I would also owe them for employee time, their time, and a payment of something like $5,000.

I listened to it all and then left without signing. I said I wanted to review the contract further though I knew that I would not agree to it. The elderly owner gave me a deposit check for $2,000. They had set the amount. They told me I could sign the contract and mail it back. I did not cash the check. I called and told the son that I would not be signing.

Later in the week, I got a phone call from the old man. He was angry that I had not cashed the check.

I destroyed the check rather than send it back as I have done with all such deposits.

That way no one could cash it and then claim that I had cashed it.

- **Commercial printer.**
  The owner wanted an annual statement for each employee showing everything that the company spent for employees. It included employer payroll taxes, benefits cost, and the cake that each employee got on their birthday. Internal costing included the floor space cost per employee. The ultimate in monitoring costs to maximize profit. Cutting costs was his business life. However that same man owned and piloted a single engine World War II fighter-bomber airplane that burned an incredible amount of fuel per hour. He loved to brag to everyone how costly it was to operate.

- **Housing authority.**
  There was a big push to hire women as executives. A former waitress

was hired to be the executive director. One day the fee accountant was in when I was there. We both worked in the conference room. He showed me what he had found. There were a number of checks missing from the bank statements for a number of months. He noticed from the statements that the amounts were all even hundreds of dollars. I noticed that the dates were getting closer and closer and the amounts were getting bigger. He asked me what I thought. I said that I was sure it was the same thing he was thinking. He got copies of the checks from the bank and sure enough they were all the same payee. She knew so little of business that she thought she could just open the statements, remove the checks to her, and that no one would ever know. She spent a year in prison. All the details were in the newspaper.

- **Capsules and tablets filler distributor.**
This company had an interesting business. It sold 29 different items that were grown worldwide that were used mostly as filler for pharmaceuticals. These items were commodities but they had to be grown and then had to be available when and where they were needed. Rotterdam was where it had most of the product for Europe come in. My charter was to set up a control system. Compliance with import laws was most important. Brazil had one that was most unusual. Every shipment and invoice had to have signed certification from the local Chamber of Commerce that the company was a reputable company and a member in good standing of the Chamber. The owner was always most dignified in every respect. While building the company he had travelled worldwide. The building hallways were full of framed high mileage certificates from airlines. I had never heard of many of them.

The owner had some kind of thing about water. The last person out each day had to turn a wheel and shut off all water into the building. Three walls of his office had large built in aquariums. He did not come to work when it rained or snowed though he only lived three miles away in a castle on a mountain top. He had a built in garage in the building for his Rolls Royce. He had spent an additional 50% for custom upgrades on the car including a superior type of windshield wipers and windshield washer. In the garage was a robot car wash. As he left the garage, he would push a button to activate the car wash.

He told me that when he bought the car he went to England to learn how to operate his Rolls Royce. He had a question at one point in the demonstration.

"I don't see a place for trash. Where would I put a gum wrapper?"

"Why sir, you give it to your chauffeur," was the answer.

He became ill and could no longer work without it being a threat to his health. He moved to his house in Bermuda.

Before leaving he hired another man, equal in education and experience though not in character. This man had a large carved wooden hand with a raised middle finger. He told me that was a graphic of his philosophy of life. When he got my knowledge, plans, and strategy he replaced me with one of his sons. The controller was replaced by another son. I was glad to be gone.

I have always done my best to only work with those that practice what was called *Honest Business* by Michael Phillips. When I have been involved with someone else, which has been too common, I have done what I set out to do for them and then left as soon as possible.

- **Office supply business.**
This was a simple application. I used one of the first PCs. There was an on/off switch. Turn it on and there was the C prompt. Give a command for the name of a program and it would execute. I used a bookkeeping program called DACEASY. QuickBooks did not exist at that time. I did learn some interesting things about about the office supply business. The store stocked a number of really expensive items.

"Who buys these things?" I asked.

"Nonprofits and government," I was told.

"They all have plenty of money."

I also learned that in June and September office supplies had the highest prices. The nonprofits in June and government in September spends what is left in the budget. Use it or lose it.

- **Sub shop.**
This sub shop business was cash only. Credit cards were not in use yet. There were two cash registers. The sales on one of them was never posted in the bookkeeping system. I was curious how it handled expenses. I found it was common practice for bakery drivers to leave two invoices. One, paid in cash and was not posted in the ledger. The other was paid by check. I set up a basic system. I told them the right thing to do.

- **Emik Avakian.**
  Though he did not become a client, I met Emik Avakian. He had come from Armenia not speaking English and with no money. His resume was thick like a book. At the time I met him he owned two companies that developed new products. A brilliant man who graduated magna cum laude in physics and mathematics. He had many patents, mostly involving helps for the disabled. Yet he could not feed or dress himself. Emik had cerebral palsy. He died in 2013 at the age of 90.

We buy a new Mercedes Benz and get rid of the Pinto.
We bought a new Mercedes Benz 240D 4 door sedan 2.4 liter diesel, hence 240D. The purpose was not to be a high spender for a luxury car. It was for a sturdy low cost per mile workhorse for high mileage. Mine did not have air conditioning, which was an option.

In Israel I had seen how these vehicles were used as taxis, sheruts, short for monit sherut as these service taxis were called. Today the sheruts use the high top stand up vans that carry eight to ten passengers.

A Mercedes 240D would not accelerate fast. 2.4 liters displacement is 146 cubic inches. Not a dragster engine. On the other hand it was a comfortable, roomy, and maintenance free car. Really and truly maintenance free so long as you changed the fuel filter and the oil regularly. Those diesels were new in the U.S.

I went from a Ford Pinto to a Mercedes and for the first time was able to build equity in a car that I bought for no money down. I was driving a lot of miles and it was a good investment.

We had our home heating oil tank in the garage.

The delivery man said that if we were going to use heating oil for the car to let him know so he could change the degree day setting so we would not run out of oil.

The only difference between heating oil and diesel fuel is the Federal and State road taxes.

I told him we would not be doing that.

I receive the baptism of the Holy Spirit.
I had a very clear experience that the Lord was suggesting that I give up my way and try His. Since age seven I had been serving Christ on and off. As an adult mostly off. I experienced the baptism of the Holy Ghost with speaking in

tongues. The book of Acts is full of tongues speaking starting on the Day of Pentecost.

I find the following passage quite simple and fully consistent with what Jesus said about sending the Holy Spirit:

Acts 19:2-7:
He said unto them, Have ye received the Holy Ghost since ye believed? And they said unto him, We have not so much as heard whether there be any Holy Ghost. And he said unto them, Unto what then were ye baptized? And they said, Unto John's baptism. Then said Paul, John verily baptized with the baptism of repentance, saying unto the people, that they should believe on him which should come after him, that is, on Christ Jesus. When they heard this, they were baptized in the name of the Lord Jesus. And when Paul had laid his hands upon them, the Holy Ghost came on them; and they spake with tongues, and prophesied. And all the men were about 12.

I knew what opponents said about it, even from churches where the Day of Pentecost was celebrated every year. I knew what the Apostle Paul said about it. I knew what the book of Acts in the Bible said about it. From that day I knew what it really was and what I could say about it. It has continued to be a part of my prayer life. I did learn that giving a tongue in church and having an interpretation, what Paul wrote about in I Corinthians 14, was not the same as tongues as a prayer language. I have never been led to use tongues in church. Some things have to be believed to be seen. This applies also to secular things, which are in fact spiritual. It is why some people become CEOs and others become unemployed.

I did not become a saint.
The apostle Paul wrote of himself as the chiefest of sinners. What he did not want to do was what he did. Me and every other Christian have the same testimony. It is the conflict between our sin nature and our saved soul. I did not become a saint after the Baptism but did have more assurance of my eternal salvation due to forgiveness of sin. I learn more and more that God does not give up on me.

I became active in Christian ministries.
I became active in Christian missions and was quite open about it. I did not do it as an income source or as a full-time activity. I did a Bible study I wrote called *Action Faith Through Bible Study*. The full text of each class is in my writing files at home.

I was a member of Full Gospel Businessmen's Fellowship International (FGBMFI)

Josh McDowell was speaking at one event. McDowell has an interesting way of presenting Jesus.

Since Jesus said that he was God, there were only three possibilities.

1. Jesus in truth is God.

2. Jesus could have been a liar knowing that he was not God.

3. Jesus could have a lunatic and thought that he was God.

We have to believe one of these three by default.

One speaker I heard at an FGBMFI meeting was a long time airline employee from England. He was from a poor section of London. He wanted to get out. He noticed that the men he knew all smoked cigars and drank gin. He decided not to smoke cigars or drink gin. He became unwelcome and had time to do other things. Soon he was out. I don't recall the point where he accepted Christ as his Savior.

The lady that wanted more newsletters.
The pastor of a church was a young family man. He had a real let down one day. He published a monthly newsletter, 8 ½ x 14, on mimeograph paper. Every month one lady at church asked for extra copies. He was most pleased. No doubt she was passing them around the neighborhood while inviting people to church. He visited her at home one week. While in the living room, he noticed a basket near the fireplace with church newsletters. He made a comment as he knew what they were. Her reply was:

"My son uses them to start fires. With the long paper it burns more to get the kindling going."

My favorite Christian song.
My favorite Christian song at the time was *Sometimes Alleluia*. Maybe still is.

A real commitment to Christ.
A professional couple, he a teacher and she a nurse, accepted Christ as savior at the Bible Study.

They became missionaries and later wrote a book *You Don't Know My God,* their memoirs of getting saved, of living in North Carolina, of becoming missionaries, and of finding a location and building an orphanage.

A copy of that book is in my glass bookcase at home. I acquired several other copies while writing this book.

Some travel experiences.
I had a number of unique, to me, experiences. In one case on a Sunday morning I saw a church van. It had stopped at a convenience store. I asked the location of the church.

"Follow me, it's close by" said the driver.

While sitting in church the pastor came up and told me the Lord wanted me to preach. No sleeping during the sermon for me on that day. I had a number of similar events occur, all last minute. At one church where I preached, the pastor asked if I could come back in the evening and continue with the theme. I went home with him and his family for the afternoon.

One thing I learned has been through Hispanic churches. The Bible says in Ephesians 3:11:

"And he gave some, apostles; and some, prophets; and some, evangelists; and some, pastors and teachers;"

I had always wondered how there could be senior pastors and associate pastors. And for that matter why would "Pastors" be capitalized when it was not that way in the Bible. I Timothy chapter 1 gives qualifications for bishops. Scholars say that today that means pastors. Could it in fact be that bishops are man-appointed positions and pastors are called by the Holy Spirit? It has been my observation that in Hispanic churches that pastors arise in neighborhoods to counsel as needed and to provide transportation to church. There seems to be no hierarchy in their churches.

Traveling.
A lot of my travel has been at night. One night around 2:00 AM I was on I-95 just outside of New York City when I passed the Pelhams. I had a sudden desire for some White Castle hamburgers. I knew of a store in the area. I turned around and went back. I got in line. White Castle can be busy 24/7. The man in front of me turned around and abruptly said :

"I need to get saved."

We went to a quiet corner where I told him the gospel and led him to Christ.

There can be many things happen while traveling, good and bad.

I have often picked up hitchhikers or walkers though would not pick up single women. Discrimination yes. But what can one do?

Willie.
I picked up one man that was standing on an interstate bridge looking over. I stopped and he had a shocked look. As we drove he told me that he had just gotten out of prison for murder and wanted to make a new start. His name was Willie. He was an ex-boxer. He said he had been standing there and had given a prayer:

"God if you are real could you have someone give me a ride?"

At that instant I had stopped. I told him the gospel and led him to Christ.

The two men with the knife.
Once I picked up two men during the day. One of them pulled a knife and wanted money. I stopped the car and screamed at them to get out. They obeyed and walked away.

Nepenthe.
At Big Sur, California, I have always stopped at the bookstore at Nepenthe and have bought quite a few books at a time. They have really good books in many subjects that don't exist at most places. And not just books. I bought a Gene Autry wind up alarm clock for Cheri at Nepenthe. At Christmas 2017, we passed the clock along to our grandson Jacob since he liked Gene Autry.

A trip to Tulsa.
There was some trip with several of or children where we took a little detour and went to Tulsa to see the home of the boys in the group called Hanson. It became quite a detour but we did find their house. Years later, one daughter says that she still likes Hanson.

I'll have to ask her if she still likes Dalmatians, the dogs, not the people in the Croatian region. Growing up she loved Dalmatian dogs. I had explained to her that a Dalmatian needs plenty of running room that in turn needs plenty of time from the dog owner.

Two steak dinners for the price of one.
I stopped at a restaurant in West Virginia.

On the table was an ad offering two steak dinners for the price of one.

I told the waiter that I would like to have one steak dinner and then start over with the second one.

He saw no problem with doing that.

I complimented him on his waiter skills and attitude.

I found out that he was just doing it part-time.

His main job was with the FBI where he was a technician at the national fingerprint laboratory in Charleston.

Senator Harry Byrd had arranged for a number of federal government agencies to move to West Virginia.

The rack jobber.
In my travels I bought good books cheap from racks in truck stops.

One day I met a rack jobber refilling one of his racks. We had a nice chat.

We were both Christians. His specialty was Christian books.

He told me that it was easier to get a rack of Christian books into a store owned by a Jew than in a store owned by a Christian.

The Christians were afraid of offending someone that might think he was pushing his religion.

The Jew was only concerned about providing what people wanted to buy and revenue per square foot.

Baseball experiences in Massachusetts.
We were pleased to be able to send one of our sons for two week sessions for several years at the Ted Williams Baseball Camp in Lakeville, Massachusetts.

Ted Williams came to the camp frequently. A few quotes:

"Baseball is the only field of endeavor where a man can succeed three times out of ten and be considered a good performer."

"If you don't think too good, don't think too much."

"A man has to have goals — for a day, for a lifetime — and that was mine, to have people say, 'There goes Ted Williams, the greatest hitter who ever lived.'"

I frequently took our son David to Red Sox games at Fenway Park in Boston. We had an interesting experience after picking up our son one year from the baseball camp. Only 42 miles from Boston.

I had bought two tickets for a Red Sox game on Friday night at Fenway Park and two tickets for Saturday afternoon. The plan was to take our oldest daughter on Friday night and son on Saturday afternoon.

Cheri would be coming and would have the daughter and the younger children with her on Saturday. For some reason Cheri did not go.

I took our daughter anyway. Worst case, none of us would go to the game on Saturday.

On Saturday, with both children, I parked and we walked to Fenway Park. En route I bought a ticket from a scalper. Normally a scalper has two tickets and there is a big markup. In this case the scalper had one ticket and let me have it at face value even though it was a sold out game. A single ticket is not worth too much in most cases.

The seat was in the same area as the other two tickets but about 25 rows down. So far so good. I got the kids seated. The two tickets were on the aisle. I sat in the third seat in to see what I might be able to do.

A group of young men arrived. They took all the remaining seats in that row. It was close to game time.

An elderly man came along and said I had his seat. I looked at his ticket and it was for a seat three in from the other end. That seat was occupied by one of the young men in the group.

I made a deal with him to take my seat further down towards the field that was a much better seat. The young man was happy to keep the seat he had.

I gave the elderly man the ticket and did not ask him for his ticket. I wanted him to feel secure.

Is it a coincidence that in a sold out stadium I got the one seat I wanted?

A trip to Monterey, California.
At a hotel in Monterey, California, I got a room at a discount rate that was at first refused. My discount coupon was only good if occupancy was less than 80%, reserved or occupied. The clerk said that occupancy was just above 80%.

"Would you get mad if I asked you a few questions?"

"No, go ahead."

"How many rooms does this hotel have?"

"341" she replied.

"It's 10:00 PM in Monterey. I wouldn't like for you to get in trouble but are you likely to have 68 walk-ins yet tonight? "

She smiled and registered my room.

Lucia, California.
I guess I have to tell about Lucia California. I was driving down the coast of California at Big Sur. I needed to make a few phone calls. This was before cell phones. I stopped at a small store, the only store around, and went to the pay phone in the back of the store. It turned out that this store was also the office for a motel that had several rooms over the hill and directly facing the ocean high up. While I was on the phone the counter clerk got several calls.

"Hello. How may I direct your call?" I could not hear the caller but in all cases he said:

"I believe I can help you with that. What date would you be arriving?"

He then went on to book a room for each caller. After my calls I decided this guy was worth talking to if he could spare the time. I asked him if he was the owner.

"No, but every morning I give the owner my permission to tell me what to do."

He was the owner of himself though not the business. A great outlook and attitude.

I found that he lived in a shack across the road and up the mountain. He kept chickens. I learned that he was also an actor and that he often performed *Little Black Sambo*. I said:

"I thought that could no longer be done."

"You can't do it but I can," was his reply.

He was talking about what would later be called cultural appropriation. He told me that *Little Black Sambo* was a positive story with a black hero and he felt that every black child should know it.

The couple with money that rarely travelled.
One client contact was a vice president at a large company.

His wife held a similar position at another company.

He spent most of his time in his office checking the value of his 401k account.

They had one child in his thirties who still lived at home. They still had the first house they had owned. They never travelled except for business.

He was in shock when during one conversation he learned that alone or with my family that I did not make hotel reservations in advance even when traveling out of the country.

He thought everyone always made reservations. Too much risk otherwise he thought.

Later he did say that he might be willing to try but he knew his wife would never even consider it.

Faith works all the time.
I could write a book just on all the ways that I have gotten tickets to events and rooms at hotels. With hotels I have not only gotten rooms at sold out hotels, I have gotten huge, sometimes really huge discounts. Some would call it good luck. Some includes Christians that do not believe that God would be involved in such things. I am a believer in faith as it is defined in the Bible in Hebrews 11:1:

"NOW faith is the substance of things hoped for, the evidence of things not seen."

Now is capitalized, at least in the King James Bible. NOW especially means now, not sometime in the future. Faith is a substance. It is not some philosophical intangible. As a substance it is evidence. According to the dictionary, evidence is "the available body of facts or information indicating whether a belief or proposition is true or valid." Faith works for good or for bad. I often hear people say "I believe I am coming down with the flu." The next day they are not at work. That belief is the substance of things hoped for, the evidence of things not seen. Some will say:

"I believed I would win the lottery but I did not win."

I'm reminded of the farm area drought. A prayer meeting was to be held. Opening the meeting, the pastor asked of the attendees: "Where are your umbrellas?"

Church denominations.
What has been a puzzle to me over the years is that denominations can say with certainty that unless you are a member of their denomination, not necessarily that you are someone who knows and diligently practices their own doctrines, that for sure you will go to hell. Discussions of their numbers compared to the number of people claiming to be Christian does not have any effect. If anything it proves that not everyone will go to heaven.

There is one denomination that is split into two opposing doctrines. Ironically the geographic divider seems to be I-95. Those on the west side claim that speaking in tongues is essential for salvation while those on the east side say that speaking in tongues is a one way ticket to eternal damnation. Both sides are opposed to drinking any quantity of alcohol. Smoking is fine and is done outside between Sunday school and the worship service in the presence of children.

There is one denomination with one name and multiple splits.

I knew of one of the pastors that had come back from a denominational meeting and told his congregation that, for doctrinal reasons, he did not stand for any of the prayers. Those prayers were given by pastors that were not of his small and fairly recent split. Does that mean that he viewed that those prayers would not be heard by God?

I recently ran across a relevant quote. Since it was said by a Jew, though the subject was not about religion, I guess that all Christians can still ignore it.

"When someone is honestly 55% right, that's very good and there's no use wrangling. And if someone is 60% right, it's wonderful, it's great luck, and let him thank God. But what's to be said about 75% percent right? Wise people say this is suspicious. Well, and what about 100% right? Whoever says he's 100% right is a fanatic, a thug, and the worst kind of rascal." — An old Jew of Galicia.

I was asked to teach a church how the Bible says to deal with the sick.
One church, of a different denomination than any of the others mentioned, asked me to come and meet with its board on the subject of publishing the names of those that were sick and needing prayer. They were concerned about missing someone even though their bulletin always said to notify the church office if they knew of anyone sick. I told them that I had no special knowledge.

I did know that their statement of beliefs was that the Bible is the sole source.

I quoted to them James 5:14-15:

"Is any sick among you? Let him call for the elders of the church; and let them pray over him, anointing him with oil in the name of the Lord: And the prayer of faith shall save the sick, and the Lord shall raise him up; and if he have committed sins, they shall be forgiven him."

I pointed out that most importantly those verses teach that the sick should call for the elders. Not his family or friends calling the bulletin editor in the church office.

The first reaction was that this church had no elder because their denomination did not believe in elders. I told them that the general interpretation of elders is that the Bible might be referring to those that are not young, not a bureaucratic structure, though the Bible does not suggest any ages.

There was more discussion and a decision was made to leave things as is. The pastor agreed.

As I've gotten older, and have learned more, I have gotten to where I no longer try to change hearts and minds. I leave that to the politicians.

Faith works in Israel in our time.
The day before taking a trip to Israel I was talking with Marshall Sternberg, my life insurance salesman. He told me of the flautist, a flautist is one who plays the flute, James Galway. I had never heard of him or of the word flautist. He told me that if I ever had a chance, to see Galway in concert. Today he would have said: "Look him up on YouTube."

I arrived in Tel Aviv. I looked at a list of things going on that day. There was a recital that afternoon with James Galway and Zubin Mehta. I called the concierge. No tickets. I called the visitors center. No tickets. They said usually they would have tickets but not for a performance by someone like James Galway. I decided to go to Gaza for the afternoon. As I was nearing the bottom of the stair into the lobby a man was rushing up to the front desk. I hear him say to the clerk:

"My aunt is sick. Do you know anyone that would want Galway tickets?"

I stepped up. He would only sell his two tickets in the balcony, though just at face value, about $10 each.

Off I went to the recital with two tickets.

As I was walking across a large plaza, I was heading toward a crowd entering the concert hall.

I was interrupted by a woman that asked if I had any tickets to sell. I was thinking that of all the people here do I look like a scalper?

She told me that she and her friend were looking for tickets. I sold her one of mine at what I paid, face value.

She asked if I would be willing to trade if they could get another one. For sure.

"You know where I'll be" I said.

Minutes before show time they arrived and traded me a front orchestra seat for my balcony seat. They were happy to make an even trade. Galway was great.

There were 12 encores.

A second trip to Israel.
The second trip I stayed at the King David in Jerusalem.

There are many group tours of Israel particularly involving senior citizens. I feel sorry for them having to be out front at 5:30 AM with their luggage standing in the cool weather waiting for a few stragglers or maybe even for their bus to arrive.

At the King David I was in the breakfast room and there was this elderly woman looking very distraught. I asked her if she was ok. She said:

"I just want to go home. I've been lied to and cheated so many times here."

I did my best to cheer her up. She was thankful. We prayed together.

In Tel Aviv I went to a lecture by an American rabbi. He was doing a weekly series. That week it was Isaiah 52-55. I was not the only Christian there.

When he was at the end someone asked why he had skipped Isaiah 53.

"Isaiah 53. Ahhh. The missionary chapter. There are some that say that Isaiah was talking about Jesus as being the Messiah. I have read that chapter many times and I cannot see how there could possibly be any connection to Jesus."

In the Bible look at what Jesus said in John 3:3:

"Verily, verily, I say unto thee, Except a man be born again, he cannot see the kingdom of God."

Note the verb is "see." The rabbi could not "see." Man says: "Show me, then I'll believe."

God says: "Believe, then I'll show you."

The ancient Jewish commentators all have said that Isaiah 53 refers to the King Messiah and is a prophecy.

Recent commentators either skip the chapter, as did the rabbi, or they say that while the chapter speaks of a person, that it refers to the whole nation of Israel that will be the savior, not the saved.

After the lecture I was standing at a bus stop with a couple that sounded American. They had been to the lecture.

In talking with them I found that they were American and that they were Christadelphians. I asked them about their beliefs. The wife said:

"Where the Bible speaks we speak; where the Bible is silent we are silent,"

That sounded pretty good. So I asked a question:

"So then you believe in speaking in tongues?"

They both turned their backs to me.

False teaching.
Over the years, I gained a lot of knowledge of "ministers" that skip parts of the Bible. I learned the truth of Coleridge's quote that:

"If you love Christianity more than you love truth, you will soon love your sect or your church more than you love Christianity, then you will love yourself more than all."

In early 2017, there was great shock when Hank Hanegraff, the Bible Answer Man, left evangelicalism and joined an Eastern Orthodox church.

A few months later he explained that he could no longer put up with the pastor-preneurs that branded their own particular set of beliefs as absolute final truth on how to get salvation and made money on it.

When Cheri and I traveled by car back when many radio stations carried religious programming every day of the week, I would turn to a program service mid-preaching.

In a few sentences I could tell Cheri the denomination of the speaker.

We would listen all the way to the end, most programs were 15 minutes, and the announcer would name the church. I was always right.

In 2017, one week in April or May, there was a cartoon in *The New Yorker* of a minister in the pulpit. He is saying,

"Today I will be cherry picking from the book of Deuteronomy."

All too often Christianity is presented in a way that salvation comes from the church or that salvation comes from baptism. No minister will dare risk his job otherwise.

Martin Luther once said that he had never seen a Christian call on his baptism when he had a need.

Salvation comes from God, the Lord, Jesus, and Him. Most everyone has heard John 3:16:

"For God so loved the world that he gave his only begotten Son, that whosoever believeth in him should not perish but have everlasting life."

Every denomination adds to this verse.

They change "believeth in him" to "believeth in him and does not do all or some of the following":

Drinking, smoking, gambling, drugs, sex before marriage, women wearing wrong length head covering, fellowship with those that do not believe exactly the way we do, failure to attend church, failure to partake of the Lord's Supper even if we don't let them, going to movies, watching tv, believing in Sunday sabbath, standing when someone from another denomination or sub-denomination prays, dancing, speaking in tongues, not speaking in tongues, played musical instruments in church, etc.

Some of the denominations simply change the basics of believeth in "him" in John 3:16.

They substitute church, baptism, the Lord's Supper, pastor's teaching, seminary teaching, trying to be good, etc.

What amazes me the most is the church people that don't know what it is that they say their church believes.

The lady that did not know what her church believed.
The bookkeeper at one of my clients was the wife of the pastor of a church and was really active in the church.

One day I asked her what were the major beliefs of her church.

"If you want to know what we believe you'd have to ask my husband. He knows all about it."

I would hope that the pastor would know.

As for her she must have great faith to believe and not know what it is she believes.

The lady that thought I was a student.
I have attended many churches while traveling. And there have been many times while traveling that I did not attend a church.

I always carried my Bible, a habit developed while growing up.

After one service at one church in rural New Hampshire a lady figured me for a student.

"I see that you have a Bible. Are you a student?"

I did not reply with a yes, or she would have asked what school. I said: "I do my own study."

CHAPTER 10: NORTH CAROLINA

"God can change circumstances or supplies power to change." -Anonymous

A mutually exclusive decision.
We made a decision to move to a small town in North Carolina. We knew no one in that whole area. We felt it to be a leading of the Lord. From a practical standpoint we were looking for a better life for ourselves and our children. I was well aware of the disadvantages, disadvantages that I will group into long term financial considerations.

At that time there were still a large number of people that had adapted the keep the same job for your whole career and wait out retirement then you can do things.

I did not subscribe to that very definite and workable career plan.

We made the move from Connecticut to North Carolina to our second owned home, an old farmhouse with no heat. We bought it for $14,000 with an acre of land. We loved our house and yard and that we had what was an ideal country residence away from the hustle and bustle of the city and suburbia.

Midpoint of our time in North Carolina, we lost our house and two of our children in a house fire during the day time. Life has not been the same after that. Still, I know that the Lord is in control.

A neighbor, a volunteer fireman, and one of our sons attempted to get the two out of the second floor window. Cheri called our pastor who lived in the town where I was working. He picked me up and took me home. We never determined the cause of the fire. A project had just been done to upgrade our wiring relative to expanding the house. The electrician had not told us about smoke detectors so we had none. I had never heard of them. They were new. There was not a ladder to reach the second floor so no one could get up there.

Some of the events below were from before the fire, others after. There was what became transition time where I had to be away from the family going back and forth, though I took children along as much as I could. I regretted the family separations for travel and work that but did not know what else to do.

Aaron and Paul……We loved ya.
published on page one of our newspaper 8/15/84.

You came to us at home during a snowstorm. Your brothers and sisters met you almost at the moment of birth. One of your brothers wanted to know how long we could keep you. Forever we hoped.

Right from the start you were alike but you were different. Paul, you were smaller but you could kick the best.

Even though there had been seven others, it was still a delight to see you make each little discovery about yourselves and the world. You knew the love of your family. When you cried for something, you knew that life was not all happiness.

I'm sorry, far more than you know, that I couldn't be with you every day. I hurried back from my trips as quickly as I could so that I could see you. Sometimes though, even when I was at home, I was just too tired to talk to you.

The times that we could talk I really enjoyed. It's no easy task to give equal time to two boys. I didn't want either of you to feel that you were being slighted.

Some of the best times together were in the early morning when it was the two of you in bed with me and Mom. We would take turns holding you. Monday morning, the last time I saw you, was no different. I commented to Mom that since it was exactly six months since you were born that we should have a party since you were one year old together.

Monday night, Mom told me where you were. She said that you were sitting, one on each side of Jesus. He had His arms around you and was saying, "Boys let me tell you how I made this world…"

We don't know how long we'll be on this earth. But we've got something more to look forward to when we leave. Shortly after you were born, I dedicated you both to the Lord. On June 19th, I had made a notation in my prayer list book to pray for your salvation and Christian growth. I have now marked those lines as completed.

The couple that had come from someplace else.
One of our first acquaintances was from an elderly couple that lived close to us, about a quarter mile away. A really nice couple. They came to visit.

"We're not from around here either," they said.

"Where are you from?" I asked.

"Do you know the dirt road that goes past the brick church? We both grew up down that road."

That road was about a mile away.

The lady that could not leave.
On another occasion I was walking downtown when an older woman sitting on a bench asked me how I liked the town.

I told her how great it was and how much I liked it.

"You can say that because you can leave anytime you want. The rest of us can't do that."

She could but did not know she could.

Social change in rural North Carolina.
Shortly after we moved in we had some work done on the house.

I engaged a carpenter that would be buying materials at a local building supply store, the only building supply place within at least 50 miles in any direction.

Before the work was completed I had to go on a trip. When I returned the work had been completed.

No bill had been dropped off or mailed. The building supply store manager had paid the carpenter. When I got back I was given the bill for the materials and the labor.

It was customary to give an invoice or ask for payment only to the man of a house unless it was a single woman.

By the time we left North Carolina, the building supply store not only had a woman advising men carpenters about technical matters but the same woman had become general manager.

All of that was my doings. More on that later.

Our goal was to raise our family away from drugs. Little did we know that the problem was worse in the rural areas of the Bible Belt. It continued to get worse. Children even of good families were convicted of trafficking in cocaine.

Hands Across America.
On May 25, 1986, our family was in Washington DC to join with six and a half million others to hold hands for 15 minutes in a line across the United States.

We were only a few hands away from Ronald and Nancy Reagan who were just inside the White House fence.

We consider buying a ship.
We found an old wooden schooner in Hampton, Virginia in a waterway off the harbor. The hull was sound and there were no leaks. The ship was powered by two Caterpillar J2 engines, both ostensibly in good running condition.

The cargo area was big enough for a basketball court. The ship had been used for carrying freight to and from the Caribbean. At one point it had carried coal. At another time lumber.

Our plan would be to moor it in a nearby river, live on it, and have a business location there.

Unfortunately the draft was a little too much for that river.

We would go to familiar places.
We would drive for several hours to Raleigh.

A frequent trip would be to stay at the Holiday Inn on Saturday nights and then go to the brunch buffet on Sunday mornings. The kids loved the circus atmosphere and the variety of good food that they liked.

Trips by air.
When living in North Carolina, we had to drive for several hours to Norfolk to the airport when we flew anywhere.

Raleigh did not have as many flights as Norfolk. New York and Boston were my most frequent flights. Sometimes Philadelphia. Norfolk to New York City was $19 one way. From Norfolk to Boston was $23 one way. The bus was $55 to New York.

Blacks took the bus. Whites flew. I was not happy about this.

We start a newspaper.
Cheri and I started a weekly newspaper as a one page 8 ½ x 14 paper with a grocery ad on the back. We mailed to everyone in two counties. Looking back I can see that by sending the paper at no cost, we were operating like Facebook and other social media. The recipients paid nothing so they were not customers. The recipients were our products that we sold to our advertisers and to government, churches, and nonprofits.

When it looked like we had enough advertisers and news we moved up to a four page tabloid and then it kept growing to a normal 16 to 24 pages. Because of the long lead time in developing film, we had to make do with Polaroid camera pictures so that we could have current news stories. We had to find ways to quickly have the articles typed and set-up for printing. Cheri did all of the set-up alone. On Monday afternoons we would drive to a city where the negatives and plates would be made and the paper printed. The paper was well-liked and provided something that had never existed yet filled a great need in a remote rural area. Here is one letter:

Thank you…. November 8, 1982.

All of this letter was handwritten in cursive.

November 8, 1982

Dear Publishers,

Your weekly issue of the newspaper is greatly appreciated, being delivered and absolutely free. You are doing our county a great service.

I like the grocery store ads, along with tips on mending, diets, and suggestions that are helpful on many topics. Thanks for keeping people informed as to what is going on.

Yours truly,

The New York Times has a slogan "All the news that's fit to print." Our slogan was "All the news that fits we print."

After upgrading to a tabloid we continued to distribute free by mail weekly to every address. The grocery store ads were our bread and butter. The grocery ads were handwritten and each store had the same page location each week. Two stores would take out a full page per week. Two more would take out a half page per week.

At the same time that we were getting the paper going, the journalist Russell Baker had written a book, *Growing Up*. I heard him on a radio program interview. There were callers of course. One was a senior at one of the best journalism colleges in the United States. He was asking how he could get a job. Baker said that there were more graduates in journalism every year than there were total jobs in the industry. He did not really answer the question. He was leaving it up to the listeners.

I wrote many editorials.

One in particular was an editorial about the coming details of gentrification of the county. I did another about the subject of gentrification in general starting with the price of hamburgers.

Much was happening at the beach towns but nothing that impacted our inland areas.

I learned later that one person had framed the article, hung it on the living room wall, and watched it all come to pass exactly as I had written, impossible though it may have sounded.

$200,000 homes in our county.
by David Sneed, 10/14/1987.

In the next 20 years, county real estate will escalate to the point where the starting price on homes will approach $200,000. This price will be for existing homes that presently are selling for $15,000 to $25,000.

While this may seem impossible, one need only look at what is happening in other areas. Within the last two or three years, the Raleigh and Norfolk areas have seen the coming of houses over $300,000. With real estate generally doubling every six years, these homes within 12 years will be reselling for over $1 million. This escalation is creating paper wealth that can and will be used to buy property in areas two to three hours away. Areas in New Hampshire and Vermont that 20 years ago were offered at $80 per acre with no takers are now sites for 3,200 square foot condos selling for $400,000 each. Buyers are usually young people who have no problems paying. North Carolina will experience this same growth.

Specifically how will this happen? This writer has been an observer of this growth over the last 25 years in a number of areas on the east coast and to some extent on the west. Here in summary is what happens, tailored of course to the local situation:

An area is "discovered." Exactly what causes this is not known. One sea coast community only 35 miles from Boston was not "discovered" until two years ago. Houses which locals laughed at for $45,000 are now selling for over $300,000. The town has been on the edge of discovery for some time and seems to be right at the edge.

Retail business will continue to decline and will appear to be on the verge of going away. Growth in larger towns will even more strongly attract people to shop in those areas. Because of labor shortages and declining business, retiring business owners will mostly opt to close down operations.

Approximately 30 properties will change hands and be purchased by outsiders at steadily increasing prices. For a period of time, there will be two-tier pricing, depending on whether the buyer is from here or from there.

The distinguishing features of the areas will be noticed and emphasized. The waterfront development and the concept of one or two industrial parks will prompt that emphasis here. A number of new businesses will appear on the scene. These businesses will primarily have as a market tourists and other non-local customers. They will not require much labor to operate and will create very few if any local jobs.

Other businesses will be created as sideline ventures and tax write-offs for people who operate elsewhere or who deal in markets elsewhere. These businesses also will not create jobs but will be heavily communications oriented.

State and Federal governments will take notice. The landfill will have to be closed, crime will increase, and teachers' salaries will have to be increased dramatically. Drug usage which presently is heavily marijuana will advance to cocaine and heroin. Local government will be pressed to provide more and more. The landfill closing alone will increase costs by $450 per person per year. Tax rates will increase and will prompt movement from the area by many people.

Tax increases will make farming unprofitable and many existing farms will revert to woodlands. Those who doubt this possibility need only visit areas of the northeast even as close as Maryland and New Jersey and talk to old timers still around who have memories of what used to be. Throughout New England there are forests of 60 year old trees and stone walls where farms used to be.

There will be a period of relative quiet. Locals will be asking prices that are a little too high. These properties will be unsellable. The first condo development will be built and will have its own sewage treatment facility.

An offer will be made to develop by an outside developer who specializes in rural and inner city development. Most of the "downtown" area will be condemned and taken by eminent domain. It will mostly include closed down properties but as a part of the deal will include operating properties.

There will be considerable roadside development. There will be perhaps four more gas station/convenience stores and two or three motels. Food Lion will build. There will will be a franchised restaurant and two restaurants with average check price of $50 or more. Liquor by the drink will be allowed as it will be in most of the state. Staffing will mostly be by people moving into the area.

This area by the year 2000 will be totally different. Some will find it scary. Many others will deny the possibility of the above scenario. Change is inevitable whether we like it or not. Oddly enough it is usually the lack of vision on the part of those directly affected that accelerates the change. Those who allow their environment to stagnate actually create the rapid change which is to their own disadvantage. What we need to do is to understand what will happen and make sure that we and our families and neighbors can all benefit.

David Sneed
Publisher

The MAC computer.
We had the first model MAC computer and used PageMaker 1.0. We never upgraded the software as it did what we wanted. Sometimes we had different color inserts with multiples of four pages.

We get an award.
The National Newspaper Foundation designated our paper as a National Blue Ribbon Newspaper. The credit is to Cheri as she did all the backroom work.

I did an editorial that same week we did the announcement below. An important excerpt from the editorial: "We are grateful that the review board also sent a critique with some suggestions for improvement both in technical production and also in the methods of news gathering and presentation."

Your local newspaper wins award.

Congratulations.

Your newspaper has been designated a National Blue Ribbon Newspaper. A certificate stating that your newspaper has successfully completed the Blue Ribbon Evaluation is enclosed. You will also find a Blue Ribbon decal and a photostat of the Blue Ribbon logo for use on your newspaper's masthead.

The National Blue Ribbon Evaluation is an assessment, by a panel of professionals, of your newspaper based on the high standards of community journalism. You have been awarded the Blue Ribbon designation in recognition of the alert, progressive, and community-minded newspaper you publish.

Once again, congratulations for successfully publishing a high quality newspaper. We thank you for your participation and hope you'll feel free to write us with any comments or suggestions you may have for improving this program.

Sincerely,

Vernon R Spitaleri - signature
President

National Newspaper Foundation
1627 K St., N.W.
Washington D.C. 20006

I hit a horse.
One early evening in the winter, the time of the year when it gets dark early, I was returning with the papers for that week. Cheri was not with me on that trip.

There was only the light from the headlights of the car. We're talking country with a lot of trees right up to the highway.

Three dark-colored horses in a line suddenly came out of a dirt road lane running full speed.

I only saw them at the last moment when they entered the road. There was no way to avoid a collision and no time to brake. The three horses occupied both lanes. I was doing maybe 60 miles an hour.

I hit the horse that was in the middle, second in line. It went up and over the car. There was heavy damage to the front end, the windshield was out and the roof was bent down. The right rear door was dented and the window broken. I came to a stop in front of the horse.

Two of our children were with me. They were sitting on the back seat eating M&Ms. They were thrown to the floor. This was before seat belts and car seats. They were not injured but were bewildered. I had one tiny glass knick on one finger. I did not let the children see the horse. They took it all in stride and wanted to resume eating candy. I said no because the candy was on the seat and floor along with plenty of broken glass. Someone in a car soon passing by went and called the highway patrol from the nearest house.

The patrolman finished off the horse as it was not quite dead. He did say that he had expected to find me dead and the car totaled with a horse in the car. He said that was the usual outcome. He felt that me having a well built Mercedes sedan made a difference, to our life and to the fact that the car was repairable. As it happened all three horses were valuable.

Because the horses had gotten out, the horse was the owner's loss and he was responsible for my car repair. I learned later that it was not the first time the horses had gotten out, though there had been no prior injuries of people or horses.

An opportunity for our oldest daughter.
I don't remember the details but we felt that senior year for our oldest would be a waste of time. She was ready for college.

We decided that if she got a G.E.D. she could simply start college. G.E.D. at her age required approval of the local high school principal. I went to see him.

"If I approve that and everyone finds out, I won't have a senior class."

He eventually gave approval.

Our printing company.
The general rule of printing has always been that you can have any two of low price, quality, and turn-around time.

We decided for the customers that they could get low-price and good turnaround time. If they wanted quality we could increase turnaround time and cost.

We jobbed out business cards, wedding invitations, and some forms. We would take 50% down payment on outside items which was our cost.

We also had worked out a pricing scheme so that the cost per sheet was the same no matter what the quantity. What we did was have different production methods for different quantities.

Our quality was not the best and that was intentional. We were in a small rural community with low volume of everything. We enjoyed making folks happy.

Did we have the first UPS store?
We may have started the first UPS store.

So that people would not have to wait for UPS to pick up a package we set up that they could leave the package with us and we would give it to UPS. Our pickup fee was less than what UPS charged. We could do that because the UPS fee was once a week for a location. So the people saved money, did not have to wait for the truck. We made money and UPS had less revenue. UPS had less cost because of having one pickup point right along the highway.

Immediately the UPS lawyers did a cease and desist. We had some discussion.

The lawyers acknowledged that UPS could not stop us though it could insist that we not imply that we were UPS. That was easy to solve.

Wedding invitations.
One day several young ladies came in to pick out and to order wedding invitations. One of them was soon to be married.

They spent plenty of time looking at samples. Then it came time for the text. The bride gave us data.

When she gave the church name, her sister said.

"We don't go to that church."

"We don't?"

"I thought we did. What church do we go to?"

I said nothing and asked no questions. She put down the name of the other church.

Colorful Characters.
There were many colorful characters that I met at various places.

All of these folks as well as so many others made an impression on me in some form.

I owe gratitude to all of them.

- **The firewood sellers.**
  There were the firewood sellers. They always wanted to be paid in advance. Once paid they would never get around to making delivery. I think here was a difference between the north and the south.

  In the north the seller/non deliverer, of firewood or whatever, would never be seen again. In the south they would remain in high visibility, though still in non-performance.

- **Andrew.**

Andrew may have never gone to school yet he was a well educated man.

I don't think that either I or Andrew knew of the concept of living off the grid. Even today I'm still not quite sure. Is it a way of being independent from control by big corporations? Is it a necessity for living in remote areas? Is it a political statement? Is it a religious practice?

Living off the grid does not necessarily mean giving up electricity, or anything else for that matter. It usually means a different way of getting electricity. There are generators. There is solar and wind. The bad part of solar is that it may not be adequate during the winter and other times of little or no sun. Wind may not be reliable at any time of the year. Andrew had a solution.

The power company had refused service to Andrew because of his location in such a wet area.

He lived in the swamp in an area that he had filled in with all kinds of solid matter including a school bus.

Not only had he built his house, he had cut the trees and hewn the lumber. A saw mill was one of his streams of income.

He had lights, wall light switches, incandescent bulbs that looked like any other bulbs, and other electrical devices including a sewing machine, all running on 12 volts.

By his back door there were maybe 20 car batteries and a one cylinder diesel engine that powered a car alternator. The diesel engine was started by an electric starter motor from a car. When time to recharge, he could turn a key and it all started up.

Later the power company wanted to pay him to run a high tension power line across his property. He refused for the same reason they refused him.

He built his own car with a one cylinder diesel engine like the one that generated his electricity. It was inspired by Mr Magoo's car in the cartoon. He was most resourceful. In building the car he used coat hangers as welding rods. The state approved the car as meeting all of their requirements and he was able to register it for highway use.

He was plain, toothless, always wearing old ragged T shirts and ill-fitting pants. For some reason women liked him and he had plenty of lady friends. Where they came from who knows. One of them was there at his house, and wanted to go home to Oregon. From the account he gave me, he said:

"I'll drive you home right now."

Andrew had always wanted to go to Las Vegas and so had the woman. They made a stop in Las Vegas and tried out gambling. I can only imagine the sight he made on the Strip. The car made it fine all the way from North Carolina to Oregon and back.

He had spent a lot of time on a perpetual motion machine. I figured if anyone could make it work it would be him.

If he had lived longer, who knows, he might have succeeded.

- **Frank.**
Many of the colorful characters were philosophers. Frank had never held a job. In his proposal to his wife of many years, he had said that "if she would make the living he would make life worth living."

They had no children and got along well.

Frank was quite sure that every Monday morning in New York there were 13 Jews that would sit down and decide interest rates, stock market ups and downs, commodity prices, and all other matters of finance and economics.

At his own financial level, Frank said "I'm playing poker tonight. I hope I break even. I sure could use the money."

- **Larry.**
Larry, a hard-working man, seven months younger than me, has been a client for many years. For the past 30 years it has mostly just been doing his personal and business tax returns.

At the time I am writing this he is retired from his job at the school and is full time with his maintenance business and store. He has a part-time job driving a school bus.

His home and store is built on a small piece of filled in swamp.

His house had been totaled in a fire so he replaced it with a new manufactured home.

A few years ago he went out the back door of the store and there was an alligator, the largest one ever seen in the state.

His only distant trip out of North Carolina had been a trip to go elk hunting in New Mexico. He did bag an elk.

- **Mike.**

Mike had come to town as a young man as an engineer on a crew installing a communications antenna. He liked it so much he stayed. He had no money but there in a poor county in the state he became a multi-millionaire with honest dealing.

He built many FHA houses. For his first one he ordered all of the materials at once and lived on the lot until the house was done. He went to FHA at that point and asked for his money. They laughed and said he had to build the house first. They quit laughing when he said it was done and they could come see it. FHA did an inspection and found nothing more that needed to be done.

Mike lived in a room back off the office at a motel that he built. He totally wore out, over many years, a Ford pickup truck. Wore it out with one part as an exception. The ignition key. He put the key in the day he bought the truck and never removed it no matter where he went. The truck was never stolen.

Mike was foul-mouthed and for a while a heavy smoker and drinker. One day he simply quit smoking and drinking. He and I became close friends.

- **Marvin.**

Marvin was the co-owner of a hardware store. He had never married and was devoted to his work and to helping others when he wasn't working. He prepared meals for people and delivered them.

One year he gave a single mother money to buy things for her children for Christmas. She then went to a town 45 miles away, bought bicycles, and asked Marvin to assemble them for her. Marvin sold bicycles but his were too high priced for her budget.

Many people spoke badly of Marvin. He would not go down on his prices and they felt they were being gouged. They did not understand that margins on appliances and lawn mowers went for overhead expenses. Stores of all kinds need margin dollars.

That law of business was not negated by having grown up with the business owner.

The business owner had grown up with all of his customers. I knew Marvin was a character when I first met him. He, an elderly man still working, asked me if I was retired. He was serious. I was 36 at the time.

As I learned later every rural North Carolina town had its share of the early retirees and of the even earlier retirees that never started working. Living was cheap so it all worked out. Kale grows year round. Step outside the back door and pick your next meal. Every rural North Carolina town also had its share of those that lived a very long time.

- **Henry lived to be 108.**

Henry was a man in his 80s who did handyman work. I gave him as much work as I could. He had his own way of doing things. I guess there are times that it makes sense when you need another 2x4 to strap together pieces. It's not going to be visible once the panelling is nailed in place.

Henry died in 2015 at the age of 108.

"I lost my daddy when I was 15 and had to go to work to take care of my family."

Henry was a logger, farmer, construction worker, worked for the Defense Department in Norfolk, Virginia during World War II, and built bridges in Washington D.C. He was there during the 60's.

He said:

"When JFK got killed I was in D.C. And when his brother got killed I was there."

"When Martin Luther King Jr. got killed I was there in D.C."

One story Henry told me about living in Washington D.C. was about people being evicted from their apartments.

"The deputy and his helpers would go up and down stairs putting furniture and other belongings on the sidewalk. Once they were done and gone, the residents would bring in a truck from a side street, load up and go to their new home."

- **Margaret.**
She was known as the dog lady. She had a house back in the woods and she had plenty of dogs.

Margaret moved back to North Carolina from New England after her husband, a doctor, in a town where I had lived, had died.

At the church she attended, Margaret caused quite a stir.

In the winter it was cold because the heat was not turned on until just before the service started. Many complained that it only got warm when the service was over.

Margaret decided that she would personally pay for all of the fuel oil used by the church so long as someone turned on the heat early. The amount was over and above what she gave as an offering. The church was warm for the service but then there were complaints that she had no right to decide where her added offering went.

One time I drove her from North Carolina to New England in her car.

She brought along some of her great fried chicken. She only brought one small dog but that dog barked and jumped back and forth between the front and back seat the whole way.

After we got to her destination, I got out at the train station. I then took the next train and went where I was going.

- **James.**
James was, like Margaret, a connection to New England. James was a fishing boat crewman and a cook. He went out on Wanchese, North Carolina boats and New Bedford, Massachusetts boats.

On the boats, the skipper, the cook, and the engineer have dual functions. They are involved with the fishing and get the same share as any other crew member. They get a bonus for their other function. James could do many things. He could cook in a restaurant or on a boat, network among boats, make furniture, do carpentry, and do cleaning. I had work for him on a project basis.

One time at our restaurant on Easter Sunday I had him come in dressed appropriately as a chef, cook a steamship round roast beef, and then cut and serve it. He was reliable when he was able. James was an alcoholic. When he got any money he would start drinking until the money was gone.

When he was sober he would ask me to hold up on his pay. I did not cheat him in any way and as soon as he asked I would give him some or all of his money unless he was drunk at the time. That was per his request.

One day when I was at a client near Boston, I got a call from James. He was in New Bedford, Massachusetts. He had just gotten off a boat. He had his pay. He asked for a ride back to North Carolina. I was at a stopping point. Knowing James, I feared the worst.

I immediately headed for New Bedford. I wanted to get there as quickly as I could. When I got there, it took some time to find him. I followed a trail around the bars. He owed money at two bars. I found him almost passed out. In just a short period of time, all his pay was gone. I took him home.

- **The young man that had never been into the post office.**
We hired a young man that had just graduated from high school. Cheri sent the young man to the post office.

She handed him the mail.

"This stack is for town mail. This other stack is for out of town."

The young man was totally confused. In his 18 years of life in this tiny town he had never been in the post office nor had any desire to do so.

My children at very young ages had been all over many cities multiple times. I think of Hosea 4:6 in the Bible:

"My people are destroyed for lack of knowledge: because thou hast rejected knowledge, I will also reject thee, that thou shalt be no priest to me: seeing thou hast forgotten the law of thy God, I will also forget thy children."

- **The man who sold produce.**
I knew an elderly man with an old beat-up truck who sold produce. I

don't remember his name.

Most of the time he just hung out on the street socializing.

On Monday morning he would go somewhere and buy a truckload of fresh produce. He would come back to town and park at a set location until he had sold out. By Tuesday afternoon he was done.

He would fill up his truck with gas and put aside a certain amount to buy the produce load on the next Monday.

He would pay his personal bills.

The rest was his spending money for the week.

That man had all of the elements of a successful business with a great work-life balance.

- **The couple that was thinking about a divorce.**
A couple in their thirties told me they were thinking about a divorce.

I don't recall the reason. Maybe I didn't ask.

I did ask them if they were church members. They said that they were.

I asked them why they were not meeting with their pastor.

Why would they come to a stranger?

There was no reply.

"Could it be that you have already decided what you want to do and are looking for someone to agree with you? You know that your pastor would counsel you to reconciliation. If you have decided to divorce you could just go ahead and do it. It's not an unforgivable sin. But my counsel would be that you not get a divorce."

I did tell them to think ahead about the future with them not together.

What kind of regrets would occur as the children grew and as they aged?

What if either or both remarried and regretted that?

I don't know what they decided to do.

- **The woman who had God's approval to divorce her husband.**
  There was a Christian couple with children.

  The wife told me that she was going to file for divorce. She said that God told her that she had suffered enough.

  I told her that I would never try to talk someone out of doing what God told them.

  I did tell her that I was curious what type of suffering she had endured that would change God's stated viewpoint on divorce.

  She told me that her husband had promised her a house with two bathrooms.

  They still only had one bathroom.

- **The young man who wanted to fix cars in his driveway.**
  I helped one unemployed young man that had an idea yet did not know how to plan and get setup.

  He knew how to fix cars.

  He planned to run a shop in his driveway, a practice that was legal.

  He did not know that he would be able to buy parts at a discount. I got him set up at a local parts store with a 35% discount like other repair shops.

  He could then charge full price to his customers, a practice in use by other shops.

  I offered him free advertising in our newspaper.

  We set up a price schedule for standard jobs and an hourly rate for other jobs.

  That man did absolutely nothing.

- **The man who inherited a laundry business.**
  A man who had inherited a laundry business and run it into the ground was in trouble for writing bad checks.

Not big checks involving strangers but many small ones at local establishments where he had been known all of his life.

I took him to the court that was in another town for his scheduled court appearance. While I could not represent him in legal matters, I was there to tell the court that I was going to help him, assistance at no charge from me, to make restitution on the checks.

I knew he had income to cover them, and that once clear he would use cash for all consumer transactions.

Checks would just be for utilities, taxes, and such where he needed records.

I did, of course, tell the judge that I could only succeed with the defendant's continued cooperation.

There was quite a bit of discussion between him and the judge.

He was not fined or sentenced to jail.

- **The judge did not know about "dollar drinks."**
While I was with the man who had inherited a laundry business and while we were waiting in court there was an amusing incident.

An elderly man had been charged in some kind of altercation involving a woman.

I don't remember the details but he was telling the court about buying "dollar drinks" for himself and the woman.

The judge interrupted with a comment:

"I didn't know that you could buy liquor by the drink in North Carolina."

- **The man who was willing to pay me $1 million.**
A man told me that he needed some help.

He believed he had won $10 million.

He would give me 10% of it if I would make sure that he got the money. He had with him a mailing that he had received.

"One of these three people has won $10 million." His name was one of the three.

As gently as possible I told him that it might be a true statement but that he was not the one of the three that was the winner.

If he had read a little further he would have seen that.

They wanted him to mail back a card with him paying postage so that he could be in next year's drawing.

He would become one of that company's products. His name would be sold over and over again.

Mail order coupons in magazines where catalogs were sold for 25 cents served the same purpose. In the direct mail world a payment in any amount qualified that person's name to be sold. Buying a stamp to be in a database may have also counted.

Later Facebook, Google, and other "free" online services would earn billions and make their founders multi-billionaires from these living "products."

- **The lady who wanted her own bathroom.**
An application had been made for a block grant to do improvements in one town. I did the census. It was a small neighborhood and the census did not take long even though I had to go back to pick up those who had been missed.

Most homes were completely darkened inside with heavy curtains. Some of the homes were of women and children. Men lived elsewhere. If a welfare inspector did an unannounced inspection and a man was found to be living there, welfare could be cut off for the mother living there.

At one home there was a well-dressed middle aged woman. She had no children. It was just she and her husband.

Both had relatively good jobs. Together they made about $35,000. I would say they were somewhat above the average family income for that county. Their rent was $40 a month. Their house had no bathroom. There was a faucet outside that was maybe a foot above the ground. There was an outhouse. So there was town water and the sewer ran right past the house, maybe six to eight feet away from the building. Freezing of pipes was not a problem. The house was cheaply built.

The woman told me that she, her husband, and the landlord who lived on the same street in a similar house were hoping for the block grant so that they would be able to get bathrooms.

A bathroom could have been put in for $500, maybe less. I do not understand why there were people there who did not think that their own money should be used for things like a bathroom.

They and so many others were exploited for that mentality.

Admission to the county fair was $1.00. Saturday kids movies at the high school was 25 cents. Those amounts kept many children away. It wasn't a matter of having no money.

School breakfast and lunch was free to all. Applications not needed as the county was viewed as being mostly poor.

A grocery store was almost next to the high school. Every morning teens gathered before school, bought and ate junk food.

It was a mentality that was childlike. The government was like a parent providing necessities and "my money" is for the luxuries and other discretionary items that I want.

Regretfully many elected government people want this belief to continue.

Restaurants in eastern North Carolina.
Eastern North Carolina is not the gourmet capital of the country but it does have a number of single unit restaurants with fried chicken, barbecue, and fish as well as quaint ambience. There were few chain restaurants in the area. The restaurants in eastern North Carolina were dark, dirty, and dingy or they were places with large glass windows and turquoise booths.

Steve's.
There was Steve's, dark, dirty, and dingy.

It is of note for its business model with a simple unchanging menu and low prices. It has been in business for over 90 years.

It only serves boiled red hot dogs, usually with spicy chili, onions, and mustard.

You can add of chips and a choice of Pepsi, Mountain Dew, or chocolate milk.

Steve's now has a second store in a mall. I would not go near it. Dark, dirty, and dingy cannot be replicated. It has to grow with time.

I have heard Steve's is planning to add banana pudding. I like banana pudding, I guess the menu can stand a change after 90 years, though I ask why do it?

Steve's might be heading down the same slippery slope as the others.

Red hot dogs.
Red hot dogs, not the short, fat, spicy hot dogs called "red hots," are a North Carolina specialty.

Johnston County, is ground zero for the fire engine-red hot dogs. The county is home to two makers: Carolina Packers and Stevens Sausage Co. Many prefer Carolina Packers, with dogs that are also called Packers dogs or Bright Leaf dogs. These dogs are a mixture of beef and pork without poultry that is in some red hot dogs.

Why are red hot dogs red?

At one time all hot dogs were dyed red. In the 1960s it was found that the red dye in use could possibly cause cancer. Most hot dog makers quit using red dye. But in the south, the makers switched to the same dye that colors cough syrup and cherry soda.

Free potatoes.
Potatoes are a big crop. Planting time is always uncertain due to the rain and the flooded fields. Most of the crop is pre-sold for potato chips. At harvest time there is a brief period of high prices. As more potatoes come onto the market the price drops dramatically. Digging stops.

From that point, farmers offered potatoes free for the digging. The grocery store owners were certain that no one dug potatoes. There were potato fields that adjoined the house and trailer lots of poor people in town. Allegedly these same people were known to be buying potatoes in town at exorbitant prices. A few times I bought potatoes at the weekend farmers market in Haymarket, Boston. I would buy a bag of North Carolina potatoes and could truthfully say that I could not afford to buy them in North Carolina as they were much cheaper in Boston. I didn't dig the free potatoes either.

I do pro bono work in North Carolina.
I have always counseled others in various ways. Me, a white man, outsider, wearing a coat and tie, and owner of the newspaper, I was like a lightning rod.

The requests though were not for money. They were for solutions.

Life insurance.
I have to say some more about life insurance. while I'm still thinking about North Carolina and about Edmund. being the top life salesman for his company. Life insurance is an incredible product. It is an instant estate at a cheap price for young people through middle age. There should be classes in high school about it. There are so many different insurance products to meet all needs. I have always used term insurance and have had total coverage as high as $1 million. With term you can vary coverage to meet your particular need.

How I Raised Myself from Failure to Success in Selling.
A great life insurance book and autobiography is *How I Raised Myself from Failure to Success in Selling*. The book was first published in 1949. It is still in print. It was written by Frank Bettger who was fired from professional baseball for lack of enthusiasm.

My favorite story in the Bettger book involved a man who had applied for a loan for his business. The bank required that he have a life insurance policy for the amount of the loan with the bank as beneficiary. Bettger went to see the man. The man pointed to a stack of insurance proposals and told Bettger that he could add his proposal and the man would be reading through them soon. Bettger said that he could see the different colored binders and knew the companies.

"You could pick any one of them. They are all good companies and good premiums. But I can do something for you that none of them can do. You need the loan to run your business. To get the loan you need an insurance policy. To get the insurance policy you must pass a physical exam. Right now you look pretty healthy to me. Tomorrow morning you could wake up with a fever and might be delayed passing a physical or might never again pass. I have an appointment for you ten minutes from now and just a block away for an insurance physical."

He went for the exam then took Bettger to lunch. Only later did he even ask what company Bettger represented.

What happened to the life insurance agents?
I remember when life insurance agents were everywhere. Then they seemed to go away. One time I had gotten an ad card that I could get a free atlas by

sending back the card. The card asked one and only one question. What is your age? I used a scribbly way of writing and put down 96, figuring I would never hear from them again. Wrong. A salesman called and wanted an appointment. He got his meeting and I got my atlas. In retrospect I'll bet that other people did the age thing. They might have become good prospects that bought insurance. At Rotary clubs and other places where I was a speaker, I would often start with asking a show of hands of who had not heard from any life insurance salesman in the past ten years. All hands were raised. What better prospect for life insurance than a Rotarian?

Court sessions as free entertainment.
A form of entertainment in rural North Carolina was to attend court when it was held. Small towns usually had one lawyer. The prosecutor and judge came from elsewhere. In court the two lawyers would loudly call each other all kinds of names and accuse each other of fraud and incompetence. The judge would threaten to lock both of them up forever.

Out of court, they might be the best of friends and possibly former schoolmates.

North Carolina Rotary club.
I was a Rotary club president one year. I published a newsletter for the club. In traveling I would visit other Rotary clubs, get a makeup card for missing my local meeting, and exchange banners. On trips, I carried several of my local club banners with me. Visiting other clubs was a great time to meet others of like minds. There is no shortage of clubs on all weekdays, and with meetings for breakfast, lunch, or dinner.

We become Paul Harris Fellows.
Cheri and I both became Paul Harris Fellows in the Rotary Foundation. The requirement was to make a donation of a $1,000 for yourself or for someone else. Some clubs required that all new members make the donation. Donations like that make a difference to the recipient but maybe make a greater difference to the givers. Jesus spoke on that subject quite often. I set out to get other members to become Paul Harris Fellows. Quite a few of them did. One young Rotarian, a regular church goer, that I knew was able to give refused.

"$1,000 in a zero coupon bond buys a lot of college money."

In effect, at that time he viewed givers as fools, an attitude not unusual for new Rotarians. He had much to learn about giving and Rotary was the place to get that knowledge.

The Rotary Foundation is the largest scholarship organization in the world and a full 100% of donations go just for programs. There is no administration or fundraising cost.

Rotarians and their families could not be recipients of any scholarships.

The top executives of Rotary International and the Rotary Foundation were volunteers with no salaries. Further they had to pledge that they would do no work, paid or unpaid, in their professions for the following two years. They were expected to devote 100% of their time and energy to Rotary.

At the time I was a Rotarian, there was a polio epidemic in the Philippines. Vaccinations were costing $14 each for the US and Philippine government program. Rotary reduced the costs to 11 cents per vaccination. Rotarian doctors and nurses volunteered their time and paid their own expenses to meet this need. Rotary guiding principles include the Four-Way Test:

1. Is it the TRUTH?

2. Is is FAIR to all concerned?

3. Will it build GOODWILL and BETTER FRIENDSHIPS?

4. Will it be BENEFICIAL to all concerned?

Other principles involve Rotary's commitment to Service above Self, channeled through Five Avenues of Service: Club, Vocational, Community, International, and New Generations. Club service works to strengthen fellowship of members through training and hospitality. Clubs have serious topics to work toward, so having various social events that bring members and their guests informally and for fun, contributes to genuine fellowship. Vocational Service encourages members to serve other people through their vocations, education, and skill sets, which encourages high ethical standards. Community Service is exactly what the name implies — projects and activities each club undertakes to improve community life. International Service volunteers work to expand the Rotarians' humanitarian work around the world. This is the highest level of service as it means that the giver and the recipients will never know each other. It is truly service above self. New Generations Service, that was added in 2010, works to engage youths and young adults in leadership roles. Rotary Youth Leadership Awards is a training program for young people, ages 14 to 30. The award emphasizes leadership and citizenship. Rotaract is an International Youth Program is for ages 18 to 30 while Interact focuses on international service for youths 12 to 18.

A trip to Singapore.
I took our oldest with me on a trip to Singapore. Westbound from Washington D.C., it was a 29 hour flight each way with stops in San Francisco and Hong Kong. It was a free trip.

Holiday Inn started the Priority Club. 75 points by a certain date would get a trip for two for one week, air and hotel, anywhere in the world that had a Holiday Inn. That meant pretty much anywhere. A traveler earned one point per stay per day. Soon it became two points per stay per day at new Holiday Inn hotels. It did not take long for me, and many other travelers to get to 75. Needless to say the second year the trip award was gone.

At the time of our trip, Singapore was beginning its rebirth into the modern world. Many of the buildings and homes were still third world country types, though much reconstruction was taking place. Singapore has gold-backed currency. Alcohol could only be sold in upper class department stores. There was no crime. Tipping was illegal. There was no welfare as families took care of their own and jobs were available for anyone needing one. Elderly people took care of the small parks even to the point of removing dead leaves one by one. Chewing gum could not be sold. Jaywalking was a $500 fine. Drug dealers were executed without delay. There was two years of mandatory government service for 18 year olds, male and female alike. Business income tax rates declined as export sales increased.

During the whole time we were in Singapore there was a well-publicized trial of a man who had been charged with stealing $100. He was acquitted. The jury determined that the $100 check he had received from his employer's customer was unrelated to his employer's business.

Though there were problems, it was a breath of fresh air to sense the freedoms of Singapore. Singapore was trying to get retailers to set prices so that haggling need not be done. It was also courting the wealthy to emigrate from their countries and become citizens of Singapore. It did not accept refugees or residents of certain countries.

Singapore was on its way to becoming the highest income per capita of any country in the world from being one of the lowest. It did succeed. I have found it most interesting that junkets to Singapore by American politicians did not occur. There seemed to be no interest in studying a place where social problems, even race relations, had been solved.

I remember when there was nothing but praise for the Scandinavian countries where government had plenty of services paid for with confiscatory taxes.

Benefits, such as government run childcare and guaranteed minimum income for all, even the unemployed, were touted with the cost unmentioned.

We had stretched out our trip to Singapore a few more days. We stayed at The Raffles Hotel, where the Singapore Sling was invented at the Long Bar. Years earlier, a tiger had been shot under the pool table in the Long Bar. I think the old hotel is still there though Raffles City with at least one large building makes up much of what was the gardens. The bathrooms at the Raffles Hotel are larger than most hotel rooms in new hotels. The hallways are very wide unlike the low ceiling tunnels in new hotels. Anytime we left the room, housekeepers would come in and remake the room. Even at night they were on duty.

In the lobby I wanted to mail some postcards. I went to the counter and asked. The clerk took the cards from me and rang a bell. A little Chinaman, I do mean little, came over from the other side of the expansive lobby, took the cards, and put them in a slot right beside me under the counter. I had not seen the slot. The man went back to his place across the lobby before I could say thank you.

Our daughter wanted to go to the shopping center that was next to the hotel. I told her that she would be ok. I did tell her that an Indian man might attempt to talk to her but that he would be harmless.

"Just ignore him and keep moving."

Such an event did occur. Of the two other races in Singapore, Malay and Chinese, I told her she would not be bothered.

Our flight home left Changi Airport, Singapore at 9:00 AM and arrived in Washington D.C. at 4:00 PM the same day due to the International Date Line.

I buy a Rolex watch.
I had already planned on buying a Rolex watch, though only one with a plain case. The price was much lower as there was no import duty as when buying in the United States. I knew to look for an authorized dealer.

While the watch was still in warranty, I had a problem with the watch. I took it into the Rolex service center on Fifth Avenue in New York in an upper floor above retail shops. They gave me a receipt and shipped the watch back to me by registered mail after a spring was replaced.

There was a man in front of me in line at Rolex service with a foreign accent and appearance. He was disappointed that his watch could not be fixed that day. It would be three weeks. He pulled a large roll of bills out of his pocket. He wanted to buy what he called a cheap Rolex, which would be like mine I supposed, to use while he was waiting for his watch to be repaired. Was he to throw that cheap one away as soon as he got his good one back? He was told that there were no watches for sale in the service center. The clerk pointed out the window to a jeweler on the other side of the street that did sell Rolex. The man with the roll of cash went out the door. Hopefully he would not need to know the time before he got across the street to the jeweler.

In 2019 the watch stopped running. Rolex wants $3,150 to repair it. I'll just do without a watch.

A trip to Kuala Lumpur.
We got a rental car and drove to Kuala Lumpur, Malaysia. We had been told not to go at night because of the bandits. After daylight, off we went as did everyone else. Plenty of lorries, as the big trucks were called. There was a six inch drop off from the pavement on each side to discourage off road passing on the right. The alternative was forcing a third lane otherwise there was never a clear space for passing. I was pulled over for speeding but did not get a ticket. The police car had four men with automatic rifles. I got out of the car and at the leading of the driver shook hands with all four. They offered me a cigarette. I was not a smoker but I decided not to decline. There was talking and laughter all in whatever language they spoke. After we all finished our smoke, the leader told me in English that I would not get a ticket. He said that as I was a foreigner that it would be too much trouble for all of us. Another round of handshakes and we all departed. I had always wanted to go to Kuala Lumpur ever since I had learned to read. Just the name was an attraction. A mystery city of the Orient. As we got closer my heart dropped. The first view of Kuala Lumpur was a McDonald's. I found that just about every fast food restaurant from the United States, past and present, had a store there. We went to a local "buffet." It was outdoors. We paid and were given a plate. Go down the row and point to what you want. Everything went into one pile on the plate. At the end throw your plate on the grass. Someone with a garden hose was washing dishes.

We go into the hospitality business.
We bought a restaurant and motel in North Carolina. We made a tabloid menu called *The Sanguinity*.

We did a good bit of remodeling. Everyone said they liked it but in retrospect I wish we had left it dark, dingy, and dirty.

QuickBooks.
I wish that QuickBooks and low cost computers had been available when I was in the restaurant business. I recommend to anyone starting out in life to pay the

cost and run all of their finances on QuickBooks, preferably QuickBooks online.

Bookkeeping at the restaurant was all manual and there was no ability to get reports and to do comparisons to past periods. As a result, I was not able to bring any greater success than past owners.

I have watched small business over the years and have seen the resulting failures due to lack of financial control. Economics, the matching of unlimited demand to limited resources, has great application in small business and in personal finances. I have always tried to build the perfect system that does not intermingle business and personal. I know that a business that is transparent and keeps meticulous books can best be successful for all stakeholders, the customers, the suppliers, the bank, society at large, employees, and the owners. This ownership of a real functioning small business was most valuable in developing future models.

QuickBooks Pro is a good way to learn the language of business and to treat personal money affairs like it was a business because that is exactly what it is. I recommend that everything be done honestly, correctly, and in a timely fashion.

Now in 2019, I have achieved the first certification level of Quick Books Online and am working on the second. I am listed on the Intuit website.

QuickBooks online can be viewed in several ways. I see it as a whole new frontier for small business.

It is cloud-based. No backups need be made and there is no concern about operating system or malware. There is no need to buy new versions and go through installation.

QuickBooks online does cost more than a desktop version like QuickBooks Pro yet is well worth it. I believe it more than pays for itself because of a new view of bookkeeping and a better understanding of finances.

QuickBooks online moves bookkeeping away from having someone just doing data entry. Each function can run its own bookkeeping using their smart phones and by-products of purchases.

I have found a most dramatic reduction in bookkeeping time using QuickBooks online with workflow changes. On the downside, this new viewpoint on bookkeeping can take some months of setup and tweaking but each month get easier and easier.

There is an investment of time and money. I do not necessarily recommend that anyone on QuickBooks desktop versions make a switch at this time.

The restaurant coffee table.
There was a coffee table at our restaurant that started each day and filled quickly at 4:30 AM when we opened. Mostly farmers.

Every day the same jokes and the same stories.

All the farmers were great guys, but there was one farmer that really stood out in many ways.

He was extremely frugal yet would go all the way to Las Vegas for gambling. He was at the coffee table every day. Like the others he would only get coffee.

On Saturday afternoons he would come in alone. His wife was not with him. He would have a Kansas City steak dinner.

He had a part of his bookkeeping and tax strategy that he had told about over and over to everyone. There was some payment that he would get once a year for about $3,000. He would always cash that check rather than deposit it. He figured that if he ever got audited and if he should be asked about something that was not in his books he could say that he bought it with the money from cashing that check.

He was knowledgeable about many things. I always enjoyed talking with him.

Ag Subsidies.
Early in the year at the coffee table, the Department of Agriculture man would be asked if the new subsidy rates were out yet.

"I want to decide what I'm not going to grow this year" or "I need to make some more money. I've got to lease some more swamp land so I can get paid not to grow anything on it." Everyone laughed including the Department of Agriculture man.

Today with the internet it is easy to see how much gets paid out. By googling ag subsidy you can find the database that can be searched by state, county, town, zip code, etc you can find out how much people get year by year. It is a fun game to see names of people in New York City or names of people in one's own town or county that get paid not to grow things. There are building contractors that will eventually build houses. There are investment firms. You can look for who gets the most in your area. The database is most enlightening.

I compete with social benefits.
The kitchen staff, like in all restaurants in the south, was all black.

I was appalled that the long time cooks, good and loyal, were getting minimum wage. I began a gradual but rapid increase to get them to $6.00 an hour from the minimum wage of $3.35. These good people began working fewer hours, still getting the same weekly pay. I looked into the reason why. They told me that if they made more money they would lose Medicaid and other social benefits, a loss much greater than the pay increase. They wanted to work full time but could not afford it.

There was a small clothing store in town.

It was to close for good as the owner was already older than most retirees and thought it was finally her turn. I wanted to hire the young lady that was the clerk. Her husband was a deputy sheriff. No children at the time. A few days before she was to start work she told me that she could not afford to take the job. FHA had told her that she and her husband would be making too much money to get a loan for a house if she took any new job.

FHA 235.
There was a program where a new three bedroom brick house on an acre of land with central air conditioning could be bought for nothing down and $40 a month. It was a 30 year loan that got a monthly subsidy. Many, if not most, of the homes went to foreclosure. Many were so badly trashed that they had to be torn down. A local agent said that if they had weekly payments and someone came by each week to collect that it might have worked.

The man that thought I had enough money.
One time that I was picking up trash in the lot in the middle of the day, a local man who was walking home with a purchase from the state liquor store across the street stopped and addressed me.

"Just look at you! You with all your money and you're doing work that somebody like me could be doing to make some money."

I told him he was hired and he could take over. It turned out that he would not be able to go to work that day. I did not hold my breath waiting for him the next day or the next.

The young man who had to take his grandmother to the doctor.
There was a young man that constantly came in asking for work as a dishwasher.

Nothing was available. I had his name and phone number. He lived only a block away. I had an opening soon and I called him.

He was so glad and would be right over. He said he was heading out the door. I did not see him that day or the next.

About two weeks later I saw him on the street. I asked him what happened about coming to work.

It seems he had to take his grandmother to the doctor out of town.

Restaurant owner woes.
Running a restaurant or any business is not easy.

I was in the lot talking with someone. I waved to a car that passed. I was asked if it was someone I knew. I replied that I was thanking them for not stopping and coming in as a customer, a prospective employee, or a vendor.

People that work in restaurants are a unique class. They can withstand irregular hours and constantly varying paychecks unlike those with nine to five jobs. They have the independence that they can quit anytime without notice and be at work the next day someplace else.

Maybe I could say that people that eat in restaurants are also a unique class.

We found that we could get flour and sugar cheaper at a *Food Lion* grocery store in a nearby city than off the truck. Yes it was a 74 mile round trip but we bought a large quantity at once and we might be going to or through anyway.

One day we were at the checkout with our cart filled high. We saw a man from our town. He greeted us. From the look on his face I thought he was going to fall over dead. I found out pretty quickly that he had gone back home and told everyone he knew that he had caught us buying things for the restaurant at a grocery store!

Sometimes we had an emergency need and would go to the grocery store that was across the street. Is buying things for the restaurant at a grocery store in town worse than buying out of town?

In rural North Carolina, I was not thinking anything about the concept of supply chains. Now the subject is a big one.

The waitresses not getting much in tips.
I came back from a trip and was in the restaurant one evening. I asked how things were going.

"We're not getting much in tips."

"Why not? How is the service?"

"The service is good but they just get hamburgers."

"We get tourists, hunters, and travelers. They have credit cards. It makes no sense that they would get hamburgers. Let me take the order from the next table."

That was quite a boast. I am no salesman or waiter. Nonetheless, they got steaks and when I went back they ordered dessert. The waitress got a nice tip.

"You were just lucky."

I took another table and they got steaks and shrimp cocktail. Also dessert. I tried to use it as a teaching moment. Another failure due to confirmation bias where they could only see customers getting hamburgers.

Restaurant failures.
There is a reason that restaurants failed so often back then, and many still do. It was an easy business to go into. People with no knowledge of business would buy an existing business. Right off the bat they had more cash in on one day than they had ever seen in a month or six weeks. It did not have to be paid out right away. The seller, a long time owner, without mortgages, wanted to a get a high enough price to invest the proceeds and get the same earnings. The new owner had the same expenses plus a high monthly payment, thus had to raise prices. Business dropped off. In about 18 months they were out of business. That was the point at which the sales tax people were demanding to get their money that had not been paid. The sellers also lost because they had a lien on at least the building. Many of them learned that they had no further recourse because it was a purchase money mortgage.

The man who wanted everyone to make good pay.
We had one customer that came in every day with his wife. The two got an extra plate and shared the daily special. This man had plenty of money. He was quite frequently on the soapbox about how anyone that worked 40 hours a week should be able to take home at least $200. He thought something should be done about greedy employers. I never bothered to tell him that it was

revenue from customers that paid wages. Two people sharing a daily lunch special generated zero for the employees.

The lady that felt cheated when we went to a buffet format.
There was a well-heeled couple that came to lunch every day. They each bought the daily special. We switched to a buffet at the same price as the daily special. The lady complained that what we did was not fair to older people like she and her husband that could not eat a lot.

The waitress who thought that prices were too high.
There was a waitress that we would never suspect of stealing. I had never thought of sweet-hearting nor knew what it was. This waitress would make checks that she thought was more of what she thought they could afford. It must not have occurred to her that no one is forced to come into a restaurant and they know the prices when they order. I wonder if she thought that cutting the bill would result in a bigger tip.

The county fair.
There was an annual fair in the county. A carnival was a part of it.

Some of the workers stayed at the motel. Since the fair did not open until late afternoon, the restaurant had a few of the ride operators and others as customers earlier in the day. A tourist couple was at the register. The man made a comment. At first I thought it was a joke.

"I've seen a lot of carnie people in my lifetime. I see now that they must come from this part of North Carolina."

Maybe it was a joke.

How the man figured out how to split a penny.
One man would come in every morning and join the coffee table. 30 cents for a cup of coffee that could be refilled unlimited times. A 15% tip was four and a half cents. One day he would leave four cents for a tip. The next day he would leave five cents. This same man traded in his pickup truck every year when the new models came out even though he only drove a few thousand miles a year and had no need to haul anything. The depreciation was still there and he did not care.

Z's Grill.
A block away from our restaurant, a lady operated from a little stand outside her home. Z's Grill made the finest hamburger and fries I have ever had. I don't know how she did it. Further, she could serve quickly. I don't think she had a license and she may have had numerous violations. I don't know if she fooled

around with the no value added expense of sales tax and income tax. No one seemed to care. No overhead. No employees.

I loved Vi's tag line that I'm sure had not been reviewed by focus groups and consultants. "Don't go 'round hungry."

The Soup Nazi.
There was a man in New York City that had been called the "soup Nazi" when he was on a TV program, *Seinfeld* I think. He had a real soup business in a prime downtown location near 57th street. He was a one man show selling soup for $8 to $14 per serving in the 1970s and 1980s. There was always a line at his counter. If a person in line was not ready to order he would send them to the back of the line. One time in an interview he told what made for his success:

"I got no overhead, I got no waitresses, and I got a cashier." While saying the cashier part he smiled and pointed to himself.

A doctor sells hot dogs.
In Connecticut an anesthesiologist quit his job and set up a gourmet hot dog cart on the street.

He had made big bucks but also had a very high malpractice insurance cost even though he had never had a claim.

He found that he could net more by selling hot dogs, had less stress, and could work when liked.

The cook that always went to church.
One of the long time cooks told me when we bought the restaurant that her church had services one Sunday a month and she would not work at all on those Sundays. That was fine with me. Later I would wish that he church had services every day. The fire department was planning a fundraising dinner. We were asked to order a few things and they would pay for it. Cheri had told the lead waitress to call her when the truck came in so she could take the hams or whatever to the fire department. Cheri went over and found that most of the order was gone. She remembered that she had seen that cook's husband parked out by the kitchen door. She went out and found the items were in his car and he was waiting for her to bring out more. We fired her. A few weeks later the owner of the grocery store in the town where she lived, told me that she had started eating meat. He told me that she had never bought any meat at his store until after I fired her. He said that she still was not buying toilet paper. He figured either she never went to the bathroom or that her son still had his job as a school custodian where she could get free toilet paper.

I teach Sunday school at a black church.
I was asked to teach a Sunday school class at a young men's class at one of the black churches. The subject got onto race. The question was why do black men get in trouble more frequently than white men? I told them that I might know part of the answer. I told them that while driving up and down the Delmarva peninsula, something I did frequently, that I might drive all night. As it got later at night almost all the cars I saw each had four to six young black men in them. I had no concern for my own security as I knew they were just riding around. At a gas station there might be one such car. The driver would buy gas. One or more of the others would buy bottles of Thunderbird or MD2020, this being fortified wine, wine with added alcohol. The only reason to buy the product is to get high, cheap and quick. Back on the road they might get stopped. A man with a little too much to drink might talk back or be threatening. They all might end up in jail. But don't they have a right to be out? For sure, but much crime happens at night.

I was able to use two Bible references.

John 3:19-20:
"And this is the condemnation, that light is come into the world, and men loved darkness rather than light, because their deeds were evil. For every one that doeth evil hateth the light, neither cometh to the light, lest his deeds should be reproved."

Ephesians 5:11:
"And have no fellowship with the unfruitful works of darkness, but rather reprove them."

I told the class that they could walk down the street at night but they might fit the description of someone that had committed a crime and they at least might be arrested. They might get convicted and go to jail. They could get shot.

I drove at night, was not seen over and over in the same town, was alone, and was not buying fortified wine. I was not likely to get into any trouble. It was not because I was white. Hopefully they got the point.

Jack the reptile man.
Jack the reptile man and his family were good long term friends that we had met in North Carolina.

The clown on the interstate in the swamp.
I drove on trips, night and day, with Jack usually when he and I had business in the same area.

Sometimes, one or two of his sons might be with us depending on the mission of the trip.

Early one Sunday morning, while I was at the wheel, Jack and I were on I-95 in a swampy area of South Carolina where there are long causeways.

I saw a car quite a ways in front of us pull over and stop. There was no other traffic.

A man in a clown suit got out.

Not wanting to miss an opportunity to say something, I woke Jack.

He was not quite awake as we passed but I said my say anyway:

"I wonder what that clown thinks he's doing?"

Why you should always get a receipt for a cash purchase.
One time during the day we had stopped for gas in Florence, South Carolina, at Starvin' Marvin, one of the large convenience store/gas stations. The store name was to let us know that the price of gas was so cheap that it was to our advantage that Marvin, the owner, could not afford to eat adequately. I was driving.

Jack pumped the gas and paid for it. The place was busy and we were there for quite a while. Four of us, waiting on lines at the restroom, and waiting on lines at the registers. Each of us buying something different. Finally we were ready to go.

As we pulled out there came a voice over the outdoor speaker. We had not paid for our gas. Despite the window being shut and talking in the vehicle I heard us mentioned. Jack said he had paid for the gas.

There were two things about Jack.

He did not get receipts and he often paid for things with quarters from his reptile farm food vending machines.

So he had no gas receipt and he had paid in quarters.

I went in and fortunately was able to work it out. Someone remembered the quarters.

I had them look back for the amount on the register that person worked.

Our amount was still on the pump as we had not moved.

The amount paid in was a multiple of a quarter.

I got a receipt.

Later I chastised Jack again about receipts.

As his accountant I had my rights.

I told him that if I had not heard the speaker, we might have been brought back by a highway patrolman.

At that point no one at the gas station would have remembered anything.

Every gas station in South Carolina had signs about a state law regarding drive offs and the time that could be spent in prison.

The pumps could be turned on by anyone at the pump.

I have always told my family about the importance of getting a receipt for any cash expense.

While maybe I'm too cautious I have said this is especially true for a restaurant with sit-down service.

Usually I recommend using a credit card at those places.

I had one case where even a credit card was a potential problem.

One of our sons and I were in a restaurant for breakfast. We were in a hurry to leave.

The check was not for items we ordered and was about $3 less than I figured we owed.

I told the waiter.

He said he fixed it so we would pay less.

I did not like the idea but paid with a card.

Then I later worried about why he did that and was concerned about identity theft with the card.

No one looked like a manager except our waiter.

Maybe he was the manager.

Non-Employer businesses.
History has showed that for independence, for income, and for security, the one person business might be the best way to go.

The Census Bureau calls them non-employer businesses.

By the mid-1990s there were 26 million non-employer businesses, growing by a million a year.

I remember a news item from when the Russians occupied Afghanistan.

There was a video showing the street vendors. It made no difference to them what government was in power. Many of them may not have known what government was in power.

They operated, they bought, and they sold.

These vendors had been operating like that for thousands of years.

There may well be something there for all of the wise to learn.

Church experience in North Carolina.
We had expectations in moving to the Bible Belt. In fact, church was disappointing in North Carolina. We went to several of them.

I did have some definable and memorable experiences at one church.

I have always been a believer in tithing though at the time I thought of it more as a requirement, perhaps even viewing it subconsciously as an essential to salvation.

I knew verses such as Ephesians 2:8-9:

"For by grace are ye saved through faith; and that not of yourselves: it is the gift of God: Not of works, lest any man should boast."

The church we attended was all about tithing.

My 10% made a big difference to the church offering, maybe not so much because I made a lot but because the others believed in tithing but did not practice it.

I was giving right off the top with no deductions.

The pastor said that I was trying to "buy the church."

There was a real easy solution to that problem. My money went elsewhere.

Further, I had not asked to be a member nor had I asked to become a deacon or trustee.

Because of my frequent travel I had not volunteered to be a Sunday school teacher though I did teach when I was asked which was frequent and last minute when I was there.

I can teach without any preparation as per II Timothy 4:2:

"Preach the word; be instant in season, out of season; reprove, rebuke, exhort with all long-suffering and doctrine."

One thing I have always included in Bible teaching is that when we go to the Bible we need to go with an open mind and not teach our own opinions.

Doing that can cause other problems.

The lesson one week that I was teaching was from I Timothy, 5:23:

"Drink no longer water, but use a little wine for thy stomach's sake and thine often infirmities."

I gave that verse as an example.

I said that churches that do not believe in drinking will say that the wine mentioned in the Bible was actually grape juice.

Then they say that I Timothy chapter 1, which is in the same letter from Paul to Timothy, that in referring to bishops, is referring to a pastor.

In verse three when it says "not given to wine" they say amen.

I told them that if it means grape juice in chapter 5 it has to mean grape juice in chapter 1.

As it happens both verses use the same Greek word.

So by placing our own meaning on it, if their pastor, Bible word bishop, drinks grape juice, Bible word wine, he is disqualified from holding his position (that the Bible says is an appointment by the Holy Spirit.)

Everyone laughed.

Then I learned from the class that their pastor bought Nehi grape drink by the case and had cases stacked up in his office.

I laughed too.

I then pointed out that this was further proof of how by putting our meanings on the Bible it could make for trouble.

This particular church was opposed to even a taste of any alcoholic beverage though had no problem with smoking that was done by many between Sunday school and church in the presence of children.

Every Sunday the pastor asked that men join him in visitation on Tuesday. I decided to do that. I was the only man to show up. The pastor asked me to stop coming.

"Dave you are making it really embarrassing for me. I've got 40 year deacons that never go. You're not even a member."

Later we found that he did not want us in his church at all.

We began to attend a new pentecostal church some distance away. We would go on Sunday morning and stay all day. Cheri would bring lunch. The whole area was really developing.

For the pentecostal church, I set up a town-wide census with small areas so that church members could all go out one day and get it done. I got them clipboards, forms, and maps of each segment to survey.

I was asked to make a $100,000 donation.
A pastor wanted to buy the lot next to his church for a skating rink for the youth. He somehow thought that I had plenty of money.

He asked me to give him a $100,000 to buy the lot.

He told me that God would bless me 100 fold.

I did some figuring.

"So that would be $10 million. Pastor, that would be more than I could handle. Who knows what I might do."

He did not know how to respond.

"I've got a better idea," I said.

"You give me $1,000. God will bless you 100 fold and you will have your $100,000."

Somehow he did not think it would work out to do that.

Women pastors and teachers.
One Sunday school quarterly covered both I Timothy and II Timothy. All of the Bible text was printed in their quarterlies. Since that denomination ordained women pastors. I was anxious to see how it handled I Timothy 2:12-15. That part had been left out. Paul wrote in I Timothy 2:12-15:

"But I suffer not a woman to teach, nor to usurp authority over the man, but to be in silence. For Adam was first formed, then Eve. And Adam was not deceived, but the woman being deceived was in the transgression. Notwithstanding she shall be saved in childbearing, if they continue in faith and charity and holiness with sobriety."

I wrote to the publisher at the denomination headquarters. I got a brief letter back from the editor, a woman. She said:

"Oh the Word of God is so wonderful and there is so much there. We just don't have space to include all of it in one quarterly. Maybe in the future we will be able to include the rest of Paul's letters to Timothy."

In my Bible, the two letters from Paul to Timothy take up a little more than seven pages. The four verses left out, I Timothy 2:12-15, take up an inch and a half yet express a doctrinal point.

This woman believes that God intended for women to teach so she actually removed part of the Bible.

Here is what the Bible says in Revelation 22:19 about removing from the Bible:

"And if any man shall take away from the words of the book of this prophecy, God shall take away his part out of the book of life, and out of the holy city, and from the things which are written in this book."

"And Adam was not deceived, but the woman being deceived was in the transgression."

Eve sincerely believed the serpent that eating the fruit was what God wanted for her to do. She saw nothing wrong with eating it. We read in Genesis 3:6:

"And when the woman saw that the tree was good for food, and that it was pleasant to the eyes, and a tree to be desired to make one wise, she took of the fruit thereof, and did eat, and gave also unto her husband with her; and he did eat."

Adam ate though he knew it was wrong. He was not deceived. When they were caught, Adam blamed Eve for his sin. Adam included God for blame because God had given him Eve. We read in Genesis 3:12:

"And the man said, The woman whom thou gavest to be with me, she gave me of the tree, and I did eat."

Eve had an excuse. We read in Genesis 3:13:

"And the Lord God said unto the woman, What is this that thou hast done?"

And the woman said,

"The serpent beguiled me, and I did eat."

Men pastors and teachers.
A man has the ability to teach the truth even if he does not live it. Men still must be wary. Note that it does not mean that men will.

The first two examples of men not living as they teach are from the Bible, Noah and Lot.

We do know that their righteousness came from faith not from their works.

The Bible says that the Holy Spirit sets pastors in the church.

God sees things about people that we cannot see.

Contrary to what is often taught, I Timothy 3 does not apply to pastors.

It applies to bishops, church administrative officers, that are appointed by man.

Noah and Lot would not have qualified to be bishops or for that matter deacons.

They qualified as pastors by standards that we do not know that includes faith.

There are many men preachers that are intentionally doing false teaching.

This has been true from the beginning of the church age and has been written about in the Bible.

The Bible tells us that the Bereans "searched the scriptures daily to see if these things were true."

Spiritual discernment, a God given ability of born again believers, is needed to know when false teaching is happening.

There are men preaching and teaching that are not saved.

Because they are not saved they can teach the logos Word of God, the words as written, but cannot teach the rhema Word of God, the words that have been made real by the Holy Spirit.

Spiritual teaching.
My spiritual gifts, gifts in the area of serving others, as opposed to the gifts of sanctification, have been teaching and administration. I Corinthians 12:28 and many other verses.

Spiritual teaching is not the same as secular teaching in schools, colleges, or in seminars.

If one of these teachers became saved, they would not necessarily be able to teach as a gift of the Holy Spirit.

Spiritual teaching cannot be taught. It is a gift.

Spiritual teaching includes proclaiming the Word of God, usually within the context of the local church, and with customization to the hearers' lives.

It is not defined as the telling of Bible stories but of explanation, context, and application.

Take Psalms 68:6:

"God setteth the solitary in families: he bringeth out those which are bound with chains: but the rebellious dwell in a dry land."

There are many intellectual commentaries on this verse, done by analysis of word meanings. In spiritual teaching there is a great responsibility to teach the truth and not one's own opinion.

What the Bible says about a virtuous woman.
Here is what the Bible says about virtuous women. Men would have a tough time living up to standards like these. My wife Cheri qualifies as a virtuous woman. I can look at each verse and see how it applies to her.

Many years ago when we lived in rural Connecticut, Cheri would go to a distant town for groceries instead of going to the supermarket in Newtown. I teased her about verse 14, "… she bringeth her food from afar." Proverbs 31:10-31:

"Who can find a virtuous woman? for her price is far above rubies.

The heart of her husband doth safely trust in her, so that he shall have no need of spoil. She will do him good and not evil all the days of her life.

She seeketh wool, and flax, and worketh willingly with her hands.

She is like the merchants' ships; she bringeth her food from afar.

She riseth also while it is yet night, and giveth meat to her household, and a portion to her maidens.

She considereth a field, and buyeth it: with the fruit of her hands she planteth a vineyard.

She girdeth her loins with strength, and strengtheneth her arms.

She perceiveth that her merchandise is good: her candle goeth not out by night.

She layeth her hands to the spindle, and her hands hold the distaff.

She stretcheth out her hand to the poor; yea, she reacheth forth her hands to the needy.

She is not afraid of the snow for her household: for all her household are clothed with scarlet.

She maketh herself coverings of tapestry; her clothing is silk and purple.

Her husband is known in the gates, when he sitteth among the elders of the land.

She maketh fine linen, and selleth it; and delivereth girdles unto the merchant.

Strength and honour are her clothing; and she shall rejoice in time to come.

She openeth her mouth with wisdom; and in her tongue is the law of kindness.

She looketh well to the ways of her household, and eateth not the bread of idleness.

Her children arise up, and call her blessed; her husband also, and he praiseth her.

Many daughters have done virtuously, but thou excellest them all.

Favour is deceitful, and beauty is vain: but a woman that feareth the LORD, she shall be praised.

Give her of the fruit of her hands; and let her own works praise her in the gates."

The quaint old house on the beach.
A lady offered us the use of an old beach house that she owned any time we liked.

We had some good family times there.

It was a quaint house almost hidden in amongst the sand dunes some distance back from the ocean. It was over 100 years old.

One of our sons sees a parrot for the first time.
I remember one time that we were at a gift shop at the beach.

There was a live parrot. That son had never seen a parrot before. He called it a chicken.

The ladies that sold us feathers.
We met some old ladies that ended up selling us a large quantity of feathers.

We paid them $150 for the lot. We never did anything with the feathers. I knew that selling the feathers was important to these ladies and for that reason alone I was glad to help them.

Why I put kerosene into my Chevrolet Chevette.
I had business in one town and sometimes went without the whole family.

We had a Chevrolet Chevette with an Isuzu diesel. We bought it new from a Chevrolet dealer for $6,800. It was Chevrolet's first entry into the growing diesel market. I needed to refuel before going home. Nothing in between but swamp.

There was one station with diesel but it was closed. I knew of a store that had kerosene. Many people in that area heated their homes with portable kerosene heaters. It did not get that cold and not for long even when the temperature dropped. It was winter time and I knew it would be ok to substitute. Anyway it would mix with what diesel I had. I went in the store and there was one customer at the register. The clerk asked me if I wanted kerosene. I said "yes." She said she would be right out to pump it.

"Where's your can?" she asked when she came out.

"Just put it in here," I said. I was standing next to the open tank of the car.

"In there?" she asked.

"It'll be ok," I said. "It's a diesel."

She pumped the $3.00 worth as I had requested. I paid her and then left.

She watched me as I went down the road.

In 2019, I guess we would call that action on my part as trolling. The word has become frequently used. Recently one of my daughters accused me of trolling her!

The boy that would not cut the grass for $25.
A section of a bridge was knocked out by a barge. A ferry was put in place to carry cars and trucks.

On the ferry I met the manager of a bank at the beach.

He was having trouble getting someone to cut the grass at the bank. There was not a lot of grass and it was easy and quick to cut. There was a fee of $25 for doing the job using the bank's lawn mower. Good pay for the work. This manager had tried to get his son to do it.

The son would not cut the grass because he might be seen by his friends while doing it.

The real reason why the county commissioners were always white.
As a newspaper publisher and as someone from outside the community, I commanded a certain respect where I had visitors and was consulted for various reasons.

One of the regulars was Walter, the unofficial head of the local black community. One day he told me that there had never been a black county commissioner. He wanted my thoughts on why not. "Has a black man ever run for county commissioner?" was my question. Walter thought for a moment. "Mr Sneed, you may have a good point there." He didn't think a black man had ever run for office.

I told him that in every precinct in the county there were more registered black voters than white. All of the county commissioners could easily be black. I gave him some tips and at the next election the county got its first black county commissioner. It all started by getting a black man on the ballot.

All white county commissioners had nothing to do with racial discrimination.

There was no need to change the culture through sociology, legislation, or court action.

The building supply business.
A man had taken a one third interest as settlement of a loan that he had made to a local businessman. He found out how bad the business was due to personal withdrawals by one of the other two shareholders, none of which was a secret.

It was known by everyone in the community that every $100 bill that was handed in at the register went straight to the purse of the operating shareholder's wife. A house had been built with materials straight from the store with no sales invoice. I know. I had tried to find invoices in the file from the time period his house was under construction. The man asked me for advice.

I told him he could either sell his third or buy the other two thirds. He chose the latter option.

Over the next year or two we did a turnaround as well as developed a unique computer system. I had started with QuickBooks version 1.0. The software had great promise. I had already been a user of Quicken. What happened was that version 1.0 got slower and slower as the database size increased. I knew that it was not going to work and I did not know when the next version would be out, if ever. The market for the product was the very small business that might never have the slowdown problem.

I wrote a completely custom system.

It was done relatively quickly because I had developed quite a library of reusable code.

The inventory worked quite well. One day we were spot checking some items. The owner was involved with this test.

We were off by one piece of 1x4. There was one piece in stock more than the computer said we should have. I checked and rechecked. There was another SKU of one by four that was a different, higher quality. It was not located anywhere near the other SKU. We counted the other SKU and it was short by one piece. I was looking at the invoices and I saw that the owner had bought some pieces of 1x4. I knew how picking was done and also knew that the owner often did his own picking. Just on a hunch I asked him if there was any chance that he had taken one of the high quality pieces for some reason. At first he said no. Then he remembered that when he got over to where the bills were made up he was one short as he had counted wrong when loading his truck. He had taken the extra piece from the higher quality stack. He shook my hand and said that I had designed a good system.

I hire a new bookkeeper.
The long time bookkeeper left very suddenly one day. I hired a young married woman with no children as a replacement. She knew little about business, even less about bookkeeping, yet had a really great attitude. She had done sales in Philadelphia.

I told her that we would hire her but she would have to agree to do exactly what me or the owner told her to do until she learned the job. There were trying moments.

She told the owner that she did not like me because every time I was there I made her cry. He told her that he did not like me either, that I made him cry, but that I knew what it took to get the place straightened out.

We were later able to move her into the general manager slot, this in an area where men had never dealt with a woman in negotiating deals. She did well.

The owner gave her a new pickup truck as he was worried that she might not make it to work one day in her old one.

He later built and gave she and her husband a house on a lot that she had inherited.

I become a non-profit executive director in New England.
I was the executive director of a non-profit in New England.

That position started while I was living in North Carolina.

I was honored that the board felt that I could do that job while living so far away.

It did mean a lot of travel from North Carolina to do the political activity, produce a newsletter, attend the monthly dinner meeting, and have a booth at an annual trade show. The pay was most meager, more to cover expenses than as pay, but I liked the job.

I do pro bono work.
I did work among the needy. I continued to do free counseling as I had done in North Carolina.

It was in line with the non-profit mission and the board thought that it was a good idea.

Many, if not all, states have some excellent forms that can be used for pro se cases, where a citizen can handle their own non-criminal cases. Landlord-Tenant disputes are common. I would get forms and help people fill them out.

The lady that wanted to boycott chicken.
I got a call one day from a lady that with others wanted to take some action. There had been a fire at a chicken processing plant on the Eastern Shore of Virginia. Several workers had died because the exit door was locked. She wanted to mobilize people to boycott chicken products because of bad working conditions primarily of women. She voiced a feeling of solidarity. She wanted my advice.

"How will a boycott solve the problem?" I asked.

"It would take away the profit from the greedy owners," she replied.

"Let's look at what else it would take away," I said. "It would take away the steady jobs of women. How will they earn money for their family? It would take away low price, good quality food from you and your children. Will you substitute high price steak?"

There are many do-gooder things that sound good on the surface. What is needed is a practical approach. While it may sound like a compromise chicken business operation was out of their control.

I think of the Serenity prayer:

"God grant me the serenity to accept the things I cannot change, courage to change the things I can, and the wisdom to know the difference."

The couple that would not work.
There was one most difficult case that I could not solve.

A young couple with two small children lived just across from the waterfront fish dealers. Neither of them had a job. They thought that welfare should pay for cable tv and it was a big expense.

They really had to economize. Thy drank beer rather than hard liquor. They smoked marijuana rather than use cocaine. They did not smoke name brand cigarettes.

The man had a simple philosophy about working "I'm not gonna bust my butt making money for someone else."

His last job had been as a carpentry apprentice getting on the job training. He found out his billing rate and noticed that it was somewhat more than he got paid.

He quit because his boss would not raise his pay to equal the billing rate. I had tried to explain to him about the difference was not profit to his boss. All to no avail.

The new immigrants would really work.
The really hard workers were the new immigrants. There were differing levels with the Italians and the Portuguese.

I remember one young Italian man that arrived with nothing. He could barely speak English. 10 years later he owned a fishing boat, a nice house, and a new car.

The Cambodians were fish cutters. A great perk for them was that they could take home all of the fish heads they wanted. They were paid by production and did quite well.

The Vietnamese were industrious yet not well-liked. They would buy leaky old junked boats and do day fishing just offshore. One man could make an average of $640 a day based on fish prices at that time.

The Cape Verdeans were at the bottom. Partly because they were so new, often uneducated, and because they were a small and separate demographic they did not speak English.

The agents would provide a certain number of fish cutters per day though with no guarantee that it would be the same workers. They would be brought in by van and picked up by van.

Names were not known. There was little paperwork if any. Employers at least claimed that they did not like the arrangement and only did it when they could not get enough other workers. A lot has changed.

The problem now is not being able to get enough fish due to overfishing and in this time of permanent cutbacks in days of legal fishing and the setting of legal limits.

The Waterways Commission.
I was a member of a Waterways Commission. I became the one to vote no to accepting free government money.

There was a grant to add six more slips to the city marina.

In part of the discussion there was the question of whether or not an environmental impact statement would be needed. The answer was yes. It was viewed that the cost would be prohibitive. The city attorney said that as a government entity we could just vote it through. After a great deal of laughter over a process that was legislated to protect the environment, a process that was heavily enforced by all government entities, one member proposed a facetious motion. The attorney wrote it in a more serious manner and it was passed.

The four picnic tables.
Working waterfront was the term often used to resist any idea no matter how much sense it made.

One wholesale fish dealer had a retail store on his wharf.

Some items, such as lobster, were available cooked. The the owner, decided it would be a nice idea to have four picnic tables on the wharf for tourists and others to be able to eat their lobster or whatever.

Some viewed this as the end of the working waterfront. The city council demanded a drawing done by a licensed engineer that would show the exact placement of the four picnic tables.

A year by year permit was granted. Each year the city council would have to re-approve.

Gurry.
Waste from fish cutting, known as gurry, was an issue in all fishing towns.

Processors would carry it to a barge and the barge, when full, would be taken out to sea and dumped.

I was able to get a grant for the development of fish fertilizer.

Several firms made the investment for the proper equipment, and created new businesses.

I became controller of a frozen seafood company.
I was asked if I could fill in as controller for a few weeks at a frozen seafood sales company, while the regular man was having surgery. I had some spare time so I took the job. The controller did not come back and the CEO left. I would be staying indefinitely.

The business was owned by two men from other countries.

The margin in frozen seafood is very small and the cash required to finance accounts receivable is quite large. It can really hurt if a customer does not pay or pays slowly.

The sales manager spoke of the company as of a certain size in dollars of sales. I spoke of it in terms of the margin. Saying that:

"We can suffer a write-off of $50,000 because we are a $50 million company" was invalid because the write off is against margin not sales.

The fish does not physically change hands. There are warehouse receipts. The same fish might change hands a dozen times before it actually goes where it is consumed.

The business was operating at a loss. There was no good financial system. I was starting from scratch.

The main supplier decided to sell direct. With the direction of the owners I met with the lawyers in Boston regarding a breach of contract suit against the suppliers and a chapter 11 bankruptcy filing. The lawyer said he wanted:

"To build a war chest to fight this thing."

That of course meant prepaying for legal services while cash was available.

How one son became suave and debonair at an early age.
Cal and Kate sold their large house and bought a place that was originally a theatre playhouse. Cal divided it up into apartments. His plan was to make rental apartments, mostly for the summer people and to keep one apartment for a personal residence.

There was a period of time during remodeling when Cal and Kate temporarily took an apartment on a small island connected by a causeway.

At the same time I had a waterfront apartment near Cal and Kate's.

The island is an artist's colony. The ambience is artsy with small old buildings and houses. The old buildings that were built on stilts into the mud flats, were restaurants and art galleries. The streets are narrow and there was is little room for parking. It attracts tourists during the season yet the whole place is quiet, day and night.

A favorite place for at least our two oldest children was Bertha's Candy Store. Bertha was an old lady running the candy store out of a room in her house directly accessible from the street. I don't recall when she passed away but of course the candy store died with her.

Directly across from Cal and Kate's first floor apartment, in a small building, was a restaurant with a piano bar.

He was quite young at the time, generally wore a coat and tie like me.

Sometimes when we were visiting, I would give him several one dollar bills and send him to the restaurant.

He would sit at one of the stools around the piano and order a Shirley Temple. That was one dollar. Another dollar was for the waitress.

He would ask the piano-man to play *Satin Doll*. The third dollar was for the pianist's tips jar.

I could keep my eye on him the whole time through the window of the apartment and the window of the restaurant, a distance of maybe 30 feet.

A seagull is caught in some plastic.
There was a seagull incident involving two of our our children.

They came in one morning early while playing before going to school to tell me that a seagull was caught in some plastic.

I went out and saw that the bird was caught in a six pack can holder. Feet and beak. I held the bird it so it could not move its wings. I got all of the plastic off.

When I let the bird go, it made a slow take-off across the water and headed east.

Something like this is better for making Dad a hero than if he brings home expensive toys.

The dangers of marijuana as told by an acoustical tile manufacturer.
There was a local man who had developed a translucent acoustical tile. He and his brother manufactured it at a location in an industrial park on the outskirts of town. The problem had been that light fixtures did not absorb sound and soundproof tile did not reflect light.

In addition to having a profitable business, this man had some little-known knowledge about the dangers of marijuana. He was always ready to share.

He said that our brains record everything.

The problem we have is not loss of memory. The problem is inability to recall information. As we get older our judgment improves because we have more experience to use in making judgements.

While we are smoking marijuana our minds are laying down bad tracks of experience that can never be corrected.

He said that this can lead to serious bad behavior often expressed in domestic violence and physical abuse of children.

In effect marijuana, because it does not put us under like drunkenness or use of heavy drugs, it causes permanent brain damage.

I did work for a fence company in New England.
One job I had was for a small family-owned fence company. It sold materials and did installations. I was trying to get them to do correct accounting.

They were quite far behind on their sales taxes. They received many notices. They were sued in the local court for the unpaid taxes and were of course served papers. They did not show up and there was a default judgment. There were more letters and notices. All of this was ignored. Then something happened and it was on a day that I happened to be there. A letter came to them from a collection agency in Florida. There was a demand to pay the judgment.

Their whole operation halted.

All of the family members gathered in the office. They asked me what they were going to do as they could not pay all of it at once.

I told them that if there was anything to ignore it would be a collection agency. I explained to them that a collection agency has no authority to do anything except call them and write letters.

What I could not explain was why their state government with a judgment and with power to attach bank accounts and other property was using a collection agency in Florida to pursue collecting on a judgment.

Did state government know that many people fear collections agencies?

Deliveries to New York City.
I had two other events related to that fence company.

On a Friday afternoon there was a need for a Saturday delivery in New York City to a toy manufacturer in a show at the Toy Center. They could not get a trucking company lined up that could do the job. I saw that it was only a small quantity of materials, the largest being some 4x8 sheets of lattice board. I offered to make the delivery as I was on my way south. I could go into the City on the way. I offered to take the same fee the truckers would charge. Saturday morning early I parked in front of the Toy Center and went to the door. I told the security guard why I was there.

He told me to go back to my truck and someone would be out shortly.

One man soon came out. I asked him where he wanted me to put the materials. He looked at me in a strange way.

"You stand in back of your truck off the sidewalk and you hand it to me."

I reached for the lattice board. "All of them at once?" I asked.

Again the strange look.

"Are you kidding me?" he asked. "I'm union. You give me one sheet at a time. You wait here by your truck and stay off the sidewalk."

He took each sheet into the building one at a time.

There was one more time of making a delivery to New York City.

This time to a house in the East Village. The customer was a Russian woman.

I carried everything through the house and to the walled in backyard.

She was quite pleasant and was pleased to get the delivery with exactly what she ordered, all with no damage. She told me her story.

She had left Russia to come to America two years earlier. I had always thought of people in Russia standing in line to buy bread while wearing rags.

I was curious what she was doing in this big house in Greenwich Village.

She was somewhat bitter about American and the banks.

She could not get a mortgage loan as she had no credit experience.

So she had found this fixer upper for "just" $850,000. She paid cash. She had then put in over a $1 million also in cash, to do the restoration and remodeling.

She felt it had all worked out well as the house was then worth about $4 million.

While doing the house remodeling she had started a business teaching Russian. For teachers she had sponsored degreed young men from Russia to come to America as teachers. These young men lived in her large Greenwich Village house even as construction work was taking place.

Trips to Europe.
I have made trips to Europe a number of times.

I had heard all of my life that going to Europe was a once in a lifetime dream trip best taken late in life.

My experience has been that it is cheaper to go to Europe than most places in the U.S. and that getting there is more pleasant because drinks and snacks on an international flight are all free and virtually unlimited. There can be unexpected events.

I was profiled in London.
On one short trip to London, I had exited immigration and customs at Heathrow and was heading for the building exit.

I was grabbed by two most polite security men, Mutt and Jeff, one man tall, the other short, and escorted to a back room. I was told that I would be searched and questioned and that I could ask for a supervisor. I said there was no need.

Clearly I was profiled. I had no problem with that.

There I was a man alone, only one very small bag, and not quite certain which direction I wanted to go.

They asked for my passport and ticket.

My shoes were sent out for X-ray. I was patted down.

I was asked if I had more than $5,000 with me.

They took my wallet and searched it through and through.

Then they wanted to know why I had no money.

I told them that I would be going to the first ATM I saw and would use my credit card to withdraw a small quantity of British money.

Hotel and everything else would be put on my VISA card.

They asked about why I had come and how long I would stay.

That day being Saturday I told them that on Sunday I would be attending church.

They asked where. Roman Catholic might not be so good.

The truth was Westminster Abbey for Matins and St Paul's in the afternoon, both Anglican.

They asked about my hotel.

Salvation Army Hostel, Buckingham Gate, Westminster was an ok answer and also true.

My shoes had come back all ok.

They both shook my hand, thanked me for cooperating and wished me a good day.

A trip to London, via Iceland.
On a trip with two of our daughters we had a few days stopover in Iceland.

We rented a car and drove 70 miles to see Snæfellsjökul.

That is the volcano in the Jules Verne novel, *Journey to the Center of the Earth,* that was the entranceway to the center of the earth.

We went to the top on a snowy and icy dirt road. We had seen no one since leaving Reykjavik.

When we were leaving we took a voluntary bump, got $150 cash each, and a guaranteed seat three hours later.

The airline gave us a taxi to Reykjavik and a hotel room.

All this for a three hour delay most of which was spent riding to and from Keflavik, where the airport is located.

In London, we took the underground from Heathrow to Piccadilly Circus.

We had rented an apartment in a quiet Mary Poppins neighborhood, in Knightsbridge, just a few steps off Brompton Road, not far from Harrods.

One daughter was most impressed with the lights and sounds of Piccadilly Circus when we came out from underground.

When we got to our apartment, two real estate agents were waiting to let us in.

They were a little disappointed that they would not be collecting a fee.

I told them that the owner of this pied-à-terre had told me personally by phone that he was no longer charging the let in fee.

The agents took me at my word.

We had a great time in London that included several West End shows at sharply discounted ticket prices.

We went on the Jack the Ripper tour. On another trip with another daughter we also did the tour.

The tour ends in a pub that was a key piece of the whole story.

Everyone except the children had a beer.

As I was sitting there I realized that in trips to Europe I drank little, if any. No bar visits. Maybe one glass of wine at a meal. Maybe none.

Maybe it was because I was too busy.

A trip to Scandinavia.
On a trip with another daughter to Denmark and Sweden, we climbed the 400 foot steeple of Our Savior Church near Copenhagen that was used in Jules Verne's book as a place to practice climbing.

No one was in the church.

I took a tip from the book and went to see the caretaker in the cottage across the lane.

Just like in the book, I got a large old iron key to open the steeple door at the point where the climb was outside.

The lower part of the steeple climb is inside.

The remainder is on a copper covered stairway, that goes around and around the steeple.

It gets smaller and smaller as the top is approached.

Near the top where there is no railing we had to put our arms around the steeple.

We took the train from Copenhagen to Stockholm.

At a point right next to Kronborg, Hamlet's castle, the train goes onto a ferry that has installed tracks through the middle.

The ferry crosses Öresund, a strait between Denmark and Sweden.

The locomotive stays behind and the train is picked up by another locomotive on the other side to take it through the dense forest to Stockholm.

We took that trip in the winter when it is dark. Being near Christmas there are plenty of lights and seasonal markets.

We were in Stockholm for the Nobel Prize ceremonies that take place in Stockholm.

In Oslo, Norway Anglican Bishop Desmond Tutu received the Peace Prize for his opposition to South Africa's apartheid government.

He was in Copenhagen to preach.

We went to the small church and took communion from Bishop Tutu. He had some good humor.

He said that the missionaries came to South Africa.

"We had the land. They had the Bibles. The missionaries told us to kneel for prayer. After the prayer, we had the Bibles and they had the land."

Trips to Paris.
I'm not saying much about Paris. I love Paris and have been there several times.

Paris is a subjective and experiential city.

To do Paris justice would require a book of its own.

There is a book out now called *Paris All Your Own* edited by Eleanor Brown.

I have not read it.

The book contains 18 essays by women, each essay a combinations of memoirs and travel guides.

On one trip to Paris, one of our daughters and I went to see the show *Feerie* at the Moulin Rouge, an expensive tourist trap.

It was fun to go anyway.

I'm glad we did.

We stayed at a clean and well-maintained 500 year old hotel, on the fifth floor, no elevator, in a very narrow street.

The rooms were quite small with low ceilings and small doors. There were no bathrooms in the rooms.

We each had separate rooms.

The breakfast room was great.

For dinner we stepped out of the hotel and directly across the street, maybe 20 feet wide, where there was a tiny fondue restaurant with gas flames at each table.

We went to another restaurant where most people were eating horse tartare. We had fondue there, beef of course.

The Louvre is a waste of time for a tourist except for recognition of something popular.

The Mona Lisa is better seen on the internet.

Rush Limbaugh said that the Louvre would be better if there were golf carts so people could go through it faster.

One daughter wanted to see the Eiffel Tower.

I took two of our daughters.

One thinks of drinking wine in Paris.

How about one flute glass of ordinary champagne all week?

Maybe the $10 per glass had an effect.

And the champagne was not very good.

I'm guessing the cheapest since in service by the glass, the customer does not see the bottle.

I had noticed that in grocery stores a two liter bottle of wine was cheaper than cola and there was more variety.

None of the fancy high-priced bottles of French wine like we get in the United States.

On that trip we stayed at the Marriott Hotel on the Champs-Elysées.

The hotel has 19 feet on the street and the whole building above the first floor.

Street level on the Champs-Elysées is said to be the highest price space per linear foot in the world.

CHAPTER 11: NEW ENGLAND

"...for some of the ablest sailors in the world were looking at me and my wish was not to appear green, for I had a mind to stay in town several days." - Captain Joshua Slocum.

I moved my family to New England full-time.
For a better future for our children, to seek a better life, and to cut down on family separations, we moved from North Carolina to a small town in New England.

Drugs was becoming an ever bigger problem in North Carolina and children were getting older.

I had become a fixture due to my work with fish dealers and with the trade group. My first interest in New England was in 1962 while I was in high school.

I had attempted to get a summer job through contact with the Chamber of Commerce, which was not a good move.

I realized too that even though I travelled we missed much of what was happening. So that became an issue with the children.

Shortly before leaving North Carolina I discovered that I did not know the meaning of "paradigm shift."

An elementary school teacher answered my questions about that matter.

He was most kind helping with my ignorance.

We sold the newspaper, the restaurant, and the motel though had little equity.

In New England, housing cost more.

All local business was down because of cutbacks on fishing limits.

We figured we could work something out.

We rented a house in an outer section that was way too small.

One regret I have is that I was not able to make a shower for Cheri and one daughter in particular.

The bathroom had only a bathtub.

We again consider a large boat for living.
We seriously looked at the possibility of buying a motor cruiser for a home.

These larger boats had become quite cheap for a variety of reasons.

One of the school bus drivers had raised his large family on a boat. He offered encouragement.

I already knew of the boat house communities in Mill Valley, California where the boats, barges, and other floating residences had been in place for many years.

Since we were looking elsewhere due to lack of sufficient space, it seemed illogical to move to less space.

Instead of the boat, we moved to another house.
We moved to a big house.

That house was too big.

The children mostly all slept in one room.

In stories from history and from touring historical sites in many places, large families seemed to live in small houses.

Trips to a tiny island.
We had a green rowboat that we kept in the woods by the shore.

I would take four daughters, the Gang of Four, and row over the reef to a tiny island, a short distance from the mainland.

On the island we would play, relax and have snacks or a picnic. There are walking paths and the island is open to anyone though the lighthouse is not.

There are shallow shoals to the east of the island that limit access. A row boat works well.

We lost the boat during a most severe storm that flooded quite a bit of the wooded area. I had thought that I had it far enough off the water that it would be safe. Knowing the high waves that were on the ocean that we watched from a hill, I can only imagine the water depth in the wooded area where we kept the boat. That small island appears in paintings by Winslow Homer and Fitz Hugh Lane.

I ran for mayor.
At the urging of the then mayor, who was at the term limit and could not run again, I ran for mayor.

My opponents were all city council members and were better known than me. I am not a politician. I did learn why I would never run again for any public office.

My campaign flyer.
I had designed a four page tabloid flyer as my campaign ad piece.

I had a trunkful of bundles that I had picked up from the printer in North Carolina. I was in a rental car that day.

We decided to take a quick trip to Montreal. I left all of the printing in the trunk.

Going through U.S. Customs and Immigration on the way back, there was a red flag since we had only come for the day. I explained as best I could. The inspector wanted to see in the trunk. As soon as he saw the bundles he radioed that there was a commercial importation. He told me to go to a certain area to the side. Another inspector came out, took one look, and said ok.

I asked him to tell the other guy that all was ok.

We lived downtown.
We moved into a building that had survived two town fires, in the 1800s.

We did not have a car at that time. I used rental cars for trips. Commuter rail was a short walk away as was the supermarket, beach, library, and everything else in town.

A travel agent was on the first floor. My office was on the second. Our third floor apartment there was mostly one large open space that included the kitchen. There was a small room, used for one child's bedroom, and a bathroom, both with no windows. There were balconies and great views of the harbor and beyond. The rent was incredibly cheap. It was a beautiful building in great condition opening right onto the sidewalk.

An artist from out of state had done a painting with our building and doorway in the center. I did not have the money to buy it though regret not finding some way. I would have given the painting to our son who was born in the building. As consolation, I knew that he could always make a picture. Today it turns out he can find the photo online. From that he could have an artist make a painting from that.

Everything we needed was within walking distance including the beach. A bakery was close by. Always great bread, pastry, and coffee. Stores of every kind lined the street. There were many restaurants including a Dunkin Donuts. One nearby restaurant served cod cheeks, even better than cod fillets. Yes the cheeks of the codfish. They are very meaty and tender. Served as cod cheeks and chips they look the same as fish and chips. Same texture and taste, only somewhat better. A supermarket was four blocks away. There were maybe 15 bars nearby though it was not a dive neighborhood. Everything was always clean and neat and crime-less. Tourists were in the area seven days a week during the 100 day season, on weekends the rest of the year.

Our daughter liked the "Our Story."
The library, just a few blocks away, had story hours like most libraries.

One of our daughters, now a Ph.D., called it the "our story."

She did not know the word "hour" and so it seemed we called it the "story our."

That sounded like Greek to her so she switched it to the "our story."

How our son's bike was recovered.
One of our family bikes was stolen from the place where a son of ours worked.

A few days later I was en route to see a client in a distant town.

As I was driving slowly on the curvy road in a town about eight miles away, out of the corner of my eye I spotted the bike on a street to the left about 100 feet away.

I don't remember the details but the bike had a unique coloring. I went back and confirmed what I saw. No one answered the door.

I contacted the police and showed the policeman. He wanted to know how I knew it was ours.

The lock and cable were on the bike though the bike was not secured. I tried the combination and the lock opened.

The policeman told me that I could take back the bike.

One son gets his first car.
I got one of our sons a van. It was on its last legs and did not last too long.

I felt so bad for him as this was a first step towards independence.

A trip to Astoria, Oregon.
I had a chance on several trips over the years to take some of the kids to Astoria, Oregon where they saw the Goonies house and the Haystack Rock at Cannon Beach that plays a big part in *The Goonies*.

There is a large tide pool at the base of Haystack Rock.

The Goonies movie was played seemingly hundreds of times at our house.

Trips by ship to Nova Scotia.
We took the M/S Scotia Prince from Portland, Maine to Yarmouth, Nova Scotia on a number of occasions.

The ship made the full round trip every 24 hours with one day off per week. There were a variety of package deals starting with the 24 hour trip with a cabin both ways.

Many people would take the cruise just for the gambling as there was a full casino and slot machines were everywhere in the ship. Except for Cheri spending and losing $10, we did no gambling.

The full ocean cruise experience was there. The food and the service was good and cheap. The crew was exactly like on the tv series Love Boat, that ran from 1977 to 1998.

There was about an hour and a half layover in Yarmouth. That was enough time to walk around the town and to grab a bite at a restaurant.

Other deals would have one or more days in Nova Scotia and could include a rental car.

The party boats that went fishing were converted to gambling boats that would go three to five miles offshore for a few hours in international waters where gambling was not prohibited.

There were at least three uses of basically the same size of boats:

- Fishermen would go out in fishing boats, catch fish and and return with the fish to sell to consumers.

- Consumers would go out on fishing boats and catch their own fish.

- Consumers would go out on the converted fishing boats and would be caught, like fish by the "fishermen" running the gambling.

A trip to Bath, Maine.
We went to the launching of the first of the Arleigh Burke destroyers in Bath, Maine.

At the opening of the launching day program we were told not to worry about the ceremony running too long. They said that because of the tide and the water depth that the launching had to occur on time.

The ship was launched and went almost to the other side of the river before it stopped. The only hitch was that Mrs. Burke was too weak to swing the bottle hard enough to break. She was given help.

Our daughter was not allowed to start school.
The public schools would not make an exception for age so that one of our daughters could start school.

The cut off was midnight and she was born 41 minutes later. It did not matter that she was ready for school.

I brought her with me to a school board meeting so they could see her. The board unanimously voted no.

To make a long story short, we homeschooled her for kindergarten and first grade. For second grade we enrolled her with no problem. At that point all that mattered was completion of kindergarten and first grade.

At that same school board meeting, there was a presentation of the progress on implementation of something that the board had already approved, the elimination of report cards. It was most touching to hear one lady say that no longer would a child with C and D grades have to feel bad sitting next to a child with A and B grades.

The sports awards banquet.
Later in the same school year we went to a sports award session.

Every child that participated in sports got the same trophy. One child did get a really big trophy.

She had gotten an injury at the first practice and could not participate for the rest of the year. For that reason it was felt that she should be especially honored simply because she had wanted to play.

I guess these kids were being prepared for the view that talking about something is the same as doing it.

How our son got a work permit.
One of our sons wanted a job at McDonald's. As a minor he was required to have a work permit. To get a work permit required a physical exam. To get a physical exam required $150.

I looked up the state law on work permits. The law had been on the books for a very long time and came about as a result of children working in the mills of New England. The law said that the physical exam cost was to be paid by the school board. Next stop the school nurse. She read the law and laughed hysterically.

"David there is no one but you that could have found this out," she said. "This will cause quite a stir."

It did for sure. The principal, the school board, the mayor, and the city council all became involved. I heard personally from the mayor and from one of the city council members. It is one thing to require a family to pay $150 for a physical exam. It is much different for a school board to do so. He got his physical exam at no cost from the school dietitian. She had the word doctor in front of her name.

A trip to Chibougamau.
I made a trip with one of our sons to Chibougamau, the end of the roads to the north in Quebec.

Now there are other dirt roads that go much farther connecting many communities.

Chibougamau is 430 miles north of Montreal, Quebec.

We found the town to be quite modern and the location of a number of sports including snowmobiling.

The real end of the road was at Mistassini, a Cree Indian town, 54 miles northeast of Chibougamau.

At the time we went there were two types of homes in Mistassini, Tipis, or teepees, and square flat-roofed plywood shacks.

The town has advanced and now is like any other modern town.

Agricultural high school.
Two of our daughters and one of our sons attended and graduated from an Agricultural high school. At the time they went it was an original multi-story brick building on a 200 acre farm.

There was hands-on and classroom agricultural studies as well as the usual high school subjects. There was work in the apple orchard, with cows, chickens etc.

It was a stress, and caused many problems, to make this work out but we did it.

The overall goal was always to find the best opportunities for the children.

It was never to give them all the same thing as time and circumstances were different over the 50 years from when the first child was born until the last one graduated from college.

Leaving town.
The owner of our building wanted to take it back at a time convenient to us as he had some new plans related to gentrification. We felt we would need to leave the high cost part of the state.

We found a way to make that happen in a way that we could contribute to low income housing creation.

Things began to turn around for us after we moved out to a small town near the corner of several states though it would take another eight years.

I turned my business over to an associate. I felt that I would be having a major lifestyle and work change, which in fact did happen. I did some work for her with a project that we did together. It was ok but took too long and there were considerable unreimbursed expenses, especially travel.

I made several big mistakes in going into my own business.

- Did not do incremental rate increases.
- Did not specify an extra for travel expenses.
- Flat fee development projects.
- Did not understand that level of expectation rises. I had to do much more than I was paid for.
- Did not progressively build up cash.
- QuickBooks not available.
- Took on too much work at the outset.
- Inadequate capital.
- Got worn out over time.
- Not good at hiring people.
- Not enough available time to think and to standardize.
- Too much time away from family, not just for work, but for travel.

CHAPTER 12: THE BERKSHIRES

"A new labor force needs a new paradigm." - David Newton Sneed.

We move to the Berkshires.
We moved to a small town in the Berkshires to be a part of a scattered site cohousing project that was getting underway. There were 16 houses. None of the houses were close together or even of similar construction. The legal format was a housing cooperative, common in New York City. A housing cooperative is a membership-based housing corporation where each shareholder is given the right to occupy a particular housing unit.

We got heavily involved. At one point I was the only nominee for both President and Treasurer. Effectively I was doing both jobs. At the meeting where the election was to be held, I was doing what I could to find other nominees. Nothing was happening. No one was taking any initiative. I finally decided that I would exhibit leadership. I announced that I was taking myself out of the running. Then I named two women, one for each position. I called for a vote. It was unanimous as they were the only candidates. This was not a failure on my part. It was a move of the Holy Spirit to get us ready for the west.

The cooperative needed good management though the residents, also known as shareholders, were not overly excited about any loss of freedom and principles.

A trip to the Mount Washington Hotel.
I was able to take some of the kids to the Mount Washington Hotel, now the Omni Mount Washington Resort, at Bretton Woods, New Hampshire, a place of similar construction to the smaller hotels though much larger. Meals were included in the price and took place at set times in the large dining room. The bedrooms were all small rooms that all had connecting doors to other rooms in that side of the hall. We were told that in past times that families would come for the summer and bring their servants. Arrival was by train as there were no cars.

Berkshires happenings.
Our four youngest daughters were quite close in many ways. I did a number of things with just them.

One daughter, next in age above the last four, studied a lot and did not go with us all the time. We made a room for her as well as a family room in the unfinished, high ceiling, most unique third floor typical of Victorian houses.

Many good things happened in the Berkshires though one of our proudest moments was when one of our younger four daughters became carrier of the month for the newspaper.

There was a lot to do in the area.

There is plenty of music in the Berkshires. Pat and Tex LaMountain were my favorites. Their song, *Ten Below Zero,* was, to my mind, the best. It tells of working hard, setting goals, and having to endure hardships of the weather in the Berkshires.

We were in a parade. One daughter had a large stuffed bear, Poley, that she pulled in a wagon.

On one occasion I engaged a barbershop quartet go to our house and provide some entertainment for Cheri and the kids.

We had a baby opossum for a while. It did not make a good pet.

There was a place where we could drive deep into the woods, park and then take a long hike. The trail would lead to a mountain overlook. A very elderly couple, both retired college professors, lived out there with no electricity, no phone, and no running water. They had donated the property subject to being able to use the property for the remainder of their lives. They welcomed the visitors to the area and were good conversationalists. On the path near their house they would leave excess garden produce for the hikers to take home.

Jacks in North Adams, Massachusetts.
At North Adams, Massachusetts, there is a hole in the wall called Jack's. Eight stools at the counter and no tables. Jack's has been in business close to 100 years. Like at a bar, each customer has a running tab to easily add on more food or drink. Fresh french fries. Hamburgers with fresh hot dogs of course. The grill is original from when Jacks started in business. There is a weekly, monthly, and annual contest and prize based on how much each customer spent.

Maple sugar season.
In the spring during maple sugar season, the restaurants at the farms serve all day breakfast with pancakes and locally made maple syrup. There are of course gift shops. For maybe four or five weekends these places are packed. The rest of the year you can always get a seat whenever you want.

Curtis Barbecue.
Just off Exit 4 of I-91 was, maybe still is, a summer barbecue place. It is on a lot next to a gas station and adjoins the exit ramp of the interstate.

Curtis Tuff is a black man from Alabama, like the rest of us, getting older all the time, that lives just a long stone's throw from the outdoor restaurant. There are two school buses, some picnic tables, and the big concrete block homemade cooker with grates for the chicken, pork, and beef to cook.

Curtis makes the best barbecue I have ever had.

Battle of Lexington Green.
One year we went to Lexington, Massachusetts for the annual re-enactment of the first battle of the American Revolution. To be historically correct the re-enactment takes place at 5:30 AM. We left home at 2:00 AM. There was heavy rain the whole time. Quite a few people were there.

Mount Monadnock.
We lived close to Mount Monadnock in New Hampshire, one of the most climbed mountains worldwide. In years past women in crinoline dresses, with who knows what kind of shoes, would be climbers.

We have climbed Monadnock many times since moving north from Georgia. It is an easy and safe climb on marked trails, provided that climbers are down before dark. It is possible to get lost in the lower wooded areas and nights can get cold. The mountain rises 2,000 feet above the surrounding area.

I remember one time when our youngest son was about three years old. I carried him on my shoulders at the lower part of the mountain that is tree covered. As soon as we got into the open area with the long views, he immediately wanted to walk. He walked the rest of the way with a better attitude.

Another time, shortly after cell phones came out, we were climbing and ran across someone in a small group with an injured leg. I made a 911 call. It was answered by someone near New York City. After they understood where we were, they were able to get me a local phone number to call. Help was soon on the way. A downside to cell phones even today is that a call to 911 may not get you to anything local as a landline can do. The downside extends to anyone using VOIP. I have given this info to churches and other places that plan on saving money by taking out their landline.

One time when our oldest daughter's two oldest children were with us, we climbed Monadnock. Later in the day I called our daughter to tell her about it. I jokingly told her that their favorite part was when the helicopter came to pick us up after we got lost.

My involvement with community currency.
I was the treasurer for a community currency in the Berkshires. There have been, and presently are, many different community currencies all around the United States. There were actual printed and serial-numbered bills that could be used as money, though many merchants would limit the percentage that would be accepted for a given transaction.

Wikipedia defines community currency as "a type of complementary currency that is used by groups with a common bond, like members of a locality, or association, and designed to meet their needs. A community currency may be geography-based, making it a type of local currency, or it may be used within a business-based, or online currency."

Marguerite Dolan.
One woman from the Berkshires that made history was Marguerite Dolan. Her husband owned a newspaper. I first met Marguerite around the time that she and her husband divorced. Marguerite died in 2009 at the age of 89.

Marguerite became a lawyer without going to law school. She told me that she went to Boston and asked around about some good books to read to pass the bar exam. She passed the bar exam on her first try. Immediately the Legislature, made up of lawyers, passed a law requiring a law school degree to take the exam. Marguerite did two pro bono cases to get going.

One involved a proposed high tension power line that residents wanted to stop. She found someone living in the area that knew a better way. The power company agreed, changed the route, and the case was dropped.

Another involved whether or not to pull the plug on a brain dead patient. The patient died before the case could go to court. Marguerite settled into regular law practice until she got an interest in mountain climbing. Marguerite and the wife of a former Massachusetts governor traveled to Nepal and other countries to climb mountains. It's all a matter of vision and execution what we can accomplish.

Cooperative.
One thing I was able to do was to give some education into business. There was a lot of misunderstanding about many things. McDonald's wanted to open in one town. Many people in the area believed that 95% of the money that came in would leave the community. I explained to them about jobs created, taxes paid including sales tax, payroll tax, property tax, and excise tax. The cost of sales was a little harder to explain until one cooperative purchase provided the best example.

The cooperative maintenance man had bought a shower adaptor that could be used in an old bathtub. He had bought it at the local hardware store for $180. I felt he had paid too much. I went to a big box store and bought the identical product for $35. Everyone was amazed. I explained how the local store that might buy one or two units would have to buy at a higher price, money that would go out of town. Big box stores were buying many thousands in one nationwide purchase. In many cases they could tell the suppliers what they would pay. Take it or leave it. Since nothing much was made in our area except for maple syrup in the Spring, purchases from local stores would send a lot more money out of town than a big box store. Further the local stores mostly only made jobs for the owner's family.

Residents of the area loved the farmers' markets. There were plenty of small farmers so it was good for there to be a venue for the matchup of buyers and sellers. The weather and growing seasons were still factors. Lettuce did not grow in the winter yet demand remained. Lettuce grown in heated greenhouses and brought to town in small quantities in small pickup trucks was considered better stewardship of the earth and energy than lettuce brought in by train, from California. Trains and ships are the cheapest possible means of transportation as they are so fuel efficient.

I became an IT director.
I became Director of IT and then added Acting CFO at a community mental health organization. I developed a concept known as *People Helping People Helping People*. I revamped the accounting system and upgraded the computers. I also set up the compliance needed in order to do electronic record-keeping. During that time I took a formal course in clinical record-keeping.

Church in the Berkshires.
We attended an evangelical church. The church had been started by A.B. Simpson who was a strong believer in divine healing. When I went to men's meetings at the church the only subject of conversation was the pills they were taking, their surgeries, and their doctors. No mention of Doctor Jesus. There were small group home meetings with dinner, fellowship, and Bible study. I led our group though the meetings were not held at our house. The lady of the house where we met said that I was their pastor for these meetings. I did not agree because I felt that I did not have the patience needed by a pastor.

A trip to Key Largo.
I remember one motel that I had stayed at when we lived in Coral Gables. Before the internet one daughter was able to find the name of the place in Key Largo from clues I had given her. It was the Hungry Pelican. It is still there and just like it was in the early 1950s. Up by the highway was a local restaurant, cheap, with plenty of seafood as well as other items, and with informal Key

Largo ambience. The sides were open.

I know our youngest was on that trip but I don't remember who else.

On another trip to Key Largo we went snorkeling on a reef we reached after about a half hour boat ride. The reef is about 15 feet underwater. We were advised that it was illegal, under Federal law, to even step on the sand bottom around the reef.

On another trip, another daughter and I went out to the reef but were not allowed to get out of the boat as the water was too rough. The boat returned to the shore.

The original boat from the Humphrey Bogart and Katharine Hepburn movie African Queen is at Key Largo. We rode in that same boat in Old Saybrook, Connecticut just four and a half miles from where Katherine Hepburn lived, in the Fenwick section of town. She visited the boat but declined a ride. She was surprised that the boat, built in 1912, still existed. The area where the boat took us looked quite similar to where the boat was in the movie in the reeds with only a narrow space to navigate.

A trip to the Dry Tortugas.
In still another trip, me and two daughters, took a four place seaplane from Key West to the Dry Tortugas. The rest of the family stayed in Orlando.

From the air we could see reefs and sunken boats and ships. The pilot flew quite low.

In the Dry Tortugas, there is a large old brick fort, Fort Jefferson, that was built to protect New Orleans, many miles to the north. The fort was built by the channel where ships had to pass. The reef is at the shore because the islands are actually sand on the reef.

One daughter, age three took pictures with a disposable underwater camera.

The pictures did not look like they were taken in one to two foot deep water.

A few days after that trip the seaplane we were in crashed and killed the passengers and the pilot.

A trip to Big Bend National Park in Texas.
I have visited Big Bend four times. Once with Jack the reptile man, once with one of our sons and one of his school friends, once with just me while en route from a meeting in New Orleans, and once with another son.

When NAFTA had just been passed, I got a picture of me standing in the middle of the Rio Grande. I was heading to Mexico to see if I could get my job back! I don't know the future of NAFTA. Everybody has an idea of what increasing exports to other countries means. The promoters of NAFTA did not say otherwise. Later we found that the U.S. shipped wire to Mexico as an export. In Mexico harnesses were made. Then the U.S. imported the harnesses, also known as wire with the labor added.

As adults on their own, two of our daughters have been to Big Bend and to other places in the area though not on a trip together and not with me. When one of our other sons was with me, we first went to Tyler, Texas, then to Big Bend. Marfa, Texas was a good stop after Big Bend.

The Marfa lights are a mystery. They were seen before the time of electric lights. Indians showed them to white settlers. The state built a viewing center on the road to Alpine. Across the desert the lights can be seen most nights. Not knowing otherwise, they might be ignored or thought to be on a ranch. The most lights I have seen are three. Sometimes all are on. Sometimes just one or two. The duration varies.

After Marfa, we went to Tombstone, Arizona, and from there to Bisbee, Arizona, very close to the Mexican border. Bisbee, is where many hippies went after the movement died down. In Bisbee, our son that was with me bought me a large framed black and white photo of the launching of a commercial fishing boat from a small New England boatyard. That photo is a prized possession of mine on the wall in our hallway.

Boquillas del Carmen, México.
Some time after we moved west, Pat and Tex LaMountain decided to do a performance tour around the country. I suggested to them that they take a detour at Marathon, Texas, go south through Big Bend National Park, and across the Rio Grande to the town of Boquillas del Carmen in Mexico.

Pat and Tex did as I suggested and they were very happy to have gone to Big Bend. They sent me photos of themselves on burros.

The whole town is most unique. Real hitching posts in use. A man sitting on a wooden sidewalk with a big Mexican sombrero. A bar where they set a glass and an unlabeled whisky bottle in front of you regardless of the age of the customer. There is no ice or electricity. The streets are unpaved. Boquillas is a stereotypical town from the wild west. The industry there is collecting plants that are used to make the wax for votive candles in Roman Catholic churches. I do not care for Mexican food, with one exception.

Tacos in Boquillas are really great. Cooked on a small charcoal stove. Why can't the high overhead national chains duplicate this? I have often said the same thing about home-cooked food and food from very small single unit restaurants. I have even added a question. How can the large restaurant chains make money with such bad food?

A trip to Marathon, Texas.
On the trip with just me, I stopped at a small bookstore in Marathon, Texas. Marathon is on U.S. 90 north of Big Bend and is where the turn is made to go to Big Bend.

This trip was during one of the times was when Paris Hilton was causing so much trouble. She was sentenced to a certain amount of time in the county jail. What brief time she was there was spent in the jail clinic.

The bookstore lady asked me if I was looking for anything special.

"Yes" I said. "Do you have *The Prison Writings of Paris Hilton?*"

She was a little bewildered.

"For a moment there you believed that such a book might exist didn't you?" I asked.

She admitted that she had. We talked about some of the books that were on the shelves. I bought a book but cannot remember which one.

Trips to Boston.
When I had business in Boston I would often take the four younger daughters. The oldest would lead and they would go all kinds of places on the subway and walking. It was completely safe. It was not at all unusual to see unaccompanied children going places, going to school and otherwise. There were no cell phones but we still felt connected.

In Iceland, where people are the descendants of the Vikings, there is such independence that very small children can be on the street late at night. I never went that far with my children. I wanted to protect them but knew that they needed to learn to make it on their own. The oldest as the leader benefitted the most but there was an effect on the other three that can be seen today.

Somehow, Cheri had gotten all four of the girls purple winter coats that were exactly the same. One day, near the State House after going to Boston on the train. Bill Weld, the Governor, was walking past. He stopped and talked to the girls.

There is no governor's mansion in Massachusetts. Governors live wherever they choose. I remember that Michael Dukakis lived in the house that he grew up in. He rode the Green Line to work, set his garbage cans out on the street for pickup, cut his own grass, and took the subway to the airport.

I may have some disagreement from both Democrats and Republicans but Mike Dukakis might be the last of the old time Democrats. Today the ideology is gone. Wall Street is the God, and the Democrats are as wealthy, if not more so, as Republicans.

Locke-Ober.
Locke-Ober was an old high class restaurant in an alleyway right downtown in Boston. Until 1976 it did not allow women, accompanied or not, into the restaurant. A law not of the state but of the restaurant. When they first made the change the ladies restroom was located on the third floor accessible by stairs. The waiters were all elderly men. Many of the customers were elderly men. Often the customers had set times and a set seat at a set table where they would dine. The same order every day.

There are now three condos in the building. The restaurant is shut down but there has been extensive restoration. I understand that the current owners are looking to have another restaurant move into the Locke-Ober space.

The Bronx Zoo in New York City on a bad weather day.
One day we set out to go the Bronx Zoo in New York City.

It was cloudy when we left. As we got closer to the city the rain increased and we heard radio reports of flooding. We, or perhaps just I, decided to keep going.

The Bronx Zoo can be miserable in hot weather, times that it is also very crowded. This day was just the reverse.

I figured it might be a better day than usual for a zoo outing.

It was nice temperature wise and the zoo parking lot was empty. I could not tell about public transportation or walkers.

We heard that there were due to be a number of scout groups. Only one group had showed up and then had left right away. I think it is quite possible that we were the only visitors as we saw no others.

The zoo staff was there. In one building they told us that it was a good day to visit. They told us that on days like that the animals were curious about the lack of guests and would come up close.

I can't remember which but one of the children cried about being wet. Years later one of them said that:

"We all cried."

To me it was such a great event and an opportunity to step out of what we normally did. Like a water slide park with no slides. It would be safer. It was warm and there were no raging flash floods. Stores and streets were as normal.

When we got home that night, I told the children that our clothes were so wet that we would have to put them in the dryer first as they were too wet to go in the washer.

Brattleboro, Vermont.
Brattleboro, Vermont, another bastion of hippie economics, is where Walmart wanted to build.

There was resistance from the local government and from the vocal few.

Walmart did not build in Brattleboro but did build a Super Walmart directly across the Connecticut River in Hinsdale, New Hampshire on a hill overlooking the river and Brattleboro.

The Silent Majority was able to buy at Walmart with the added savings due to sales tax free New Hampshire.

For the sake of ideology, Brattleboro got no sales tax, no property tax, no unemployment tax, no workers' comp premiums.

Brattleboro Film Festival.
We went to the Brattleboro Film Festival that had a series of films, mostly ones that I did not know.

One was *Stop Making Sense*, a concert with David Byrne and Tina Weymouth.

Their group was the Talking Heads. It was part of the punk rock scene.

I had never heard of them but was quite impressed.

For many attending it was a nostalgic time.

These people would frequently stand, as if they were at the live concert that took places years earlier.

Even before going, I liked the term "stop making sense."

In effect that had been said to me many times over the years.

The songs had meaning to me for that reason.

The film festival was another way to expose the children to new things.

A trip to New York City on Amtrak.
We took Amtrak to New York City early one morning from Springfield.

We arrived at our hotel, the Marriott Marquis, about 9:00 AM. We had two reserved rooms.

Since one of our rooms was not ready, we were offered a suite on the 50th floor at the same rate.

We let the kids have that room. It was most elegant including two bathrooms and a ten place dining room table.

I went to Dannys Hideaway, a nightclub two blocks away and popular with the movie star set. Cheri stayed at the hotel with the children. Blossom Dearie, her real name, was singing.

I was quite pleased as I had always loved her singing and her piano style.

When she was not at Dannys she was in London.

I lease a Ford Aerostar.
I had leased a Aerostar van so that I could get to work in Boston and other areas. We bought the van after the lease expired. The van just got us to Cheyenne and then it bit the dust and had to be junked.

A trip to Philadelphia.
We went to look at colleges for one of our daughters.

We went to Lehigh University at Bethlehem, Pennsylvania.

We visited Drexel Institute in Philadelphia, Pennsylvania. A guide took us and others around the Drexel campus. We learned that all of the class notes were available online. I was curious and asked some questions. He gave us the website that was completely, open to anyone. No use names and passwords required.

"Why would there be any need to pay big bucks and go to class?" I asked.

"So as not to miss the college experience," the guide replied.

"You mean alcohol, drugs, and sex?" I then asked with a grin.

Everyone, including the guide, had a good laugh.

Another trip to Philadelphia.
I took one of our daughters to the Philadelphia Museum of Art. I showed her one of Van Gogh's Sunflowers that had most recently been sold to the Meiji Yasuda Life Insurance Company of Japan for $39.7 million, triple what it had sold for two years earlier. The painting was in a large gaudy frame. I told her that when I had showed the painting to her brother that was with me on another trip and told him the sale price he had asked,

"Did that include the frame?"

After somewhat of a long pause looking at the painting and the frame, she then asked,

"Well, did it?"

Most high value paintings were done before 1803. Sunflowers was from 1888. Allegedly Van Gogh only sold one of his paintings during his lifetime.

Philadelphia Museum of Art.
I think that all of my children have gone into the fountains outside the Philadelphia Museum of Art at least once. To my way of thinking that is at least an equal experience to the high-valued painting.

A trip to Ojai, California
At another earlier point we visited Ojai, in California, as a high school for one of our daughters.

It was looking like rural North Carolina was fine when the children were young but as they got older it was looking like a dead end. It was not yet time for a complete move.

On that trip to California we went to see Ronald Reagan's house in Bel Air. 668 St. Cloud Avenue. It was 666 St. Cloud Avenue before he rented it but he had the city change the number so his critics would not make an issue of his address as being the address of Satan.

A mile or so after we passed his house, while heading west, we saw a Lincoln limousine heading our way. We turned around and went back though did not stop. The Lincoln was just turning into the driveway. A Secret Service man gave us a look.

A 24 hour trip across country to Los Angeles.
On another occasion there was a $49 deal to take a 24 hour flying trip anywhere on New Year's Eve. I took one of our daughters and one of our sons. We stayed at a hotel in Hollywood. We had a rental car and did a variety of things. A lot can be done in 24 hours. I really regret not taking the time to find the Hollywood sign. Our daughter that was with me really wanted to see it.

A trip around the country.
At a school break, I took two of our our sons, on a trip. We were going to visit my mother in Denver but then decided to drive around the country. We drove 8,500 miles starting in New England.

We visited Niagara Falls then decided to continue through Canada to Detroit. At the border crossing at Detroit, we were quizzed thoroughly about why the boys were not in school. We had no paperwork but finally we were allowed through.

As a result of that trip, I always got notarized letters with agreement from Cheri that kids take a trip and have thrown in explanations.

We went west on I-80 from Chicago. We dipped into Denver on I-76 to visit my mother. From there I-25 up to I-80 at Cheyenne. One son got his first winter driving experience at the Donner Pass. We had to buy chains as they were mandatory. He did well in the deep snow. At the summit the rest area buildings were covered in snow. We went to the restroom through a snow tunnel.

We visited San Francisco then down through Big Sur, an overnight stop in Morro Bay, and on to Los Angeles, then San Diego, where one of my brothers lived at the time.

After leaving San Diego we drove east on I-8. In Calexico California we walked across to Mexicali, Mexico. Coming back into Calexico, the youngest son with me was pulled aside and questioned by the U.S. Immigration officer separately from me and an older son.

We visited the Meteor Crater, and the Petrified Forest. At the exit gate, the man exuberantly said "Well boys, how was collecting today?" Any collecting was illegal and he was trying to get us to confess unawares if we had been collecting which we weren't.

We got to New Orleans for Mardi Gras. From there I-95 in Florida and home.

We did get some criticism from some other family for doing such a rush trip. My view is that there is no such thing as a once-in-a-lifetime trip. What we don't see this trip we can do on another trip or maybe never.

A trip to Camp Pendleton after the first Persian Gulf War.
After our oldest son returned from his U.S. Marines service in The first Persian Gulf War, I went to visit him at Camp Pendleton. It was a weekday afternoon, I found him sitting on the balcony, a number of floors up, that was Marine living quarters. All rooms opened to the balcony like a hotel. He asked where I was headed next. "San Francisco," I replied. "Can I go with you?" he asked. "How can you get away?" He said it was no problem. He quickly packed a bag. We stopped by the company office. He stood in the doorway and waved. "Going somewhere?" He was asked. "When will you be back?" He deferred to me. I wasn't planning on coming back that way so he said he would fly. He gave a return date to the U.S. Marines and we left.

A driving trip to Alaska.
With two of our daughters and our son, I took a driving trip to Alaska, 10,500 miles round trip.

We decided to go via the Upper Peninsula of Michigan while heading west. After crossing the Mackinac Bridge we soon came to the town of Paradise, Michigan on the western shore of Whitefish Bay on Lake Superior. It was so nice we stayed for two days. The water was quite shallow and calm. All of us could wade way out. The Great Lakes Shipwreck Museum at Whitefish Point was quite close so we went. We learned quite a bit about the Edmund Fitzgerald. The museum played Gordon Lightfoot's *The Wreck of the Edmund Fitzgerald* over and over and over. At one point on Lake Superior we walked out on a ledge close to the water to see some ancient petroglyphs. Going there was quite safe for all of us.

When we got to somewhere past Saskatoon, Saskatchewan we ran into the most fierce thunderstorm that I have ever seen. Our younger daughter was crying and our son was was praying. The other daughter was holding on.

I think that the water slide park at the West Edmonton Mall in Alberta, Canada may have been the best part of the trip for the kids.

In Alaska, there was effectively only one radio station as they all broadcasted the same content. We must have heard the George Strait song *Write This Down* a thousand times. *Write This Down* was like a theme song for the trip. A middle part of the lyrics is:

"Baby, write this down, take a little note; to remind you in case you didn't know; tell yourself I love you and I don't want you to go, write this down. Take my words, read 'em every day, keep 'em close by, don't you let 'em fade away; so you'll remember what I forgot to say, write this down."

Watson Lake, Yukon, is at Milepost 635 on the Alaska Highway. The mileposts are most important to know where you are and where you are going. Everything is designated by name and by milepost.

My favorite restaurant on the Alaska Highway was Mukluk Annie's at Teslin Junction, Milepost 804. No matter where I was on the Highway, traveling in either direction, I knew the distance to Annies. The restaurant is now closed as are many of the old time places. Pancakes cooked on an open fire were available at all times. There was a car wash at Mukluk Annies. The price was dependent on whether or not you at bought a meal. Mud can accumulate and harden on a vehicle. Washing a car was not easy. It takes a lot of water and the whole family could join in on working the mud loose.

Much has changed on the Alaska Highway, even during my lifetime. It is now one of the finest roads anywhere. In years past it was a hazardous trip with plenty of mud. Broken windshields were a certainty. Rock is quarried along the highway and each year the highway has gotten better.

There are no long distance power lines in Alaska. The local communities now have their own diesel generators. There are power lines just like in any city though just within the few blocks or less of that community. During my time on the Alaska highway, each gas station had its own generator for the gas pumps. The generator had to get started before gas could be pumped. Even today, during nighttime hours there are few places open and they are long distances apart.

From the Alaska Highway at Watson Lake, we headed up the Robert Campbell Highway, a distance of 362 miles with no houses or stores except at Ross River and Faro. For the first two or three miles out of Watson Lake, the Campbell highway is wide and paved. After that that it is narrow, paved, and was pretty much a one lane trail through the woods. In recent years it has been widened and paved with gravel. Ross River, Yukon is 225 miles from Watson Lake, Yukon. At Ross River we went down a narrow road to an Indian village with one really old gas pump powered by a generator.

From Faro to Carmacks the highway is in pretty good shape and needs to be for the mining trucks. The end of the Campbell Highway is at the Klondike Highway in Carmacks, Yukon.

One daughter got a lot of driving practice in Yukon. Our youngest son was too young then but in later years he got his driving start and plenty of time driving my F-250 crew cab diesel truck with a manual transmission.

Dawson City, Yukon, Canada.
From Carmacks to Dawson City, Yukon it is another 220 miles, again through wilderness. We had no reservations but easily found a place to stay in one of several rustic hotels. At Dawson, there is a Chinese restaurant that has breakfast with whatever one might find on the breakfast menu at any American restaurant in the United States. Dawson City, population 2,000 was the first fully electrified city in the world. During the gold rush days it was known as the Paris of the north. The ferry across the Yukon River only runs about 65 days a year when there is no ice. The current is very strong. I have been told by boat crew that the ferries can work with one engine in an emergency.

I meet a real Democratic Socialist in Dawson City, Yukon, Canada.
On another trip, I was waiting for the ferry in front of an RV. I was talking to the RV owner. He told me that he was from California. He had retired, bought an RV, and was traveling as much as he could. He told me that he was appalled at how every state but California neglects taking care of its people. When I got a chance to speak, I said to him :

"Why do you have a Montana registration?"

"The registration fee for an RV in California is so exorbitant I register it at my brother's address in Montana."

In all of his conversation about California he did not seem to comprehend a connection between high taxes and government freebies and other benefits.

"Oh, well," was my unsaid thought.

"Democratic socialism is fine for him and for states taking care of their people so long as he can limit paying for it himself."

A trip to Chicken, Alaska.
Across the Yukon river is the Top of the World Highway that goes to Chicken, Alaska, 108 miles from Dawson City, that takes four to five hours of driving.

There is a border crossing on the Top of the World Highway. A new building has been built that houses both the Canadian and American Customs and Immigration offices and checkpoints. I don't know if it has changed but border crossings in either direction were only from 9:00 AM to 5:00 PM and only for the days when ferries could run from Dawson City.

The town name Chicken comes from the bird name ptarmigan. There are plenty of ptarmigan in the area and along the highway. Since no one could spell or pronounce ptarmigan the name Chicken was chosen. The population is 23 in the summer, seven in the winter. I had no occasion to eat ptarmigan there.

On another trip, in Reykjavik, Iceland, at the Christmas buffet at the Pearl restaurant on top of the hot water tanks, we had ptarmigan stew. Not too bad.

A trip to Tok Junction and Delta Junction, Alaska.
From Chicken the road goes down 80 miles to Tok Junction and the Alaska Highway. Tok Junction is at Milepost 1314.

A son and I explored a glacier off the Richardson Highway near Delta Junction. We knew to avoid the crevasses where one can slip, disappear down a slide, and never come back.

I had a bit of fear when I realized that if we kept going we might not find our way out. Climbing the icy walls is not an option. We turned and worked our way to our starting point.

The girls had not ventured out on the glacier.

We had to drive through Yukon, Canada on the Alaska Highway to get home. At the border going south, the kids were pulled aside for questioning as to their relationship to me and what we were doing. I had a Massachusetts driver's license and a car registered in Massachusetts and we were headed south. We had to go through part of Canada to drive home.

I work in the insurance industry.
I did work in both the Life, and Property & Casualty insurance industries developing new ideas.

A most important achievement was that for several years in a row, I was able to take four of our daughters to several annual Take Your Daughter to Work Day.

I worked with three insurance companies:

1. Property and Casualty company
2. Life and Health company
3. Another Property and Casualty company.

A plan to use only one temp agency.
One of the insurance companies used plenty of people temp agencies. The powers that be decided to narrow down to just one temp agency. They believed this would get them the best price and the best employees. A schedule was set up covering a full week to have a dog and pony show where temp agencies salespeople would do a proposal showing why their agency should be the one chosen. I went to some of the sessions. I could hardly stand the platitudes. All of the proposals were voluminous. One company in particular had one that was fully 12 inches thick. All boilerplate material. Who would read all of this. The next week the evaluations started. Everyone involved had a different idea of how to rank the companies. I went to see the V.P. in charge. I told her that everyone was missing the basics.

- Having one temp agency would be no guarantee of having the best people or even having people available when a call was made. There should be alternate agencies.
- Insurance companies have plenty of cash because money is collected in advance of the insured period and accumulates for future claims.
- Temp agencies are always short of cash because their service is rendered, expensed to them, and paid out by them well before their invoiced cash is collected.
- The best service from a temp agency is given to whomever pays the quickest.
- The insurance company could set up a payment procedure using time sheets rather than invoices. The rate is known. Invoices would be required the next week.

The next day all of the handout material was shredded. No visible change was made. I do not know if they implemented my plan. Sometimes conflict just makes the status quo prevail.

The executives would never ride a train.
One of the companies had executives constantly going to New York City. These people would travel to their airport, fly to New York, then take a taxi into the city. From their office an Amtrak station could be seen close by. I did a comparison of time, money, stress, and comfort and showed that they would be way ahead to take Amtrak to New York. My contact VP laughed.

"There is no way that our people would ride a train no matter how much it saved."

HACCP.
I have done many things where I have adapted technology or ideas from one industry for use in another. One of these was HACCP. HACCP, Hazard Analysis Critical Control Point, was originally developed by NASA for quality control in the space programs. HACCP is a systematic preventive approach to safety hazards in processes that can cause the end result to be unsafe, and designs measurements to reduce these risks to a safe level.

HACCP was found to be of value in processing of seafood, then in restaurants.

I found HACCP to be of value in developing new insurance plans and in writing new coverage.

In insurance two big hazards are anti-selection and moral hazard. People that are likely to have a claim want to buy insurance. Those not likely to have a claim do not want to buy insurance. Moral hazard involves a variety of ways that the likelihood of a claim is increased. Today insurance companies have many more ways to assess moral hazard. Can you say Facebook?

Sometimes when I have used the internet in gathering information about a prospect or client, several of my children have accused me of stalking. LinkedIn is stalking? On all of the social network sites the data is put there for the purpose of others finding it. There are growing resources that will do the searches rapidly and compose a dossier in less than a minute. With artificial intelligence specialized analyses can be done at the same time.

At one insurance company, I used HACCP principles in developing a way to measure outstanding risk and type of risk by county in Florida. When a hurricane is coming, the uninsured rush to get coverage. It was good to be able to know up to date at what point before the storm the company should stop writing insurance.

I get formal insurance education.
I gained a large number of insurance certifications in classroom and self-study work:
- Massachusetts Insurance Brokers' License for Life, Health, and Accident
- LOMA Fundamentals of Life and Health Insurance
- LOMA Associate, Customer Service with honors
- LOMA Associate, Insurance Agency Administration

- LOMA Associate, Insurance Regulatory Compliance
- LOMA, Fellow, Life Management Institute, with distinction
- LOMA Underwriting Life and Health Insurance
- ICA, Associate, Life and Health Claims
- HIAA Health Insurance Associate
- HIAA Managed Healthcare Professional
- HIAA Long Term Care

Toastmasters.
I earned a Competent Toastmaster certification. I did the basic Toastmasters' program that meant a certain number of major speeches and a lot of shorter ones. There were table talks where several people would speak successively for two minutes each. They would be given their topic when they got to the podium and the meter started. Other people critiqued aspects of each speech, short or long.

A trip to Panama.
Two daughters and I went to Panama for a few weeks to help some missionaries with construction of an orphanage. It was a good break and a vision extender.

There was really bad winter weather in the northeast at the time we were scheduled to go. We stayed at a hotel about 12 miles from Newark Airport the night before our flight. Many flights had been cancelled that day and the next day was not looking better. There was heavy snow the next morning. The car would not start. Time was running out. I called a garage to pick up the car. We took a taxi to Newark. There were many flight delays and cancellations.

Eventually we got to Houston though we had missed our flight to Panama. The airline got us a room at an airport hotel and gave us more food vouchers than we could possibly use. They rebooked our Panama flight for the next day at no cost to us. That was all really great because airlines do not have to give any compensation for weather delays.

The missionaries were at the airport when we arrived even though we had not been able to call them.

There were some exciting happenings once we got to Panama. One daughter's room opened onto the street. Early one morning some workers passing by killed a fer-de-lance, a small very poisonous snake, right in front of her door. A little farther down, a poisonous bocaraca snake was seen in a tree that overhung the road. At night dogs could be heard barking all through the jungle at residences. I teased her and told her that they were barking spiders.

Public transportation consisted of private services that used ancient American school buses. The drivers did not own the buses but rented them by the day. Routes were not exact and there could be slight variance in fares. There were no set bus stops. People stand in the road and the next bus or buses coming along, usually seconds or maybe as much as a minute later would stop. When boarding the bus one had to be careful not to get burned by the engine as often the cover would be missing. The buses were brightly painted to make up for rust, dents, and other defects.

One night we were coming back from Panama City with various supplies and did not relish walking from the main road.

We paid the driver a few dollars extra to take us up the mountain to our village.

The road was really bad with plenty of ruts from the frequent rain. It was very dark as there were no lights and the moon was not out. He got us up there, albeit quite slowly, and was able to turn around.

We were quite close to Panama City. There were many Kentucky Fried Chicken stores. It seems like they were on every other corner. The other corners seemed to all be Pio Pio, a Panamanian chicken chain.

I found that the Kentucky Fried Chicken product tasted like it used to taste in the U.S. It was great. I had previously, in the U.S., called national customer service to ask about the recipe.

I was told that it was the same recipe everywhere and that my taste buds had probably changed. Were they ever wrong.

The missionaries had not been going because they too did not like the recipe change. They were so glad to find out what I had found out.

I had been in Panama a few years earlier and knew the way the roads worked around Panama city, with wide one way roads.

On that previous trip I had Thanksgiving dinner at an American military installation on Galeta Island off the city of Colon.

One day one daughter and I had dinner at a hotel where I had stayed before.

The lobby was completely open to the outside and made great ambience. The steak was exactly as I had remembered it.

For the orphanage, cement was mixed by hand on the ground in a pile of sand stirred by shovels. A hose for water was used. Any other type of automation would result in work slowdowns that negated the gain. So there was not even a small mixer with a motor. Workers were paid daily $10 for a 10 hour work day.

Panama has used American money since 1904, calling a dollar a balboa. It does have its own coins and does have a one balboa coin.

Buying things is a lot easier for Americans than in most countries. Panama was becoming a safe retirement country for Americans, those with or without money. Social security alone could make one upper middle class. The wealthy could find many large home neighborhoods on the waterfront.

Credit unions are well-established and solid financially, paying good dividends on savings accounts.

Many Americans not living in Panama have savings accounts in Panama.

I meet Dr C. Everett Koop the Surgeon General.
Jack was due to be on a TV show. Merv Griffin or Phil Donahue, I think. We had to be at a studio in New Jersey near the George Washington Bridge for the filming of a show. It was not for the actual show. I helped Jack get his animals set up. Then I went in the break room. There I met Dr. C Everett Koop, the Surgeon General of the United States. We talked for awhile and then decided to go out for breakfast. Dr Koop did not know when he would do his part but he was not worried. We found a diner a few blocks away. It was a great conversation time and we both learned from each other.

Trips to Okeechobee, Florida.
A frequent destination was the exotic animal sales in Okeechobee, Florida. There was a per person ticket price that included several meals throughout the day. A sign at the gate said "Brokers, Traders, and Merchants. No Pests." Pests referred to animal rights people looking for good photo ops. With the kind of prices paid at the auction it is hard to imagine that anyone would mistreat the animals. Jack would go to buy and to sell for his snake and animal farm. The sale was run as an auction with professional auctioneers.

The sale days were long but a lot of fun. One time two Cuban men put a calf in the back seat of their car. The auctioneers were all good at humor.

On one trip I took one of our daughters. We rented a 32 foot flat deck pontoon boat with two outboard engines. The daughter was the skipper and did a great job piloting the boat through the narrow channels in the Everglades. We saw plenty of alligators and birds. Even when alone I often rented a boat and enjoyed the times exploring the swamp.

Other trips with Jack had been to the rattlesnake roundups at Claxton, Georgia, home of Claxton fruitcakes, and Sweetwater, Texas.

In Brackettville Texas we had a chance to tour the second Alamo, the one that was made for movies that is like the original Alamo. It's on a private ranch, owned by James T. "Happy" Shahan, and is no longer open to the public. Many Alamo and other westerns were filmed at the site. As a working ranch it was not difficult to herd cattle through the "town." It as a vastly different experience from the commercialized, beautified Alamo in San Antonio.

At the grocery store in Brackettville, I found that one of the products for sale was driver training to meet the requirements of getting a ticket dismissed. They gave me a set of the materials as I was involved in safety at that time.
In Florida, we stopped at a restaurant in Ortona, on the Caloosahatchee River. Ortona has to be the most laid-back town in the United States. The waitress asked where we were from.

"Up north," Jack said.

"I'm from up north too," she replied.

"Whereabouts?" I asked her.

"Ocala," she said "I couldn't stand the city anymore. Ocala was getting too big."

Ocala was 200 miles up U.S. 27 and at that time had a population of about 20,000.

I meet Tom Crutchfield and Mike Van Nostrand.
In Florida I had met some biggie reptile people such as Tom Crutchfield and Mike Van Nostrand. Tom, of Crutchfield Crocodile Enterprises, and Mike of Strictly Reptiles, Inc.

In doing their part at building the reptiles for collectors industry, both men had built large businesses and advanced the reptile mission.

Jack dealt with both men.

My involvement was strictly social except for buying from Jack a captive bred baby alligator for one of our sons.

There is a sign at Strictly Reptiles at the doorway into the back area of the store. It read:

"No Admittance, Especially If You Are A Friend of Mike's."

There is a Far Side cartoon about a skydiving school located next to Crutchfield's 40 acre crocodile farm in Bushnell, Florida. Gary Larson has made the cartoon that showed Crutchfield's Crocodile Farm as being directly next to Anderson's Skydiving School. I don't recall there ever being such a school next to Crutchfield Crocodile Enterprises but it made a funny cartoon and a 2005 Calendar Cover.

Tommy showed me the original hand drawn cartoon autographed by Larson.

One important thing to note about the reptile industry is the difference between breeders and importers or traders.

The breeders make a lot of money from captive breeding of rare foreign species.

The traders import as much as they can, sometimes even when it is illegal.

The only thing the two groups have in common is that they both make a lot of money.

Reptiles alone bring staggering prices. Drug dealers practice conspicuous consumption yet still have too much money. Paying $100,000 for a snake is then quite impressive.

A trip to Florida with crocodiles.
I took some crocodiles to Florida for Jack.

Crocodiles cannot handle the northern winter weather. With a little accommodation, alligators do ok. Every year his crocodiles went back and forth to Florida. When they got too big he would leave them in Florida and acquire baby crocodiles.

My family went with me to Florida on that trip. Or maybe I could say it was a family vacation where I took some crocodiles to Florida. I rented a 15 passenger van. The crocodiles were in five foot wooden boxes. No care was needed en route. The boxes fit under the seats by pushing them in through the rear doors. We put blankets and pillows on top of the boxes. The children had a nice sleep and play area over the boxes and the seats. We had several unique experiences on that trip.

We stopped for gas at a high volume, low price gas station I knew in South

Carolina. All of the pumps were full. I had to pick one and get in line. A black man had just pulled up and was getting out of a very nice, new looking, black Cadillac. Cadillacs were still big, prestigious, cars and not cramped little tin cans like they are today. The man had walked up to the window in the side of the store to prepay for his gas.

"This will be quick" I said out loud as I pulled up behind the Cadillac. Neither Cheri nor any of the kids asked why. No one said anything. The man came back to his pump and in less than a minute had "gassed up."

As the man got back into his car and left, we moved up. I could hear one daughter in the next seat back. Just one word in a low voice. "racist."

Why was I racist for knowing that he would buy only $2.00 worth of gas?

After taking the tape off the mouths of the crocodiles and putting them in their own outdoor tank at Gatorama, we headed for the Keys. I don't recall who was with me. Cheri and some of the kids had stayed in Orlando with Cheri's sister.

Gatorama.
The destination for the crocodiles was Gatorama at Palmdale, Florida, in the southern and central part of the state not too far west of Lake Okeechobee.

Gatorama was originally started by legendary cracker and gator hunter Cecil Clemens in 1957. Clemens said that yankees coming to Florida wanted to see the beach, an orange grove, and alligators. He would show them alligators.

David Thielen took Gatorama over from Cecil.

David's daughter Patty and her husband, Allen Register, took over Gatorama in 1989 as managers. It was not until 2006 that they bought it from David.

I had some great visits with Allen and Patty.

Among other things we had discussions about the use of QuickBooks.

Cecil was alive until January 25, 2016 when he passed away at age 94. I never met Cecil.

Gatorama is a tourist spot but also raises alligators for the meat and skins, a legal business. There are huge barns full of alligators. Most everyone has seen or knows of a frog or turtle jumping into the water when someone approaches. Imagine thousands of small alligators doing that in a barn.

I get profiled near Homestead, Florida.
It was late when we headed back to Orlando. We were somewhere near Homestead on the Florida Turnpike. There was no traffic in either direction. Some distance back I could see another vehicle approach and then hang back. If I slowed down it slowed down. If I sped up it sped up.

Another vehicle came onto the highway between me and the other vehicle. It approached and followed for a while. Then lights came on. It was the police. I was relieved but apprehensive. The car further back was also a police car. I stopped and was quickly surrounded with police with drawn guns. Some were shining flashlights into the back where the kids were sleeping. Others were on both sides of the front doors. I was pulled out of the van. What happened was that I fit the profile of a drug runner. One white man in a van with northern license plates heading north late at night. The police decided all was ok. They apologized and suggested that I be more careful in the future of when and how I travel.

During my lifetime, people have become too sensitive.
There are cultural differences among races, nationalities, religions, and parts of the country.

Being from the south, I love redneck jokes and in general any jokes about people from the south. I sure heard plenty when I moved north. I was never offended.

Jeff Foxworthy of College Park, Georgia has made a fortune off of jokes about southerners, who are his biggest fans. What I like about Jeff Foxworthy is the jokes where I can see relatives of mine.

Before Foxworthy, there were so many others doing the same humor style. Jerry Clower, Andy Griffith, Brother Dave Gardner, and so many others.

Most of the humor is outdated but the number of practitioners is increasing.
One of my best long-term friends was from North Dakota and was of Norwegian descent. He collected Norwegian humor books. I gave him Ole and Lena books whenever I found them. He was most appreciative and looked forward to reading them and was glad to add them to his collection.

For 43 years, the Lil Abner comic strip was most popular. It made fun of the hillbillies in the fictional Appalachian mountain town of Dogpatch, U.S.A. What was not widely known is that the author, Al Capp, a Connecticut native of Russian Jewish descent, based all of his characters, their attitudes and their actions, on real people he knew from Seabrook, New Hampshire.

Maybe we should all take heed of what Henry Kissinger, Richard Nixon's Secretary of State, once said:

"The only thing worse than being satirized in the comic strip Doonesbury is not being satirized in the comic strip Doonesbury."

Travel stories.
Traveling at night has always been what I like to do.

Day or night, I make hourly stops to get out and walk around the car. On the east-west interstates in particular, trucks stretch out in convoys. Each truck has a front door, the truck in front, and a back door, the truck behind. With that setup known, that trucker is in the rocking chair. All the vehicles are exceeding the speed limit. At night the truck stops are booming cities. Families with children traveling in a tractor trailer are numerous.

During the CB radio craze, I had my own CB though just for listening on Channel 19.

There was initially a radio operator's license. A court ruled that the citizens band, CB, could not require a license. Everyone got a refund of their fee, $65 per year I think it was.

I had a white collar office worker neighbor that actively used his CB.

While on the air, he had a really good southern accent though he may have never been south.

He also knew all of the CB lingo and grammar.

"Breaker-Breaker. Breaker one nine. Can I get a westbound on 84? You're wall to wall and tree top tall. Any bears out there? What's your 20 good buddy?"

As a listener only I was "sandbagging" or "reading the mail."

Our youngest son's first airplane trip.
Our youngest sons first airplane trip was from T.F. Green Airport at Providence Rhode Island.

We had barely left the ground it seemed when he said:

"I can see the whole world."

A trip to Newport, Rhode Island.
Our first child worked at a great hotel and resort in Newport, Rhode Island, a great town. One time in Newport there were two guys in town on the same day wearing cowboy hats, me and Bob Dylan.

At an outdoor waterfront restaurant I had a lobster. The waitress had asked where I was from and all that. She was clearly proud of the restaurant and its ambiance. Indeed it was a fine place.

Not wishing to run down her place in any form, I did tell her that I could go to Walmart out west, buy a live Maine lobster, have Walmart boil it, then have the same dinner as in Newport on the tailgate of my truck while looking at the mountains. Not the fine ambiance of Newport and this restaurant of course.

A trip west.
I took two of our daughters on a trip to take a car to give to our oldest son and to visit my mother.

I bought a Volkswagen bus as I had planned to do. Our second purchase of a Volkswagen as planned. In the Volkswagen We took a trip further west in a loop to the south as a detour on our way back home.

We had some car trouble that became noticeable after we crossed the mountains. I later realized that I had made the mistake of forgetting that a Volkswagen bus should not go more than 50 to 55 miles per hour.

The Lord was with us as we continued our trip. We found a Volkswagen shop in New Mexico.

It was the Fourth of July weekend start and I would have to leave the bus.

We made some phone calls and found a rental Dodge at the Farmington, New Mexico airport that needed to get back east. We got a super rental deal. Everyone was happy.

A few weeks later we went back, this time including one of our older sons.

We would have two vehicles going back and needed another driver. It was really hot. There is no air conditioning in a Volkswagen bus. We stopped at rest areas where the kids got soaking wet in the lawn sprinklers. They stayed cool drying off with wind blowing through the windows.

We stopped at a store at near Lake Eufaula in Oklahoma.
Lake Lotawata was on the exit sign off I-40. Don Garrett thought up the name

while working on a highway drafting squad that was planning signs to go along the then-new I-40. When Don's crew got to that road, he could see that it "didn't go much of anywhere except down to the water."

Don just thought up the name "Lotawata" and wrote it on the map, thinking someone would find a more proper name. No one ever did.

Our daughter had some second thoughts.
I enjoyed spoiling my children by letting them buy things.

Our younger daughter got an Indian bow and arrow set. Her older sister chose a fringed vest. Later I felt really bad for her. She liked her vest, it looked good on her, but it didn't do anything. The other daughter was having fun with her bow and arrow.

I think one of the worst parts of being a parent is when their children start making decisions and soon get to where they have to make mutually exclusive decisions.

There is more than one choice and for whatever reason, usually involving time, they cannot do but one.

At one point on that trip our son wanted some alone driving time on Route 66. I stayed back a mile or so until he was ready for us to travel together again.

A trip to Miami Florida.
I had been on a quick trip to Miami Florida and had some spare time.

I had a rental car and went to the Keys.

At a point where I needed gas I could not find out how to open the gas cap door. The store attendants could not get it open. Other customers had no luck. We searched for buttons, levers, and pull wires. Nothing. Then another customer pulled into the station.

He smiled and touched the back of the gas cap compartment door, the area near the hinge. It easily opened.

CHAPTER 13: "GO WEST YOUNG MAN"

"When a plan produces the right amount of money and is sustainable there is no longer a need for the visionary. The visionary will even be accused of doing what the opponents themselves want to do." - Anonymous.

We moved west.
It was Cheri's choice that we move west. I was just completing a project in New England.

We looked up facts about different locations.

We did want easy access to be able to travel to other places and to receive family visitors.

We considered the impact on family of moving west.
We did plenty of thinking about family impact on us and on our children and their families.

One daughter had graduated from high school with high honors. She was to start college in the Fall.

We moved west just as she moved into her dorm.

I become executive director of a non-profit.
Through someone I knew in the Berkshires, I had gotten wind of an opportunity to turn around a non-profit.

I took a quick trip west.

The interview became a working session of what I would do. It makes a tremendous difference in job search if an applicant can tell what they will do rather than tell what they have done in the past or that they would love to fill the position.

One of the applicants, in his cover letter, said that he was getting older and wanted a job that paid well, had good benefits, and would not have much stress or much work to do.

I did tell the interview committee that I viewed it as a six month project during which time I would also be learning the state.

I was offered the executive director position.

We look for a house.
Back home we searched the internet for a suitable house. We found one but were talked out of it by the agent who felt that the house across the street would be better for us and a better value. Our oldest son went to Cheyenne to look at it. He saw no problems. We made the deal. We were not going to see the house before the closing. Then something came up that delayed it to the next day. We went to drive by the house. The sellers, a policeman and his wife, an architect, happened to be there at the time. We met them and toured the house. We liked what we saw. There had been plenty of work done to the interior. There was much to be done which we did over time.

One of our daughters made two important early improvements.

1. We wanted a door going into what was to be a son's bedroom. That room had originally been a garage. Two different carpenters said that it could not be done. She did not know that so she installed a standard 80 inch door that still works fine.

2. We wanted to make a room at the foot of the basement stairs. There were cabinets along the stairs. Inside the basement there was a door into a room with cabinets. Two different carpenters said that there might be a load bearing wall and they would not touch the job. She found that the cabinets had been installed separately. She removed them all, put up panelling and a floor. I am in that room right now writing this book. That room is most valuable to us.

It has been great to have children and their families visit, often a number of them at the same time. Our house became a meeting place for them. Most have stayed at a hotel. We could have squeezed them in but it has worked out better for them to have separate space.

When I was growing up, things were much different.

Travelers often could not afford hotels.

Over time my parents had, like others, set up networks of friends and relatives.

I can remember us going to someone's home, walking right in the unlocked door, and my mother fixing dinner for the convenience of our hosts when they came in from work or wherever.

Weekend Trips.
We often did trips on weekends. It reached the point that it was me, Cheri, and our youngest.

Then he no longer wanted to go with us.

I was sad.

He was our last to travel with us as a child.

On the good side, it was me and Cheri again.

I did have one more opportunity with him.

Somehow we discovered that he needed glasses.

I took him down the line to deal with the matter. As we left the eyeglasses place he said:

"Thanks Dad."

I wish we had known sooner.

The newsletter.
We did the newsletter the same as we did the newspaper in North Carolina. Tabloid newspaper style. It went over well. As I did site visits, I noticed that people kept all of them and made a stack in their office.

I made photos for everywhere that I went. There were no boiler plate filler articles like so many publications have. We wanted to make it interesting.

Joe Kaplan.
Our most avid reader was Joe Kaplan, for over 60 years the executive director of a non-profit in Los Angeles.

Joe called me almost every month with comments.

Every Christmas, Joe, who was Jewish, was a bell ringer for the Salvation Army. He had the biggest collections as he sold people on putting $20 bills in the kettle instead of quarters. He related the donation to how much they had just spent at the grocery store or big name department store.

At the national meeting Joe and I would go hiking together just us or with others in a bigger group.

I went one time to Joe's house off Wilshire Boulevard. He and his wife lived in a quiet wooded dead-end street with only four houses, all on the same side of the street. The house was originally the home of a movie star of the early 1900s. At that time no one was building Bel-Air mega mansions.

Joe Kaplan passed away at age 95.

Hurricane Wilma.
I took a trip to Fort Lauderdale, Florida with a son and a daughter. We were there during Hurricane Wilma. We stayed at the Harbor Beach Marriott. We elected to stay during the storm. Our balcony sliding glass door was taped. During the storm the power went out. All was dark in the area except for the hotel that had its own generator.

There was an all night party on the lobby level. The Tampa Bay Buccaneers, a professional football team, was staying at the hotel. The kids were impressed.

We went just outside during the storm as did others.

I told the kids to face away from the wind and blowing sand.

There are hurricanes and there are hurricanes. The wind was about 90 miles an hour. We did not go down to the ocean but stayed on the upper beach just outside the building.

There was an open passageway from the building to the outside.

As the eye of Wilma passed there was calm. I told the kids that the wind would soon be coming from the other direction. It didn't happen.

We found the next day that the storm had reversed course at the Marriott, went back down the Intracoastal Waterway then turned west. A1A was impassable due to about six feet of sand.

Planned activities at the Swimming Hall of Fame were taking place. We attended some of the diving competition.

The sand went only as far as A1A.

All other streets and roads were cleared of branches and debris very quickly.

Power had been restored.

We started a subsidiary non-profit in Wichita, Kansas that quickly became sustainable. One daughter did a tremendous job of setting up the office and staffing it with good people.

Conferences.
We did a series of eight conferences in various locations that followed a pattern I had planned:

- 2001 - Building a New Paradigm
- 2002 - Expecting the Unexpected
- 2003 - Communicating.
- 2004 - Creating a Culture.
- 2005 - Sustainability.
- 2006 - Designing - Do it Now!
- 2007 - Best Practices for Incident Control
- 2008 - Innovations.

At each conference there were two dinner banquets. The first night was always full. The second night was uncertain because it was the final event. Most attendees were too far from home to go home that night. Nevertheless, last minute decisions might be made not to attend due to work situations. Those attendees had to drive back at night.

Estimated counts, with dinner price guarantees for the hotel, had to be made in advance. I took action to minimize our loss from uneaten dinners.

At the last moment point when people were seated and we knew our reservation gap, I went out and offered free dinner and entertainment to other hotel guests passing by in the hallway. I told them they could sit with others or by themselves at a vacant table. I noticed that most chose to sit with others.

I told them they could leave when they liked but could also stay for the casino night fun.

The first time I did this, the board President questioned me about the strangers in the room.

"They are our guests for dinner," I said. "We have a mission to the community not just to a special group.

He thought it was a good idea. It was a social event. There were no trade secrets discussed. The hotels may bank on charging for no shows though the amount of extra profit is questionable as the food and staffing had to be available for our guaranteed count. Anyway I told them we were doing this.

Aidan.

At one conference, I surprised the BP attendees with Aidan, a Group, Corporate, Director for BP from London.

I had first visited Aidan in London to learn about BP's new program that held promise for every company and I had asked him in person to come to the U.S.

He attended part of our board meeting. While we continued our meeting, I loaned him my truck for some local area sightseeing and reminded him to drive on the right.

Aidan was the keynote speaker and also was able to hold a separate meeting with the BP people in attendance.

Jim Fowler of the Mutual of Omaha TV program Wild Kingdom.
For the 2001 conference, held in Casper, Wyoming that year, my very long term client, Jim Fowler, the naturalist, of Mutual of Omaha Wild Kingdom TV program was the keynote speaker.

Jim brought live animals. The state only had objection to his bringing a bear but because of his reputation and experience they allowed it. A full grown tiger, a really big snake, a large fennel cat, several birds of prey, a bear, and some other animals were on the scene.

We had engaged a college student to open with the U.S. national anthem. At the last minute she could not make it. We got a substitute from a high school. Surprise surprise! This young lady's hero was Jim Fowler. This was not known until she got to the conference venue. She and her mother both shed tears of joy. Jim spent a good bit of time with her and her mother and many photos were made.

Jim brought quite a message as an holistic keynote speaker. He said that we are wired to fear being scratched, bitten, or clawed by an animal yet we do not fear going down the highway at 75 miles an hour in a 7,000 pound truck. He also said that we need to think 500 years ahead for anything that we do to the environment.

Jim passed away in May 2019 at home in Connecticut.

Dr Gene Howard.
At one conference we had Dr. Gene Howard as keynote speaker. Gene is a John Wayne look-alike that dresses and talks the part, an ordained minister, and is an academic that has done studies and is an accomplished expert on such subjects as attention spans.

He wanted to schedule some evangelistic services so we covered his added expenses to do that. We had unique and interesting speakers at all of our conferences.

A good repair shop and tire store.
Across the street and a block away was a tire store that also had a garage and a good mechanic. The customer service there was great. I started a relationship there that has continued to this day. One of many surprises happened there. One morning before the store opened I left one of my trucks in front. I meant to call at 8:00 AM but forgot. At 10:00 AM I called.

"Your truck is all set," said the manager.

"What do you mean all set?" I asked. "You parked in front of the tire center, your truck looked like it needed tires so we put them on. You always like the best 10 ply so that's what you got."

I was most pleased. Tires are really important. A vehicle is connected to the road by four little squares of rubber and not by four big tires and wheels. Lives are at stake with dependence on those little squares.

Positive Living Breakfast Club.
I became a member of the Positive Living Breakfast Club. The club had been in operation since the 1940's. There was a weekly Wednesday morning breakfast meeting. I attended every Wednesday that I was in town for 15 years. We each bought our own breakfast. We each had a saying that we shared. Then there was discussion of positive events and ideas. Over the years attendance had dwindled.

I found the breakfast club to be a great inspiration. We all had vastly different viewpoints on everything yet we were able to talk together about anything with no one taking offense.

A fake REDDI call on a trip to Montana.
One Sunday afternoon I left for a trip to Montana. It was a nice sunny day. I was going north on I-25, driving a rental car with a Colorado license plate. I passed an old pickup truck with Wyoming plates traveling quite slowly. A number of people were in the truck and it was loaded down with all kinds of things. It reminded me of the Beverly Hillbillies. Now don't get me wrong. I'm sure they were all fine people. I have never met a Wyoming native that I did not like. There is a certain rivalry with those that are known as the "Greenies." The driver began blowing the horn at me constantly and there was shouting. I continued on my way and soon they were far behind even though I was going a little under the speed limit.

Some miles further I went over a hill and there was a highway patrol car in the median. After I passed the car pulled out and stayed the same distance behind me. I got off at Orin Junction to take a rest break and visit the men's room at the service area. The trooper got off behind me. I did not notice immediately notice that he had pulled into the rest area behind me and that after I had pulled into a parking spot he stopped behind me. As I got out he had gotten out and approached me.

"Sir, this is not an official traffic stop but can I ask if you've been drinking?"

"I've had an iced tea that I got in Wheatland," I replied.

"You don't look or smell like you've been drinking. And you were driving ok. I had a REDDI call on you." REDDI is "Report Every Drunk Driver Immediately."

"Could it be my Colorado license plate?" I asked.

He then went on to tell me that he had seen cases of REDDI calls on cars with a Colorado plate that was not a real case.

He and I chatted some more. He had not asked for my ID but I told him who I was and where I was going. He then remembered that he was in a class I had taught a year or so earlier.

There was something really funny.

He did not stop me because there was no probable cause.

He told me that usually in less than a mile he can find a probable cause to stop anyone.

When he saw me get off the interstate he figured I would not do a proper turn. There are long white lines on both sides of the lane. A driver of any vehicle is expected to stop and make the turn at the end of the white lines. That is so that there is adequate sight line under the bridge. He said most people didn't do it properly.

He said I caused him some worry because he had just gone off duty and was afraid he would have to follow me to Lusk. He said he was glad I pulled into the rest stop.

We both went our separate ways.

A visit to Lava Hot Springs, Idaho.
Our youngest son and I were overnight in Lava Hot Springs, Idaho.

Hot water is piped into motel rooms and of course is in pools around town.

We decided to climb a mountain on the edge of town. There were no trails. The mountain was higher and steeper than we had thought but we continued to the top.

Our motto of the day became: "We set out to do something and we did it."

A good motto for all of life though care is still needed.

Our son rides in a helicopter.
I had been on a driving trip somewhere. Our youngest son had gone with me. We were somewhere in Iowa heading back to Wyoming.

We saw a helicopter close by the interstate. We got off the highway to investigate.

It was some kind of a community event. There were helicopter rides in a small helicopter. Not very much money to ride. It was $25 I think.

He got his first helicopter ride.

Our daughter and the swans.
On one trip to Chicago, Cheri and five of our children were along.

On the way back, we took a break in Nebraska. One daughter got brave and went swimming with the swans.

I break my wrist in Pinedale, Wyoming.
One trip was to Kelly, Wyoming, a small town in Jackson Hole for a train the trainer class. The class was scheduled for Friday.

I got through Pinedale, Wyoming and it had started snowing heavily.

I headed back and got a room. Then I went to a local restaurant that was near closing time.

I had parked directly in front. I came out of the restaurant and to keep from falling, was holding on to the rear of my truck with my right hand. Somehow I slipped and went right down on my left hand. There was pain and I could not move my hand.

I went across the street in my truck to a gas station and asked if there was a clinic in town.

The clerk made a call for me and showed me that I was only a block away. I drove over and parked in front.

At almost the same time a car pulled in on my right and a sheriff's car on the left. The deputy shined a light into my vehicle and then said I could get out.

We all went into the clinic.

The deputy started helping the doctor, actually a PA, physician's assistant, get set up. I have found that a PA is, in effect, just one notch below an MD.

The deputy spoke.

"Sorry if I scared you out there. We have a policy that if the clinic gets a night call that a deputy goes over in case it is someone after drugs or whatever."

"Sounds like a good idea," was my reply. "I guess it's a good thing I wasn't drinking tonight."

The deputy laughed.

"Yeah. Sometimes we give some treatment after the clinic job is done."

I had a broken wrist. There wasn't much that could be done that night. I would have to see an orthopedic surgeon in Jackson the next day.

The PA asked if I had a room and was otherwise set for the night. She gave me some kind of pain pill.

She told me to stop off before going to Jackson and she would have an appointment lined up. She said that an ambulance could take me if needed.

The next morning I gave her the pill back. I figured that if I had taken it I might not be able to drive. She agreed.

I went on to Jackson.

The doctor tried to fix the wrist but could not quite do it. He made some calls and said that I could get surgery the next day. When I told him I had to be in my class the next day, he made some more calls.

We would have to go to the hospital immediately. It was only next door.

The surgery was done and I stayed in the hospital that night. A room is a room.

The next morning early I asked the nurse for a towel. I told him I had to get moving.

"There's nothing on the chart that says you can leave," he said.

"Good, then there will be a place to record that I left," I replied smiling.

The nurse called the doctor who said that if I felt like leaving I could go.

I did my class and drove about half-way home. It was late and I got a room by the interstate. Home the next day on Sunday. The story was not quite over.

I filed for workers comp insurance on Monday morning since I had been traveling for work.

I learned later that there was some suspicion that I might have been injured while skiing. The PA at the clinic in Pinedale, as a matter of practice, had already dealt with that in her report. She had recorded a lot of detail about what I had told her about my job and why I was in the area. She may have even called the school in Kelly.

It was the PA that suggested workers comp.

There were two years of therapy.

I'm a leftie and there was quite an inconvenience in not having use of my writing hand.

Initially, I had to go to Jackson for therapy per workers comp rules.

I don't recall why it changed because later I was able to have therapy in my town.

SCORE.
I spent a number of years as a volunteer with the SCORE Association counseling small business start-ups and was the Wyoming district director and the Casper chapter chair. SCORE, originally Service Corps of Retired Executives, is a non-profit organization primarily funded by SBA, Small

Business Administration. There was one-on-one counseling, seminars, and email counseling. Email counseling has actually worked out the best for me. In cities the one-on-one counseling has been better. Distance is the issue.

I wrote a booklet called *You Want Advice from Me?* and passed it out to new volunteers.

I have done some one-on-one counseling on an impromptu basis while traveling.

Sometimes I have met with a restaurant owner that I had met while dining. We would go off into a side area of the dining room and talk business. I did not work for my dinner. When I was offered a comp meal I refused.

It is a part of the SCORE code of ethics that a counsellor cannot accept even a cup of coffee from a client.

While with SCORE, I did several thousand counselings, much of it via multiple emails per client, with follow-up meetings.

There were many good cases.

One involved a creative family in Huntington Beach, California. The husband's interest in self-employment came after he lost his career job and decided that it was just as well. He and his wife and now grown children have been involved in new ventures.

I remain in frequent contact with him.

A trip to Newport Beach, California.
One time when one son and I were in the Huntington Beach area, Newport Beach to be precise, we saw a restaurant named called Josh Slocums, after the sea captain who went around the world singlehanded.

We decided to try it.

Not great but not bad either.

When we were preparing to leave there was some commotion as a group came in.

The leader began to move tables around and put them together.

I made the comment that he was acting like he owned the place.

It turned out it was Dennis Rodman, the retired professional basketball player, and we learned that he did own the place.

The unhappy dry cleaner from Korea.
There was this late middle-aged Korean guy in New York City that had saved up from his meager wages for many years to fulfill his dream of coming to America and getting rich.

He was disappointed that in four years, all he had been able to do was save up $500,000 and own a paid for $500,000 house.

Other trips.
For a meeting in Portland, Maine. Our youngest son went with me. He was about 13 at the time.

We went to the Skowhegan Fair in Maine, one of the nicest and oldest of the many New England Fairs.

While I was in meetings one day, he went out on a schooner and had a great time.

We had an interesting experience in a Portland waterfront restaurant on that trip.

The building was old and there was plenty of sea coast ambiance. We had a table by the window on the street side.

I told him that at any moment a pirate with a parrot on his shoulder might come along.

While he was still looking out the window, a man came along with a live parrot on his shoulder. I doubt the man was a pirate. He may well have been unemployed which I guess is roughly the same thing.

Another meeting was held in Nashville, Tennessee.

The conference center was right at the airport so there were free shuttles. I did not have a rental car.

One night after the sessions were over, I walked four miles to the nearest White Castle.

When I got there the inside area was closed and they had a policy not to serve walk-ups. I was wearing a coat and tie. I told my story through the drive through window but there was no exception. I hailed a cab and had the driver go through the drive thru and order for me.

Then he took me back to the hotel.

On the morning we were all to leave Nashville, I had made an appointment to meet an associate in the coffee shop just beyond the security checkpoint.

It was around 6:00 AM. I got there first and was easily able to see everyone coming through security.

There was a short elderly man wearing an old army uniform that did not quite fit right and the green foldable field service cap. I figured him to be a WWII vet either coming from or going to a military retirees meeting. He had trouble walking and was alone.

TSA decided that he needed to be checked further.

He struggled to get his shoes off. I could see that he was crying.

Four tall young Arab men easily and briskly came through, quite a contrast to the man that had defended the United States many years earlier.

The TSA person apologized to the Arabs for the old man blocking their path and causing them inconvenience.

I had no suspicions of them, I'm sure they were ok. It was the irony of who was getting the extra security check.

Indians, the American kind.
On another occasion, I remember a certain phone call I had with one of the government administrators in Washington DC. He was really a great guy that really tried his best. He and I were good friends.

In my phone call, I happened to mention something about Indians, something positive.

There was a long pause at the other end. "Do you mean Indian as in Native American?" he asked.

"No, Bob. Indian as in Bureau of Indian Affairs in Washington, D. C. Indian as in Indian Health Service in Washington, D. C. Indian as in United States Senate

Committee on Indian Affairs. Indian as in every store name on the reservation and on highway billboards. Indian as in Indian flatbread that every restaurant on the reservations sell."

Since we were friends I tried not to be too hard on him.

Capacity Building.
I customized a boilerplate capacity building program to work for non-profits. I did a presentation in Fort Lauderdale, Florida.

Originally planned for four hours one afternoon, we also went all day the next day.

Capacity building involves a variety of ways to enable an organization to do more of what it does.

Indian Reservations.
I did work on the Wind River Indian Reservation in Wyoming as well as five other reservations in Montana. All with great folks.

At my first visit to the Wind River Reservation in Wyoming. I did as any speaker does and introduced myself. I pointed out that I was a new arrival from Massachusetts.

At the break, one man, a tribal member, said:

"Can I give you a request?"

"Sure" I said.

"I heard you say you are from New England. Please don't call us Native Americans. We are Indians. We are no more native than you are and Americans are the people who conquered us."

I remember one really hot day when we were driving through the Four Corners area in New Mexico.

I picked up a Navajo hitchhiker. He said he was heading to Farmington, New Mexico, to get drunk.

There were plenty of grasshoppers around, even inside our car. Our Volkswagen van did not have air conditioning so the windows were open.

One daughter put a grasshopper on the man's shoulder. She was quite young and I know she meant well.

The Navajo hitchhiker was a nice fellow and I enjoyed the conversation.

A trip on Amtrak to Portland, Oregon and Seattle, Washington.
One time I had a need to stay over the weekend at a reservation in eastern Montana.

It was too far to go back home and eastern Montana in the summer where, from May to September, it often gets to 100 degrees and on up to 112 degrees with no wind, is no place to pass the weekend.

Winter has seen lows of minus 42 degrees.

I took Amtrak on a 54 hour round trip.

I went to Portland, Oregon; Portland to Seattle, Washington then back to Montana.

With great air conditioning and scenery I also got a lot of work done while on the train in my Superliner Roomette and at a table in the lower level lounge.

A cold day.
I had a meeting scheduled at the fairgrounds in Worland Wyoming. I had to get the key from a cook at a restaurant in town. It was 27 degrees below zero.

Since I was parking just outside, I didn't bother putting on a coat for the quick trip into the restaurant. There were six people, out-of-towners I could easily tell, sitting at a table. They stared at me as I ran past them.

On the way out, one woman said: "Don't you wear a coat?"

Desirous of maintaining a good local image, I replied with:

"Well ma'am in Wyoming we don't start wearing coats until it gets cold."

I smiled and ran out.

Hatchet Resort at Moran Junction.
I was on my way to Jackson, Wyoming for a meeting. It was mid-afternoon.

I passed the Hatchet Resort at Moran Junction, 30 miles from Jackson.

The sign said "No Vacancy." The Holy Spirit directedI me to ask anyway.

In the office the lady told me there were no rooms. I turned to leave.

She said: "I do have one room with two beds but one bed is not made up. The towels have been changed. The man had to leave suddenly. The housekeepers have already left. I could let you have it as is for $25."

"I only need one bed," I said. I took the room. I had a relaxing afternoon and then a great meal in their restaurant.

Good deal for Jackson Hole!

Svilars restaurant in Hudson, Wyoming..
Restaurants in Wyoming are not the greatest. There is one exception, Svilars, in Hudson, Wyoming, near the Wind River Reservation.

After a visit to Svilars one wonders why other restaurants cannot provide the same experience.

Mama Bessie Svilar, the founder, died many years ago but the place survives with the same good food and service.

Not much can be said for the town of Hudson, Wyoming, as it became almost a ghost town after the mining went away. The Wind River Reservation begins at the end of the restaurant parking lot.

At most restaurants, even the so-called fast food places, one has to wait to eat. At Svilars there is a basket with a variety of breadsticks and different types of crackers already on the table. Very soon there is a plate of peppers, carrots, celery and dip.

The cocktails are amazing. There is something about the glasses, the ice and the drink itself that is most pleasing. At most places one feels cheated. Not at Svilars.

For those that like wine, Svilars has the type of selection that restaurants used to have many years ago. None of this phony baloney with fancy labels on ordinary wine with high prices. Just your basics including rosé with plenty of choices.

Before the entrée is served, there is a small serving of ravioli and sarma.

Sarma is a Yugoslavian item made of meat wrapped in cabbage. Not too bad.

Svilars buys sides of beef and cuts their own. There are 10 different cuts plus three sizes of prime rib. French fries are homemade. Why is that such a problem for most restaurants? There are five seafood choices. There is fried chicken. There are seven combo items with steak and seafood. There are seven choices on the Senior/Childrens menu including three steaks. Dessert is ice cream or cheesecake. Coffee is included in the dinner price.

The décor might be original. If it was updated the place would lose character. The entrance is through the bar that is a drop back in time to the early days of the west.

There are 86 seats in the main dining room. Often the tables turn twice a night. There is another dining room that can handle several different size groups.

Svilars is a must for any group meeting in Riverton or Lander and is worth the 26 mile round trip from either town. Svilars is open seven nights a week.

The only thing I have found wrong was a few misplaced apostrophes on the menu.

A trip to Inuvik, Northwest Territories, Canada.
Our youngest went with me to the Inuvik, pronounced e-NOO-vik, Petroleum Show in Inuvik, Northwest Territories.

Flying to Inuvik was incredibly expensive and there were no easy flights available. With layovers it was going to take several days. No direct flights to anywhere close.

Further I was not sure of the return date.

I had some meetings scheduled with a number of oil company execs, in Inuvik as well as in Calgary, all tied in with planning I was doing for the extension and globalization of the non-profit, both local and national.

A driving trip of almost 8,000 miles.
I elected to do it by driving. It was almost 8.000 miles round trip in a rented Nissan Frontier truck.

Rental cars.
I told the car rental folks where I was going as I always do. No problem as they reiterated that it was unlimited mileage.

With long trips in rental cars, I have always changed the oil as needed. I also wash the vehicle before taking it back. I view that I was the owner yet for just a short time and that I wanted the next "owner" to be happy.

The business model for a car rental business has generally been that the car rental companies lease the vehicles from the manufacturers and turn them in at a certain mileage specified by the manufacturer. When a car goes back a new one takes its place. The off-lease cars are then sold as "program cars." People that cannot afford a new car can still buy a current year model car yet for a lower price.

In the fine points of the business model there is a cost per day per car whether they are out on rental or parked. There is also the matter of registration. It has amazed me that it took so long for the rental companies to include a pro-rata fee per day for registration in the rental price.

Alberta.
At Lake Louise in Alberta, I got a $450 room, for me and our son, facing the lake, for $99, as a result of negotiating at the front desk. It was quite true that even $99 was a little high for our budget on that trip but it had become a hope of our son that we could stay at that hotel. I found some other ways to make up for the cost.

The next morning we took a hike around the lake.

We went to the Columbia ice fields, the largest glacial ice field in North America.

The keeper of the stories.
We visited a First Nation, Canada's politically correct term for Indian ,reservation in British Columbia. We met the lady that was the keeper of the stories for her tribe.

There is no written language so there are people that memorize the history and traditions.

We went to some of the places on the reservation that she told us about.

Indian time.
We had some questions and went back to ask her.

We were told by the white lady there that our contact had gone to lunch. I asked if we could wait until she returned.

She smiled.

"Yes but it could be an hour, a week, a month, or even three months before she comes back. She is on Indian time."

I have found out from my work on reservations that Indian time is a very real thing that is a problem to the rest of us yet maybe shouldn't be.

On my first trip to a reservation in Wolf Point, Montana, I was ready on Monday morning at 7:30 AM for my class to start as scheduled for 8:00 AM in a meeting room at my hotel. At 9:00 AM no one was there. The hotel manager told me not to worry.

Sure enough we did get going by 10:00 AM though all were not there.

Pets can be on Indian time.
I was having lunch with Robby White Hawk at the Sherman Inn in Wolf Point.

Our table was by the window. Suddenly Robby jumped up and ran outside. I saw him pick up a dog and put it in his truck. He came back in and told me that a few months earlier his dog had not come home one day.

That day it was walking down the sidewalk.

Travel on the Dempster Highway.
We traveled the Dempster Highway, the last road stretch to Inuvik. This 458 mile highway starts at the Klondike Highway near Dawson City, Yukon. Along the way, the Dempster crosses the Arctic Circle.

The highway is built on a gravel berm that ranges from a thickness of 3 feet 11 inches to 7 feet 10 inches. It serves as an insulator from the permafrost. Without the berm, the road would sink into the permafrost.

There are two river crossings on the Dempster Highway before getting to Inuvik. In the summer there are ferries. In the winter there are ice crossings. In the one month Spring thaw and in the one month Fall freeze-up the road is impassable as the ferries cannot run and the ice is too thin for driving.

Because it was summer, there was daylight 24/7. We drove continuously as there were no towns, houses, hotels, or gas stations until Eagle Plains at milepost 229.

There was no one to be found at the hotel. The hotel is built of a number of Atco trailers fastened together. We slept in the lobby on the couches and had breakfast before heading on to Inuvik.

From Eagle Plains it is still another six and a half hours to Inuvik with nothing in between.

We did have extra gas. We did have xtra tires already mounted on wheels.

Tire problems on the Dempster Highway.
We found that both ferries had old tires and wheels of all sizes and have air compressors. There are a many tire problems due to the sharp rocks. I learned that semis traveling the Dempster Highway can destroy a brand new expensive big truck tire in one passage while a car with bald tires might make it just fine. The first time we had a flat we could not find the jack. Two RVs stopped and the drivers could not find the jack either. Finally we found that the back seat could come out and the jack was under it. When we arrived at Inuvik and checked in we went straight to bed. Later in the day we found that two of our tires had gone flat. I had to buy two new ones. There was no tire store in Inuvik but there was a trucking company that sold and installed tires. I borrowed an air tank from them, inflated the flat tires, and was able to drive the short distance to the garage.

Inuvik.
It was a long trip to Inuvik, but it was worth it.

The ground is permafrost that is 900 feet deep. As a result, roads are not paved and water is trucked in to each house and business. There are indoor sewage and waste water tanks that have to be pumped out. The town indoor swimming pool is elevated.

At a Rotary club meeting I did learn that musk ox burgers are not so good.

There was a seasonal road over ice and the frozen ground that extends the Dempster Highway another 121 miles to Tuktoyaktuk. A new all season road was finished in the winter of 2017-2018.

A trip to Tuktoyaktuk.
We flew from Inuvik to the Inuvialuit village of Tuktoyaktuk, on the Beaufort Sea of the Arctic Ocean, in a DeHavilland Twin Otter.

The Twin Otter is an airplane with two engines and large propellers that carries freight and passengers in the same cabin. Seats fold down. The airplanes can and do land anywhere. Many have pontoons for water landings.

The Inuvialuit, formerly called Eskimo, in Tuk, as Tuktoyaktuk is called for short, hunt whales from aluminum outboard motor boats using harpoons.

They are always most anxious for the summer ice melt.

There is a community ice house with access via a ladder 29 feet deep into the permafrost. There are two horizontal tunnels with family compartments for seals and cut up whales. A native who had been to college in Ontario gave us a tour of the town.

Our son was pleased that in the general store there was a Pizza Hut.

I asked our guide why the word Eskimo was no longer used.

She said the word was viewed to be derogatory.

"In English it means 'people who eat meat raw.'"

She said the name had been given them by inland Indians and that they in turn had called them 'lice carriers.'

Later when we were touring her family ice house compartment I asked her how they cooked whale and seal meat.

She said that: "It does not cook well so we eat it raw!"

Today, truth and facts can be politically incorrect.

The Inuvik Petroleum Show.
We were looking to position as a player at the top level of the companies wherever that might be.

About 800 people were in attendance at the show. I met folks from various places in Wyoming and Montana.

Plenty of good ideas. Plenty of discussion. For the meals and breaks, caterers had come from Calgary, over 2,100 miles away.

There is not much business up that way.

There were some really good speakers at the conference.

A large issue was the McKenzie River Delta gas pipeline. The Dehcho First Nation was holding out for more and more money to cross over their caribou hunting land that few of them had ever seen or would ever see.

I could foresee that the pipeline would never be built and that eventually gas would be liquefied and taken out on ships.

On the way back home, I attended a BP meeting in Calgary, Alberta. I had been invited before leaving Inuvik. I met a number of BP people from Houston.

An orientation manual revision at a factory.
At a factory in Cheyenne we did orientation classes.

Our daughter who was interning did a revision of the manual. It was really first class.

One of our board members had written the original. He was not too congratulatory.

I leave the non-profit.
I left the non-profit. I had put a lot of effort into turning things around. Both mortgages had been paid off and cash was accumulating. We had remodeled the building. With the Kansas branch all settled down, there was plenty of money and the promise of much more.

Before I left we had gone over $1 million in revenue for the fiscal year. We had a solid accounting system that was up to date and transparent.

I was ready to implement a new plan that would move us solidly forward. We had a two day board meeting. On a third day I had a consultant come in to give witness to the credibility of my plan. There was strong resistance from one of the board members.

The board then agreed to the $30,000 that I needed to get it going.

I emailed the board that I had disbursed $15,000 as a down payment. More resistance from that one board member.

I stopped payment on the check. I submitted my resignation three months in advance to end the year and to get the audit done.

I was asked to stay even longer and was told they would make it worth my while with extra compensation. I agreed to do so but wanted nothing above my existing salary.

I was most disappointed that I could not implement the next part of my vision.

I do consider it to be the Lord's will.

Council director is resigning
Newsletter article, as is, when I gave notice in May 2008.

David Sneed, who led us out of the red and through nearly eight years of steady financial growth, has decided to step down as the organization's executive director.

"I'm a fixer, and I came in to fix problems," Sneed said in an interview. "We are at a plateau and I feel that this is the right time to leave."

Sneed, 61, who notified the board on Friday April 18 of his decision, will stay around until as late as July 15.

"Joe Kaplan, my counterpart in Los Angeles, was director for 60 years. He retired at age 94 and is still going with other ventures. Joe's 60 years sure dwarfs my almost eight years. But in this day and time even eight years may be too long" said Sneed.

During Sneed's tenure, we phased out a major low-quality training product, added new ones, and outsourced the commodity training to almost 150 smaller players. "That move, which is still in progress, allows training to take place locally without travel expense" Sneed said. "It also minimizes fixed costs by not needing to have a larger employee staff of trainers."

We partner with SCORE and can provide free counseling for businesses. "A real plus here is that we have been able to help startups understand the need for safety as a mission critical value" he added. Sneed is the Wyoming district director for SCORE.

Recently we have been testing a program with a grant from UPS.

The project leader said: "A town of 242 population will be the first town in Wyoming to receive the designation"

Other American cities with the designation are Anchorage AK, Omaha NE, Dallas TX, and Springfield MO.

Financially during Sneed's tenure growth at a rate of 21% per year. We council did a major office and classroom building renovation project and have paid off that cost and the mortgage on the building. As a prudent measure used by responsible nonprofits there is now a cash reserve to allow us to weather downturns. "When I came on board it was the council was on cash with order terms with all the suppliers" said Sneed.

"There is state of the art technology primarily done with donated professional help. "Unfortunately we do not yet have the conference registration fully automated because of some other priorities." Sneed added. "Hopefully we are forgiven that they have to print, write, and fax."

Sneed said he was not sure what would be next for him. "2008 is the peak year of the Corporate Social Responsibility, CSR, bandwagon" he said. "The safety world got on it somewhat later than other industries even with such things as meeting planning but is fast catching up." Sneed indicated that he has encouraged the safety council board to go that route. Sneed said that there is plenty of CSR money and that safety councils should get their share.

Sneed said "I want to be at the forefront of the future and so I am going to go beyond CSR. It is farther than the council board wanted to go and so I need to do it another way. We will provide real value to community-oriented small businesses that want to save their community and want to save money. We will be working to set actual guarantees of incident reduction whether on the job, off the job, or in the community."

Sneed pointed out that during his tenure there was a conscious effort to avoid begging for money. "We accepted but did not even push advertising in the newsletter as we felt that with such limited and diverse circulation it might not be an efficient medium. We have devoted our resources to always be available. Programs are available with no advance registration.

Sneed then quoted some statistics and pointed out that more and more money is being spent on training but the numbers do not show any significant improvement.

"By 2010 there will be more millennials than baby-boomers. With an understanding that the majority of our population is a new generation of people who have a new approach to life, that the industrial economy with a command and control philosophy is gone and that there is global competition we can see the need for a new paradigm."

"More and more businesses are receptive to moving from a compliance focus to best practices." Sneed went on to describe a variety of provable results programs that he will be implementing.

"By taking advantage of open-source knowledge sharing, virtual community concepts, and social networking with with process and product innovation, and by understanding the new ways of learning, then incidents will decrease and safety concepts will drop dramatically. With improved distribution efficiency we will also be able to reach a large number of entities not currently reachable."

Sneed pointed out that he will mobilize collaborative resources in a variety of disciplines all around the world and will be able to quickly provide customized solutions. product in a day, PIAD, and organized tacit knowledge will be two of our competitive advantages" he added.

Sneed has a vast background in a number of industries where he has always been involved in innovation. He left the large company world in 1976 and has transferred and adapted best practices to small business since then. As a new twist he now expects to lessons learned in small business about safety to large business.

When asked for any more comments Sneed said, "This is the smallest turnaround I have done and took the longest. But it has been the most fun. "

CHAPTER 14: REINVENTION

"Now that we can do anything, what will we do?" - Bruce Mau

I quickly develop a new pattern.
I went to a meeting in Dallas, driving rather than flying.

My first night was at Las Vegas, New Mexico. I stayed at a Mexican hotel that had an entrance through a truck stop. After checking in and putting things in my room, I went to the restaurant. It was packed. There was a mariachi band and dancing. Multiple family generations were at each table. From babes in arms to the very elderly. I sat at the bar which only had about five stools. A toothless, older lady, very much an older lady, was the bartender. I got a beer. She asked me if I wanted dinner. Instead of a menu I got a plate all prepared. I don't normally care for Mexican food but I ate what was put before me.

I left early the next morning. The man that had checked me in was there and wished me a safe trip. Roswell, New Mexico was en route to Carlsbad. I took a break in Roswell. Even the Walmart has alien images on the outside.

Carlsbad Caverns in New Mexico.
At Carlsbad Caverns in New Mexico, I started at the natural entrance at ground level, went through the various caves, there are 119 total, to the end. I went up on the elevator to get out. At that point the shaft is 754 feet that was cut through rock. It was just me and so I had decided I wanted to see how quickly I could travel the whole distance. Right now I cannot remember the time but it was quick. The initial 1 1/4 miles is steep and drops about 800 feet.

A trip to Greece.
I went on a trip to southern Europe. One archeologist daughter picked me up at the airport in Athens, Greece. Her time as an archaeologist in Greece had made her almost a native. She was easily able to show me around. On my first day there, arriving at 9:30 AM, we climbed Mount Lycabettus and the Acropolis. I was so happy for her. We were the only tourists on the Acropolis that day. She was able to savor the history without crowds of tourists.

A trip to the ancient Greek city of Delphi.
Delphi is a wonderful site, my favorite We stopped overnight at Arachova, a picturesque ancient village and ski town on Mount Parnassos. From Delphi there is a view all the way down to the nearest port city. It is truly amazing how these Greek sites are built on the mountains.

A trip to the ancient Greek city of Corinth.
We went to the Corinth canal that is quite an engineering and historic work. At

the lower end there is a drawbridge that sinks so that ships can pass over. We watched it function. There is a raised section about three feet high between the two lanes of the roadway. That part comes up first. A dog was waiting. The dog walked straight onto that section as it kept rising. At the other end the dog had to jump off and did so before any of the cars had been able to cross.

A trip to ancient Cenchrea, a city where the apostle Paul got a haircut.
There is now not much at Cenchrea except the remains of the stone wharves and some stone building foundations.

In Acts 18:18: "And Paul after this tarried there yet a good while, and then took his leave of the brethren, and sailed thence into Syria, and with him Priscilla and Aquila; having shorn his head in Cenchrea: for he had a vow."

One of the residents was Phoebe, a first-century Christian woman mentioned by the Apostle Paul. In Romans 16:1-2: "I commend unto you Phoebe our sister, which is a servant of the church which is at Cenchrea: That ye receive her in the Lord, as becometh saints, and that ye assist her in whatsoever business she hath need of you: for she hath been a succorer of many, and of myself also."

A trip to the Greek island of Crete.
We took the ferry to Crete, leaving the port of Piraeus next to Athens at 9:00 PM, arriving in Chania, Crete about 5:30 AM We had to wait two hours to get a rental car from a mile away.

We visited some wonderful city-states, all different. Knossos, of course, was one of them. There are many excavated sites on Crete.

We climbed a mountain to the Cave of the Wisdom of God. There was an elderly Greek Orthodox priest who lived there. He had an altar with plenty of oil lamps. After going back down, we went into taverna. The black-robed priest was sitting at a table with his feet up on a chair having a beer and a conversation with some folks. No criticism from me.

At a hotel, the proprietor shows the room and if you like it you get the key and pay when you leave. In the restaurant at one hotel I asked what kind of fish they had. The lady took me into the kitchen and showed me in the refrigerator what she had. She pointed out the window and showed me where on the beach of the Mediterranean Sea every morning that her son would catch the fish for the day. I picked out the ones I wanted.

From Chania, we took the bus into the mountains for the 11 mile Samaria Gorge hike down to Agia Roumeli on the East Libyan Sea. There are no roads there so we took the ferry to Sougia where we could get a bus back to Chania.

Our daughter is admitted to the bar association.
One event that worked out well to get me back on track was the admission to the bar of one of our daughters. She passed the exam first time and was to officially become a lawyer. It was a great day. The ceremony took place at Faneuil Hall in Boston, Massachusetts.

Peter Faneuil built Faneuil Hall for the City of Boston and made the gift in 1742. The lower level was forever to be a marketplace of goods. The upper level was to forever be a marketplace of ideas.

We had a fine lunch at The Union Oyster House, close by Faneuil Hall.

A few years later our daughter was admitted to the bar of the Supreme Court of the United States. I did not go to that event.

We start an online business.
The Lord led me to a chance meeting in Texas that resulted in the start of an online media business in February 2009.

At this one-on-one meeting in the aisle of a thrift store, I gained knowledge that I should have had before. I guess the time had not been right. An opportunity surfaced for the ability to meet needs in a variety of areas with no advertising. I already knew how to find material and I knew that there was a need.

We started the business. Cheri mastered the art of making listings and setting prices. The business has done well but has not had the continued growth that we wanted. Our sources of supply have become our competition and taken much of our source of new listings. We do maintain an inventory of almost 12,000 used books, many if not most, that are hard to find. Often I note sales and wonder how the buyers know the titles. Used books that no one wants now become in high demand in the future. We have seen some books go out of demand and then come back.

The business continues and is in its 10th year at the time of this writing.

Our metrics.
In our online business we achieved and have continued to maintain perfect metrics in all of the many categories of measurement.

Constantly we can see exactly how we are doing. We have developed customer service techniques that stop the development of problems or complaints.

I have developed another measurement where I can see on one screen how we are doing in the current month compared to prior years as well as year to date comparisons.

Shipping policies.
We made a decision to always ship priority flat rate or first class unless the item is too heavy or too big, a rare case. Getting delivery of an online order in two days instead of a week or two makes buyers happy. We do not get expedited shipping payment premiums. We set this policy because we want to give good service.

The man who thought the book was not autographed.
There are many things that can happen in the used book business.

We had a near miss when one buyer wanted to make a return because we listed a book as autographed and the buyer said it was was not.

Cheri had made good photographs for the listings. We went back to the photos and sure enough there was an autograph.

We authorized the return, sent a prepaid return label but told the buyer about the autograph. He looked back and saw that he had missed it.

He seemed to be a collector as he had numerous books come in on the same day.

He replied that he wanted to keep the book.

I meet a future son-in-law in Chicago.
Chicago is where I first met a future son-in-law.

One of our daughters had called me. She had heard that I was in Chicago and asked if I wanted to meet him that night.

I was planning on going that night to an open house/fundraiser at a design school in Chicago.

The school mission has a simple premise:

"Design shapes the way we live. The fewer resources that communities and individuals have, the more they need great design solutions to enhance their quality of life." Our "public forums and partnership-based education programs propose a range of socially responsible and ecologically resourceful design solutions for Chicago communities."

I told her that I would buy him a ticket, it would be held at the front desk, and he could join me at Archeworks. It would be a good time and we would be able to talk in a casual, albeit crowded venue.

I bought a ticket for him and asked the ticket desk folks to watch for him and send him to my table.

I met him. We had a great meeting, though a funny thing happened.

There were some acrobat entertainers that needed a little more space than was available in the building. The school being a creative place, someone noted that an adjoining parking lot was mostly vacant, so everyone, most with glasses of wine, went outside to watch the show.

No had one questioned the legality of a large crowd of mostly young people drinking wine while enjoying an unlicensed show in public on property not owned by the school. After all, it is a free country.

The police arrived and quickly made clear the knowledge of the laws that had been broken.

If everyone would quietly go back inside there would be no further enforcement activity.

Real social problems.
Chicago is a great place though it can be a sad place.

On Miracle Mile, an upscale retail area on Michigan Avenue, there are whole families of homeless people sleeping on the street and in doorways. There are more beggars in Chicago than in any other city in the United States that I have visited. These people all have good stories.

While I only have time and money to help a few, I have taken care of some, mostly those with the good, albeit false, stories.

I deeply regret not helping one young man that asked for just one hamburger out of my sack from White Castle. I did not feel safe and my hands were full.

After that event I have given money to those that promise to buy food.

Pacific Garden Mission.
One of the greatest mission works in the world is the Old Lighthouse, the

Pacific Garden Mission in Chicago.

I did a tour of the place and was most impressed. It even has a barber shop and a free medical clinic. Evangelistic services are held several times a day and attendance is mandatory. Stanley Tigerman, the co-founder of Archeworks, designed a new building that replaced the original building. The original building, that had been used for well over 100 years, was already old when it became a homeless shelter.

How I got a front orchestra ticket to *Wicked* for $20.
One cheap hotel exception area is Chicago.

Further to that, every hotel, even when an older one can be found, a rare event, is full. Sometimes there can be a payoff.

I had such a payoff at The Talbot Hotel at 20 E Delaware Place.

Here is what happened.

I had made friends with the concierge, a long term employee that knew his stuff.

I asked him if he could get me a ticket to Wicked. While on the subway coming back from the White Castle, that is only a few blocks off the Cermak stop on the Red Line, I had seen a sign for *Wicked*.

The concierge told me that a ticket would cost over $500.

He told me that at 5:00 PM every day, there was a drawing in the theatre lobby for a seat that night in the orchestra front row for $20 a seat. It was necessary to be present for the drawing.

It was getting close to the time so I thanked my concierge friend and immediately went to the theatre, signed up for the drawing, and joined the huge crowd that was there for the drawing. The end result is easy to guess.

My name was drawn and I got a seat in the orchestra, on the front row, for $20. I did give another $20 to the concierge the next day.

I am most anxious to again see The Talbot Hotel after its 2016, $20 million, four month renovation. It was already in the top 25 hotels by TripAdvisor. Now it has the ultimate in "green" things.

I am most anxious to see the front desk in its new location behind the elevators. I loved it before with the front desk just to the right of the narrow hallway and the concierge desk across from it just to the left. I'm sure I'll like its new location.

It's a small world.

Dinner at the Cape Cod Room.
I went to a seafood restaurant, The Cape Cod Room, at The Drake Hotel in Chicago.

The Cape Cod Room was an incredible place with great food as well as high quality and quantity service. The rum and coke was fabulous. The Cape Cod Room made its own cola and that is what made the difference.

I usually got clams casino and the lobster Thermidor. The lobster was the favorite dish of Marilyn Monroe.

She and her husband Joe Dimaggio carved their initials into the bar shortly after they were married in 1954.

There was a remodel, of the restaurant and the price went way up, on the clams casino, the Thermidor, and just about everything else.

On New Year's Eve 2016, The Cape Cod Room closed for good after an eighty year run, a casualty of The Drake Hotels lower arcade remodel.

The man that enjoyed the "perks" of a cash business.
At a small store in a small town, I had met the older couple that were the owners. I had passed through several times en route from one place to another.. Each time I was there I talked with them.

I could sense that the business was not going well. I offered to help them at no cost. I would give them a computer and QuickBooks. I would set it all up and then show them how to keep it going. Were they happy with the offer? Not for a moment.

The husband told me that there were some "perks" of being the owner of a business.

Over the years as a counselor I have run across many that want to be bookkeepers.

I always ask them: "What are you going to do when a client does not want to do things the right way, and possibly wants to act fraudulently?"

A trip to Seattle.
I drove to Seattle with one of our daughters, her husband, and their children. They were taking an Alaskan cruise. I would find a place to put their truck and then I would explore Seattle. I had only been near the city, never in it, yet had negative feelings.

I decided that I would not use the truck and would only do downtown things mostly walking. I did use the trolley to/from Lake Union a number of times. I began my visit on a Saturday morning. I learned that Toots and the Maytals had done a one night show, the night before. Toots, Fred Hibbert, of Jamaica and his band were the first of the reggae groups. They did Monkey Man that I first learned about while Cheri and I were on a visit to Jamaica.

There is plenty of seafood in Seattle. The restaurants were doing an afternoon and a late night happy hour that included food items. I found that the afternoon session was great for the day's big meal. Overall I found that the best food and ambiance was at McCoy's Firehouse Restaurant. Excellent steak.

I learned of Seattle history. It is most unique how the city was built on the tidal flats. The underground tour is well worth the time.

I had a scare, not what I expected, or had ever experienced. Standing on a busy sidewalk in front of a restaurant in the daytime I was talking to Cheri on my cell phone, distracted from surroundings. An obnoxious woman, a street person, accosted me and demanded money for food. I had nowhere to turn. She pointed to a Subway across the street advertising a $5 special on a large poster in the window. She told me she wanted that. She said she was hungry and the shelter where she lived did not provide much food. I might normally have gone across the street and paid for her meal but I gave her $5 and she left though not to the Subway. A short distance down the street she accosted someone else.

I realized she could have had a knife or a gun. I revised all of my thinking on personal security. The distraction of a cell phone is a real problem anywhere and anytime.

That afternoon I went to a baseball game and had a chance to see how the stadium roof works to cover or uncover the field in the event of rain.

I took the ferry to Winslow on Bainbridge Island. A neat little town. There is a trail through the wooded mud flats. There was a thrift store where I got four boxes of books really cheap.

The problem was how would I get them to the ferry landing, take the ferry to Seattle, and get them to the truck. In town I bought a collapsible dolly with two wheels. Problem solved.

One night in Seattle I slept on an old tugboat in Lake Union. The tugboat is part of a tugboat museum. I noted that school or scout groups could spend the night on board. That night nothing was scheduled. I asked if I could have the boat for the night. The museum agreed and gave me the combination to the lock. It was a great time. A seaplane service operates just a short distance away. I got to watch the takeoffs and landings that seemed to be constant.

Right next to the tugboat museum is a wood boat museum. All the boats are in the water and all can be rented to give them a try. Most are sailboats.

A road trip with Steve.
I did a road trip traveling meeting with an associate from South Africa. He and his wife have many years with the United Nations. He was in San Francisco at a meeting. I drove to Boulder and parked my truck. One daughter took me to Union Station where I went by train to Emeryville, next to Berkeley. I stayed in a hotel nearby.

I had some spare time so I walked two miles to the subway and went to San Francisco. At Fisherman's Wharf I rented a bike and went over the Golden Gate Bridge to Sausalito. I took the ferry back to San Francisco. There were many more bicyclists than pedestrians on the ferry.

I walked all over North Beach looking for the type of Italian restaurant that used to be there. Sadly, all are gone.

Early the next morning, Steve picked me up at my hotel and we headed out.

Our plan was to drive Route 50 across Nevada, what has been called the loneliest road in the United States.

The possible hitch in the plan was the Donner Pass. Worst case we would have to wait for it to be opened, probable case we would have to buy tire chains. We happened to arrive just as the pass was opened without a chain requirement. Approaching the Pass we had passed many vehicles that were chaining up.

A road trip to San Francisco and Los Angeles.
Two years later, I went, again with a daughter, and her husband and children on a business trip they took to San Francisco.

On a Sunday we went to Muir Woods., the redwood forest across the Golden Gate Bridge. Cars were parked along the road two miles away. I let the others out. I stayed with the car. I found a space near the entrance just as someone pulled out. I was able to join the others and we had a nice walk. It was so pleasing to be able to take them to the place that held so many family memories for over 50 years.

On that trip I took a walk from Fisherman's Wharf in San Francisco over the Golden Gate and then on to Sausalito. Our daughter and her children stayed at the hotel. Her husband was at his meeting. It was raining and there was heavy wind. I had to close the umbrella. It was of no use. In Sausalito I took the ferry back.

The next day she and the children wanted to walk the bridge. I drove the rental car, let them off on the city side of the bridge, and parked across the bridge. I walked back to meet them. We got the car, drove to Sausalito, and had lunch. We took the ferry back.

Heading home we visited Monterey and drove down the coast through Big Sur. I took our daughter and her children to Monterey then went back to pick up our son-in-law husband. I had dropped the family at the Aquarium at Monterey. We all went to dinner on Fisherman's Wharf. We did see and hear the sea lions.

It is too bad that steamer clams are no longer available along the Pacific coast. Now it is all non-native manila clams that were accidentally introduced from Japan with oysters. I don't care what anyone says. Manila clams are not a substitute for littlenecks and certainly not for cherrystones.

As we left Fisherman's Wharf a whole family of raccoons was coming out from under the land part of the wharf.

The next morning we left Monterey early. I had hoped we could stop at Nepenthe that has my favorite book store. We had a ways to go to meet one of our sons in Los Angeles and we wanted to see the elephant seals so we passed Nepenthe several hours before it opened. We had breakfast at the Whale Watcher's Cafe about 65 miles down the road. I love my coffee but will not pay $4.00 a cup especially with just one refill. Maybe I need a change of attitude.

How I developed a better way of church and missions bookkeeping.
I became part-time bookkeeper, for a small church. So that I could spend as much time as I needed, and not be bound to a set number of hours as an employee, I worked under a contract with my business. The church wanted it to only take six hours a week. I averaged 18 to 20 hours a week. I did not ask for more pay.

Using desktop QuickBooks that I knew well, I developed, over almost four years, an approach to bookkeeping that allowed for a project approach to church management.

I have now migrated most of my applications of QuickBooks to the on-line version with links to bank accounts and credit cards for automatic updating.

Not necessarily in order, here are a few of the changes I implemented that I have done and refined over the years with for profit businesses:

- Kaizen, or continuous improvement.

- Consolidating various bank accounts into just one account. What had been separate physical and computer accounts became sub-accounts of the one bank account. Only one reconciliation per month.

- Consistency of postings with protocol manual. Each vendor has different types of data. In the past there might have been no description or a description that varied with different bookkeepers or with how the bookkeeper felt that day.

- Combined redundant general ledger accounts.

- Detailed descriptions of expenses so that inquiry reports could substitute for getting out original invoices. One day a trustee asked me who did the back flow prevention testing and what did they charge? Straight from the computer with search of "back flow." I printed out transactions for several years past. The report showed that every year it was someone different. To have gotten the invoices would have meant knowing who did that type work.

- Improved filing system to save time, to deal with calendar year versus fiscal year and to deal with differing retention periods. With filing by month, a box would gradually fill and then be removed to the storage area. Revenue, payroll, expenses by check number, and other expenses went to different monthly file folders.

- Header sheets for report packages.

- A crisis management detector and progress report that got some real use in one crisis.

- Checklist.

- A work schedule that for me started at 5:00 AM with sessions averaging about two hours.

- Paying bills up to date rather than one payment date per month.

- A comprehensive revenue report by week with backup attached. Partly this came about because of added ways of receiving revenue other than the Sunday offering. Many large churches no longer use worship service time for offerings.

- Set up an easy way for corporate members to make one check to cover a number of items. I have had corporate clients that clients that donate to their church a percentage of their gross receipts.

A problem in many churches is that the general offerings have a flat growth curve, often not even increasing with inflation. Older givers are passing away and the newer givers, if any, are not giving as much.

Overall what has happened is that the budget models in use, known as unified budgets, are expense oriented with prioritization. The items with the lowest priorities are reduced or eliminated. All sources of money go into the same offering income account.

One day when I was at the church and waiting for the printer in the copier room, I was reading a bulletin on the counter. It had John 8:47: "He who belongs to God hears what God says."

I was instantly aware that my chronic right ear pain was gone. When I got back to the computer in the office and resumed my work, I became aware that my arthritis was gone. I had the assurance that neither one would return. I had not been doing anything with drugs or doctor visits for either condition.

Many may wonder how that verse could have anything to do with healing. I had seen that verse many times and nothing had happened. There is the logos Word of God. That is seeing the words on paper. Then there is the rhema Word of God. That is when the Holy Spirit makes the logos Word of God have a particular meaning.

Saved, Holy Ghost filled, readers of the Bible, over many readings and many years, find that each reading brings out new meanings.

Thrift Store

Cheri and I volunteered in the book department at a non-profit thrift store as volunteers.

We organized the books, put out all newly donated books the same day they came in, got rid of non-selling books, and kept the section neat and clean. We upgraded shelves as donations of shelves occurred. We standardized the price to 50 cents for any book. Tremendous time was saved from the prior practice of pricing each book individually.

Book sales dramatically increased. From being long term book buyers we knew what buyers wanted to see.

Each day we counted the number of books that came in and we posted the number of books discarded. Each day had a card.

At the end of the month we counted the books.

We could then take the prior inventory count, the count of new books in, the count of books discarded, the end inventory count, and then calculate the number of books sold.

Every month we gave a formal report for that month and year to date.

With all books the same price we could calculate sales dollars.

The checkout register could not separate sales by item type. The register only had one number for sales dollars for the day for the whole building.

We were "persistent yet knew when to quit."
After almost five years we resigned our volunteer positions.

The culture in our building was bad and nothing could be done about it. It had gotten worse and was making it difficult for us to do our job efficiently.

Efforts were made, without the approval of management, to reduce our floor space, change our our way of furnishing the department area, change our way of using shelves, remove our tables, and dump books from boxes into carts.

A trip to Crested Butte, Colorado, for skiing or otherwise.
I went on an ad hoc family trip to Crested Butte, Colorado.

I was not the organizer nor did I do any skiing.

We rented an alpine house at Mount Crested Butte. There was a very short walk to the ski lifts.

Crested Butte, itself, is an old mining town at the foot of the mountain. Mount Crested Butte, at the top of the mountain is a small modern town built around the ski lodge and lifts.

There is one 17 1/2 mile paved road into and out of Crested Butte area from Almont. There are two seasonal narrow gravel roads of 37 miles to Somerset and 30 miles to Paonia, that are not designed, for high traffic or speed.

There is a free bus that travels the two miles between Crested Butte and Mount Crested Butte on a frequent basis. Wait time is in minutes.

I took my grandson Jacob onto the bus through the front door. He stood respectfully beside the driver and said: "Are you the driver?"

The answer was affirmative. Jacob then took a seat and proceeded to sing *The Wheels on the Bus*, a song in which the "driver on the bus" plays a key part.

The death of my mother.
My mother died.

I was at the nursing home in less than two hours after she died. I was in her room for several hours with my youngest brother, and a pastor that has been well known to all of my family for many years. When I left around midnight, the funeral home had not yet come to pick her up.

Both of my parents parents are buried in Georgia. I did not attend either of their funerals. There was a simple graveside service for my mother.

Why I did not go to Georgia for the graveside service.
I would have gone to the graveside service for my mother but had a conflict on the date that was picked.

One of our daughters and I had to be in Chicago that day.

She had made an appointment six weeks in advance, a lead time the Italian Consulate required, for a mandatory in person interview for a work visa.

Rescheduling would have required another six weeks that might mean losing her job offer in Rome.

I have no double standard. I have made it known that I do not want anyone to feel obligated to come when I pass away.

Life is for the living and all of my children have their own things they need to do. It's a time they could meet but that could be done as well at another, perhaps more convenient, time.

We all do what we can as best we can while we are living.

Jesus said in Matthew 8:22:

"Let the dead bury the dead."

The context was that Jesus had called a man to go with him. A man whose father had just died. Jesus gave him a choice.

A long hike.
I revived a long ago idea to hike the Appalachian Trail, the idea not the trip.

While growing up I had hiked small parts of it in day hikes.

Because it takes about seven months it had been impossible to even think of doing it in the past as I did not have the time.

I got the official book that is revised annually. I found that I had a connection to someone who had done that hike as well as many others. I had some conversations with him.

There are opposing views on how to do the full hike; northbound with a usual start around the end of February or southbound with a usual start in June.

Both dates are related to the end of snow.

To me the northbound route made more sense.

I did some preliminary planning and even started walking to get in shape.

Further along in the planning I realized that I still did not have the time.

As far as ability to do it, age does not seem to matter.

More and more people in their 70s and 80s are doing it.

And I believed that my health was good enough.

How I realized my plan for an outdoor office.

For a number of years I tried several variations on a backyard office.

Several involved tents that did not survive the wind. Home Depot sheds did not cut it. I was aiming for something too big.

We built a 6x9 screen house for my backyard office. This version was just what I wanted. Construction was done in 4 1/2 hours. What helped was that my son-in-law has a nail gun and a table saw unlike any saw I have ever seen before. My first impression was that it looked like a hospital gurney.

60 mph wind does not cause a problem. I am glad the screen house is not larger and I am glad that I did not buy a pre-made shed. It looks good in the garden and is a value add. I live in a cold windy area in the western United States. The studio has an intended ambiance of both a wooden sailboat and a cabin in the woods, a feeling that is enhanced on windy, rainy, or snowy days. At the same time the nine foot ceiling and the non load-bearing translucent walls remove any claustrophobic feeling

I bought 12 36x80 wooden screen doors from Meals on Wheels. As soon as I saw the screen doors I knew what I wanted. The screen doors were new, though slightly defective thus problematic in a modern house use, and had been donated by Lowe's. I got them for $2.50 each rather than the perfect price of $100 each.

We started by building a 6x9 deck. Then 4x4 posts made the corners and were placed in concrete piers at each corner. The deck was nailed between the posts. A frame for the roof was built at ground level, raised and nailed. The roof was angled and excess from the 4x4 posts was cut off. The screen doors were put in place and fastened with finishing nails. The finishing nails were my idea. Anything else would have split the wood. Three screen doors made nine feet for the sides. Two screen doors made six feet for the ends. One of the doors at one end became an actual operating door with hinges. The initial roof was tar paper over particle board.

The following Spring after building, we added a metal roof, that was part of the original plan. That work was primarily done by one of our daughters.

Initially, I made a small porch for the screen house with a skid covered with boards.

In 2017, I built a 6x9 deck next to the screen house in about six hours. Three panels of privacy fence make for deck coziness, screen house extension with no roof. The deck is furnished with a fountain that I have had for many years, a 1950s style metal glider and picturesque firewood storage.

For grandchildren, I built a 6x6 treehouse right next to the deck of the screen house between two trees. An attached eight foot ladder provides access.

All initial screen house furnishings came from Meals on Wheels except for the small wood stove that came from Barts, a flea market mall in Cheyenne.

The small wood stove is made of welded sheet steel. If both stove doors are closed, the fire stops quickly as there is no way for air to get in. There is plenty of air in the room coming up through the deck spaces and from where the roof connects on the east side. The wood stove provides more than enough heat in the screen house even in the coldest weather.

Prior to the second winter we we covered the outside with white plastic all in one sheet. That covering made has made it through two winters ok.

We got a 16x6 reed fence piece from a Kmart going out of business sale and covered the west and south sides as extra protection. It was not necessary and I only bought it because it was cheap. Now that it is installed I believe it is adding to the durability in the wind. The reed fence functions like cladding that is seen on so many buildings today. It adds to the appearance.

There is good light from inside lamps and from natural light through the translucent plastic during the daytime.

I change the furnishings in the screen house.
The ambiance gets better and better. The furnishings in the screen house have been changed and quantity reduced.

I have eliminated the half-width library table.

I got rid of the bookcase after the purchase at Bart's of an old six foot tall pine behind-the-toilet bathroom cabinet. The three shelves serve as a bookcase, the lower part as firewood storage. The cabinet is right by the door so wood restocking is convenient from the outdoor storage areas without tracking in water or snow.

I got rid of the three drawer cabinet. There is a pine seat box that I use for paper to start the fire. I have a box of small sticks. There is now a vintage folding wood chair made of the molded plywood of the 1950s. I got that chair at Bart's for $6.00.

To save on shredding time, I have a trash basket under my computer shelf in the basement office for paper to be burned instead of shredding.

When convenient I take that basket to the seat box in the screen house.

The material is not exactly top secret but it is stuff that I would not want to see blowing around on the street if it fell out of the recycle can.

The backyard is part of the office.
The screen house connects to the backyard by the translucent walls and by leaving the screen house door open using a bungee cord that attached to the top of the door and to the tree house. It is above head height so no ducking down.

There is a large firewood storage area at the end of the deck against the lot divider fence. More firewood storage by the deck along the lot divider fence and the L of the deck. This outside is always shaded. I have done a lot of work on the backyard. The grass is in great shape now. There is a spring-loaded gate between the backyard and the deck area outside the house to keep the dog out. There is an additional firewood storage area along the border privacy fence at the southeast corner by the alley.

I can bring in logs from the alley and cut them just inside the backyard. I cut everything with my two reciprocal saws. One I picked up cheap as a spare.

I had earlier built a 6x12 standalone deck for the plastic greenhouse, now gone, I had tested as an office. That deck is now furnished with a park bench and a kid's turtle shaped sandbox with a cover, accessible on all sides.

She did it the 21st century way.
After one of our daughters graduated from college with a Bachelor's degree she applied for jobs and was getting nowhere fast. Wyoming is not the greatest place to be for jobs. Many graduates leave then state and don't come back.

She wanted to work in Europe for an NGO, an acronym and abbreviation for non-government organization. What she was doing did not seem to have a connecting path.

I told her about the book *What Color Is Your Parachute*, a 40 year old title that is revised every year. The book is good no matter which year version is used. The author is a Methodist minister. He has developed a job search plan that does not involve human resources, job applications, resumes, answering ads, using a job search service or going for interviews. His program is that you decide where you want to work and what you want to do. Done correctly it can get you a job where there is no job opening. She expressed an interest. I went to Barnes and Noble right then and got her the book.

From a contact of mine she got some names of other contacts in China and in Paris. A few weeks later, she was off to France on a project job. While in France she did an interview on Skype with the NGO. They wanted her to head to Rome right after her last day on her French project.

Italy is not as liberal with immigration as some countries. It took two months to jump through their hoops even with a promised job with. The NGO was willing to wait for her. One part of the process involved a ten minute interview in person at the consulate in Chicago.

I had thought that it might work to do the interview, get the visa, and go straight to the airport. As it turned out it took another two weeks for the visa after the interview. Since she was the first visa applicant that had all of her paperwork in order, the $225 fee was waived.

She spent over a year in Rome. She did a short project in Armenia before work in that country was defunded.

She was on a one year capacity building project in the country of Ukraine. She has successfully taken on the Russian and Ukraine languages.

As I'm writing this she is returning from a weekend trip from where she lives in the country of Ukraine to Budapest, Hungary a distance of about 1,200 miles. She does not balk at travel.

From Ukraine she got a job with the U.S. Government. She married a really great guy that most recently had been a library director. He is an MBA graduate.

Next steps.
I did another quadrennial reinvention of myself.

At the time of the end of this writing I am 72 years old. I do not feel like I am anywhere near that age though I must be getting older. One day downtown a tourist called me old timer.

Cheri and I celebrated 51 years of marriage a few months after I turned 72.

I have often said that my retirement plan would be that one day I would fall over, not get up, and would not expect anyone to get me up.

Cheri and I both have advanced healthcare directives, DNR, do not resuscitate, properly set up for that purpose. It is a basic of medical care that there must be the consent of the patient, or with the consent of the parent or guardian for minor children, in order for any medical care to take place. The issue of consent for medical care and the removal of consent is a big subject. There is a condition of implied consent for medical care for children when parents or guardians are not present. Implied consent for adults it is when they are not conscious or otherwise not able to give consent. The purpose of the DNR is to withhold consent under certain conditions defined in the DNR. The DNR negates implied consent.

I fit a small demographic.
I have maintained one record over a long period of time. What it means, if anything, I don't know.

There is a very small population demographic that reads *The New Yorker*, *Harper's*, and *The Atlantic*.

I am one of that demographic and have been for over 50 years. The percentage of the Wyoming population is much less smaller. Am I the only one?

I was reading *Harper's* while sitting in Albertsons in Cheyenne as Cheri was grocery shopping. A cowboy was going out the door.

"I didn't know cowboys could read," he said.

I got a hands-on impartation from Rev. R.W. Schambach.
Shortly before the death of R. W. Schambach, perhaps the last of the old time preachers, I was in Tyler, Texas. I received a hands-on impartation from Brother Schambach.

Impartations are biblical. There are many interpretations of an impartation. An impartation can be a transfer of knowledge, attitude, or appointment. It can be to stir up a remembrance of a calling. It can be a faith recharge. The one giving, the one receiving, or both can have the same or a different expectation, conscious or unconscious. We do know that the laying on of hands can have a powerful impact.

The story of George Mueller is not unusual except for the magnitude of what he did. Without telling his wife in advance he gave up his pastor's salary so that pew rents could be abolished. He then continued as pastor for 66 years until his death.

The largest tombstone in the Granary Burying Ground in Boston is that of Josiah and Abiah Franklin, Benjamin Franklin's parents.

The epitaph reads, with spelling as it is on the tombstone::

"JOSIAH FRANKLIN,
And
ABIAH, his Wife,
Lie here interred.
They lived lovingly together in Wedlock
Fifty-five Years;
And without an Estate or any gainful Employment,
By constant Labour, and honest Industry,
With GOD's Blessing
Maintained a large Family
Comfortably,
And brought up thirteen Children and
Seven Grandchildren
Reputably.
From this Instance, Reader,

Be encouraged to Diligence in thy Calling,
And distrust not Providence.
He was a pious and a prudent Man,
She a discreet and virtuous Woman.
Their youngest Son,
In filial Regard to their Memory,
Places this Stone."

After leaving the church job, I continued on with systems development. I now have it where it is online, most postings are automatic from the bank accounts and credit card accounts, and reports are in a formal package in one PDF that is emailed. No more stapling together a pile of paper and leaving it to be handed out. Check writing goes away. Statement reconciliations are automatic. I have developed a process for having multiple people be able to keep bookkeeping.

I can do all of my work from home without going to the client on a regular basis.

I have developed a filing system that saves plenty of time.

I have developed a way to record non-monetary transactions of data that is important to have.

Document images can be attached to transactions.

A trip on Amtrak.
A few weeks after leaving the church job in 2015, Cheri and I took Amtrak to California.

The trip had been planned for and booked several months earlier. I had been worried about how I could free up the time from the job at the church to go. That was all solved.

We had the full bedroom in both directions of travel, with en suite bathroom including shower. The dimension of the bedroom is 6x9, the same as the screen house in our backyard.

The purpose of the trip was first and foremost to take care of grandchildren while the parents were away at a mandatory conference.

A trip to New England.
I took a flight from Denver to LaGuardia in New York City. I took the M60 bus to the 125th Street train station in Manhattan. From there I took the train to New England.

At the end of my trip I reversed the whole process.

I did make sure to go to The Wedge Inn in Stamford, Connecticut. for a meal of great hot dogs and fries.

The Wedge Inn was my favorite lunch place when I worked a block away in the late 1960s.

When it is easy to do, as it was on that trip, I prefer not having someone pick me up.

I like the philosophy of the German photographer Julia Nimke who says:

"Adventure has nothing to do with being a large distance from the place where you live—you have to be open to a new look on what's around you. A lot of things can be adventures; you just have to look at your surrounding differently."

In his book *Zen and the Art of Motorcycle Maintenance: An Inquiry into Values,* Robert Pirsig writes of a 17 day motorcycle trip with his son Chris, where he points out why the best way to see the United States is on a motorcycle.

The bus trip from LaGuardia to the Harlem train station is not quite six miles but I never get tired of it. It is my contention that the best way to see that piece of the United States is by bus, the legendary M60.

I stay at the St Birgitta Convent Guest House.
The guest house is on a 10 acre seafront location in a cove on Long Island Sound.

I had a room for three nights overlooking the water. Not too fancy of course. There were only a few guests.

One guest was The Most Rev. Bishop Robert Joseph Baker S.T.D., Bishop of Birmingham in Alabama.

Another was a lay person, a local, that visited every year.

A Delaware state delegate, Mary Beth Carozza from District 38C Worcester and Wicomico Counties, was there one night.

The convent chaplain, Msgr Robert P McCormick, a retired priest was there all the time.

Father McCormick passed away at age 95, shortly after I was there.

We all had some great chats around the table. I learned much from the bishop and the priest.

The bishop asked me if I knew the second largest denomination in the United States after the Roman Catholics.

Expecting a trick question, I did not venture a guess.

The answer he gave is ex-Roman Catholics.

I always appreciate those that can see the bad side of their church, their town, their job, or whatever.

Ironically the St Birgitta guest house building, built as a summer home for a wealthy family, was donated to the sisters by a Baptist woman of the original family owners.

The furnishings were all original. There was a large chapel.

The convent itself is in a separate, more modern, building connected to the guest house with an enclosed walkway above the driveway.

While at the guest house, I began the planning for my next calling, my next reinvention by the plan of the Holy Spirit.

A graduation party.
I went to a graduation party for our grandson Matt.

It was a great party and many were there. Food included, not just the usual hot dogs and hamburgers, but fresh clams.

I stayed over night at a 1920s hotel.

One of that hotel's unique features is a mail slot system that is operated by the USPS. Mail can be deposited on any floor and it drops down to the lobby level where mail can also be deposited. There is a card showing pickup times like any mailbox on the street.

On the way back, I stopped at Mystic Aquarium where we have a charter lifetime membership.

I take a grueling but educational job.
I spent three months doing retail current asset validation. I was both short on cash and in need of some variation of tasks. The work was done in a variety of locations between Denver, Colorado and Rapid City, South Dakota. The work was hard, pay was low, work time was uncertain, and start and stop times varied to all parts of the 24 hour day and day of the week. There was added pay for travel time, hotel, and per diem. Company vans provide transportation.

I worked some of the time and did planning at home the other part. It was a great experience. I recommend that type work for those just starting out and who want to aim for career independence as well as for those who need some reset time and tasks. The idea of working nine to five for 30 to 40 years is losing appeal. As it is, full time or 40 hours a week are not good ways to define a job. What is good about this project work, anytime and anywhere that there are some tough disciplines to develop where the working times are not known. Ending time is when the job is done and the trip home is done. There are great opportunities for use of time. Riding in a van can be an opportunity to sleep, to read, or to meditate. While riding there can be no interruption where one has to go do something else. All the people I met are great people. Overall I was around several hundred different people, all of whom, except for me, seemed to be heavy smokers.

I get cataract surgery and regain my sight.
I had cataract surgery at the end of 2016 and am again able to see.

The surgery is quite simple and for each eye takes only a few minutes, on separate dates a few weeks apart, while the patient is fully conscious.

I work on my business.
I began moving more on my new business.

Changes were coming in the used book business and we realized that it was not going to grow as we had expected. Volume had been dropping for several years after several years of good growth.

I had told Cheri that I was at a point where I did not know if I was really waiting on the Lord or was just lazy. I have never been a good salesman but to know how to do many things. My next venture will be a variation on what I have been doing all along.

Tipping has been of concern. We have tried variations and are not sure if we are making things better or not.

A minimum tip from the customer is is one way towards a better pay per hour than legislation. On the other hand does it really make a difference?

Consider diminishing marginal utility.

Diminishing marginal utility is the common-sense notion that an extra dollar is worth a lot less in satisfaction to those who are richer than to people with low incomes. We are perhaps richer and can afford to give a good pay for service.

One critic said that all we accomplish is to slightly increase the pay of one person for one shift where even that one person will not see any difference. Is that to say that diminishing marginal utility has exceptions?

I understand the viewpoint of the critic. Yet I see the bigger tip as convergence, where our idea intersects with what others value.

I can see that doing this opens us up to see more solutions. I'm reminded of the starfish story.

There was a little boy at the beach grabbing the poor sand-stranded starfish and hurling them back into the sea.

An old man asks the boy:

"Do you really think you're making any difference?"

The boy, bright-eyed and righteous, who holds aloft one of his rescued starfish, delivers the line,

"It makes a difference to this one!."

He chunked it into the water.

A trip to California.
One of our daughters was driving back to California. I rode with her.

We took three days by car to get there.

First night, Provo Utah. Walking distance to the Paleontology Museum of the Brigham Young University from our hotel. Great dinosaur museum.

We went to see the petroglyphs at Parowan Gap in Utah. The second night we spent in Las Vegas, Nevada.

We spent a total of $10 gambling, each with $5 on slot machines.

We went to the White Castle in a casino on the strip. We learned that a second White Castle was under construction. We made another visit to White Castle at breakfast time the next morning as we were leaving town.

I spent three days with our son.

I heard him preach and could see that he had made vast improvements since I last heard him.

He gave a great altar call.

After that service, we went to another church. A truly great service.

As I boarded the train I was greeted by Jesus, an elderly porter that I had known from a previous trip. He gave me a card with my dining car reservation for dinner about an hour after boarding. I told him how I wanted my room made up. When I returned after my great steak dinner, meals are included in first class ticket prices, everything was just as I wanted it.

I love Amtrak and hope long distance trains do not go away.

I had a good night's sleep and breakfast the next morning in the dining car.

Gallup, New Mexico.
At 8:30 AM, I got off at Gallup, New Mexico. Gallup is the capital of the Navajo nation. I had planned a two day layover. Gallup is a small town but two days was not enough. One or two days more would have been better. Gallup is said to be the most patriotic town in America. During World War II, Gallup would not turn in its Japanese residents to be put into internment camps like Heart mountain in Cody, Wyoming. Gallup is the world center for handmade Indian jewelry.

Gallup started with many Indian trading posts. There are about 150 trading posts still in existence today. These businesses hire Navajos as well as trade with them. There is great effort to avoid counterfeit product. The most recent crackdown with federal indictments had involved what are called Palestinian traders operating in Gallup that had brought in jewelry made in the Philippines. There are estimates that 80% of Indian jewelry is counterfeit.

I left Gallup on Saturday morning. Scheduled time was 8:30 AM, exactly 48 hours from when I arrived. On Amtrak long distance there is one train a day in each direction. I ended up leaving around 11:30 AM. The locomotive had broken down and could not be repaired at that point. A BNSF locomotive was put in the front of the train. The broken locomotive would be dropped off at a shop in Illinois.

While I was still on the platform, I actually got a live cell phone call from Amtrak. Kudos to the big company Amtrak. There was an apology and an explanation of what had happened. I was informed that I would miss my Amtrak connection in Raton, New Mexico to get to Denver, Colorado. There was a solution.

Amtrak offered me two possibilities of getting to Denver. I could stay over another day in Gallup and Amtrak would pick up the costs. Or, I could get off in Albuquerque, go to the Amtrak ticket counter, and be ticketed on a Greyhound bus that would get me to Denver. I needed to be in Denver by Sunday morning to get a ride to Cheyenne with our son-in-law from Cheyenne so option two worked the best. At Albuquerque, Greyhound had held the bus for me. I got to Denver at the bus station that was a few blocks closer to my hotel, what we now call the former downtown Marriott, than Union Station.

All worked out well except that getting to Denver later than I planned meant that I missed dinner at Sam's No, 3, a kitschy diner at 15th and Curtis that has been in Denver since 1927. I love the rib-eye steak, the ambience, the service, and the prices.

"Why, oh why, can these type restaurants not be replicated? Why are new restaurants so bad?" I know the answer. Restaurants today are run by accountants. I did not get to everything in Gallup. I need to make another trip.

The unexpected happens.
I have had a healthy life. To have something unhealthy occur, was completely unexpected.

I don't recall the date but sometime after getting home from Gallup in early April 2017, I developed chest pains that pretty much shut me down. The pains didn't go away.

Almost two years later, I was still going through multiple types of chest pains. The sequence changed numerous times. I am completely over it as I am finishing the editing of this book. I no longer hope that I will not wake up in the morning.

I had not been fearful that it was heart disease. I have learned that if chest pains go away with exercise, it is not due to the heart. With my type of pain, shoveling snow, cutting grass, picking up concrete blocks, exercise stopped the pain.

The quickest way to get the pain back was to have any type of conflict or stress.

I have told Cheri that whatever she wants us to do or wherever she wants us to go is fine with me.

Dinner?

"Anywhere is fine with me. Order me whatever you choose."

There is a question that no one has asked.

Do I still believe in divine healing?

The answer is yes and even more so.

Psalms 103:3 tell us that healing is in the atonement:

"Who forgiveth all thine iniquities; who healeth all thy diseases."

It is God's will that we be healed. When it happens is up to Him.

Please read chapter 17 *"Is Healing For Today?"* and chapter 18 *"Does God Heal Through Doctors?"*

I have been getting things done, albeit slowly. I am certified in QuickBooks online and have implemented three systems so far.

I have been getting things in order for the day that I do not come down to breakfast.

There is a list for Cheri. Financial matters are up to date. Cheri now has a credit card just in her name. She is using it and we pay it off each month.

Upon my death, all of my own accounts stop. Cheri will be able to continue the business bank account as it is in the corporation name.

It pays to plan ahead.

A Bible school graduate in the house.
I have finished a Bible school program that I started in the 1980s. On October 29, 2018, I became an ordained minister of the Gospel of Jesus Christ. I don't see a need to use the prefix Rev. and I am not called to be a pastor.

Plans in the works.
God willing, I have a number of plans in the works involving:

- Evangelism.
- Missions effectiveness and efficiency.
- Discipleship in areas that others do not do. Mathew 6:33 for example.
- New Bills of Material applications.
- QuickBooks online applications to make bookkeeping automatic.
- A simple way to install a small business/church financial system.
- Book writing and publishing.
- One person jobs and brochure - an upgrade from notes on the door with bad grammar and misspelled words.
- Help children and grandchildren as needed.

What is next?
"Take care of your house. It will bring you much pleasure in your old age."

I once thought of that quote as referring in some way to having a huge mansion with a swimming pool, indoors and out, and other amenities.

In observing the phenomenon in the United States and in other countries, I believe that having a huge mansion could be a detriment to having "much pleasure."

If anything, our house is too big even for Cheri and me. It does have some things that are bringing me much pleasure. I say "are" because it is happening and also I am in what might be called old age.

As I was writing this book, I got an email from our daughter who was working in Ukraine, with comments relative to my home. She sent photos.

She also mentioned what she saw in Ireland while on another trip:

"You might find this interesting. Went to my executive director's beach house. Some people live out here, some just for vacation from the city. Reminds me of all your projects and sheds and work spaces. "

"In Ireland the beach homes were trailers lined up along the coast. "

Our home.
For our home we have, not in any order:
- Low property taxes.
- Air conditioning.
- Hot tub.
- Treehouse for visiting grandchildren.
- Nice small backyard with privacy fence all around.
- Sanctuary for rabbits to feed.
- Working fountain.
- Two good reel mowers.
- Reciprocating saw.
- Tiki shack.
- Retro 1950s style glider.
- Tool shed built into house from original construction. Our youngest son got this working.
- 6x9 work area building with high ceiling and a wood stove. Backyard lights.
- Non-kink hose - a real wonder.
- Good computer work area thanks to a daughter who could see what two carpenters could not.
- Good work area in amongst book shelves.

I did do one project outdoors in the Spring of 2019 while doing the final editing of this book. I removed six large Aspen trees. It seemed impossible for me to do. I meditated on it for quite a while. I considered a number of alternatives. I began work.

I hope to never go up a ladder again. I almost could not do that last high climb as I was losing my nerve. I had to finish and finish safely.

Because of location constraints and risk of damage I took the trees down from the top in pieces. For one tree I had to make the cut while hanging in another tree.

In 4 1/2 days, not working all day, I got 'er done.

I remembered the quote from Earl Nightingale: "Success is the progressive realization of a worthy goal."

When it warms up, I plan to build a double gate, 5 1/2 feet on each side.

CHAPTER 15: QUOTES AND NOTES

"A quotation is a handy thing to have about, saving one the trouble of thinking for oneself, always a laborious business." - Anonymous.

"A great many Christians would probably give God a handful of meal after He had filled the barrel; but they would hesitate to give Him the last handful on His promise to fill the barrel when empty." - Anonymous.

"The common denominator of success --- the secret of success of every man who has ever been successful --- lies in the fact that he formed the habit of doing things that failures don't like to do." - Albert E N Grey.

"This is the result when Christians become one interest group among many, scrambling for benefits at the expense of others rather than seeking the welfare of the whole. Christianity is love of neighbor, or it has lost its way." - Michael Gerson.

"I don't want to be standing in hell next to a preacher that taught that parts of the Bible do not mean what they say." - David Newton Sneed.

"Fixing problems is a whole lot different from finding the problems to fix." - David Newton Sneed.

"Years ago shrimp was cheap bait. Today it is the same shrimp, used for food, and at a much higher price." - David Newton Sneed.

"Be nice to everyone. You never know who it is you will pass on your way down." - Anonymous cynic.

"I wish I had enough money to buy an elephant." "What would you do with an elephant?" "I don't want an elephant I just want enough money to be able to buy one." - Anonymous.

"Work less. Make more per hour." - David Newton Sneed.

"Forgiveness is not visible; healing is. How can we know that we are forgiven?" - David Newton Sneed.

"Fossil fuel is cheap because damage is off the books." - Anonymous.

"Substance costs less than symbolism." - Anonymous.

"One of the great delusions of the world is the hope that the evils of the world can be cured by legislation." - Thomas B Reed.

"Surround yourself with people who make you feel stupid." - Mick Ebeling.

"Ideas not Ideology." - Anonymous.

"Denominations can say they believe the Bible because they say that the parts they do not believe no longer apply." - David Newton Sneed.

"Value is not made of money but a tender balance of expectation and longing." - Barbara Kingsolver.

"Often has it happened and still does that devils have been driven out in the name of Christ; Also by calling on His name the sick have been healed." - Martin Luther.

"Those who have the privilege to know have the duty to act." - Albert Einstein.

"Resist the temptation to ignore your customer." - David Newton Sneed.

"Trust that still small voice that says this might work and I'll try it." - Diane Mariechild.

"Energy is a service and not a commodity." - David Newton Sneed.

"No one has ever been fired for buying IBM." - Anonymous.

"There are churches that no longer need offerings." - David Newton Sneed.

"Allopathic medicine has not been the solution." - Anonymous.

"Only marketing and innovation produce results. All the rest are costs. Only opportunities produce results and growth." - Peter F Drucker.

"Universal priesthood of the believer." - Martin Luther.

"If the server can't read the table and understand how to relate to the guests, the guests will be disappointed , even if the food is fabulous, and the service otherwise top-notch. It is so much about the understanding, the expected style of communication, and continuously orchestrating the experience to those expectations - which of course keep changing during the meal." - Anonymous.

"Don't compete with rivals; make them irrelevant." - Anonymous.

"Do fewer things, better" - Anonymous.

"Americans will save anybody so long as they are a different color, speak a different language, and live thousands of miles away. " - Will Rogers.

"If you give what you do not need it isn't giving." - Mother Teresa.

"If God lived on earth, people would break His windows." - Yiddish Proverb.

"Jesus proclaimed the Kingdom of God; what came was the Church." - Alfred Loisy.

"We do not build the Kingdom of God; we receive it." - Anonymous.

"Do things that don't scale." - Anonymous.

"It is thread, hundreds of tiny threads, which sew people together through the years. That's what makes a marriage last." - Simone Signoret.

Cease ye from man, whose breath is in his nostrils; for wherein is he to be accounted of? Isaiah 2:22.

The Lord will perfect that which concerneth me; thy mercy O Lord, endureth forever: forsake not the works of thine own hands. Psalms 138:8.

Seest thou a man diligent in his business? he shall stand before kings; he shall not stand before mean men. Proverbs 22:29.

Come unto me, all ye that labour and are heavy laden, and I will give you rest. Matthew 11:28.

Living by Faith - Author unknown
A few preachers have found a happy solution to the economic problem in the simple plan of living by faith.

No one can put the economic squeeze on such a man; for as he is accountable to God alone for his ministry, God is, by the same token, responsible for his daily bread.

It is impossible to starve a man into submission under this arrangement, for the servant of God lives on manna, and manna can be found wherever faith can see it.

CHAPTER 16: I LEARN THE MEANING OF FAITH

"The problem with people who think that God will provide is that they think God will provide." - David Maine.

What is faith?
Often in my early life I had heard the word faith. It was always loosely used like a buzzword that no one believes.

The definition of faith that I kept getting was that faith is believing in God and going to church. None of that made sense to me.

I kept reading the Bible.

I found many defining verses that did not match what I was hearing from the real world.

James 2:19: "Thou believest that there is one God; thou doest well: the devils also believe, and tremble."

Does that mean the devils have faith?

John 4:21-24:

"Woman," Jesus replied, "believe me, a time is coming when you will worship the Father neither on this mountain nor in Jerusalem. You Samaritans worship what you do not know; we worship what we do know, for salvation is from the Jews. Yet a time is coming and has now come when the true worshipers will worship the Father in the Spirit and in truth, for they are the kind of worshipers the Father seeks. God is spirit, and his worshipers must worship in the Spirit and in truth."

Does that mean that faith has nothing to do with going to church?

Could it be that the Creator of the Universe would actually base my eternal salvation on whether or not I went inside a certain type of building on Sunday morning at 11:00 AM regardless of what I did inside?

Could I sleep or listen to a ball game on a little radio with an earphone?

It was Jesus' custom. per the Bible, to go to the synagogue on the Sabbath.

If we are following Jesus should we not do exactly as Jesus did and go to a place between Friday night at sundown and Saturday night at sundown to listen to a rabbi read in Hebrew?

Where we we instructed to go on Sunday during the day? I'm not advocating one way or the other. I'm just asking.

The problem we have is that we pick and choose from the Bible, modify it, and then condemn others to hell that do not see it as we do. I have heard many sermons from Acts 20:7:

"And upon the first day of the week, when the disciples came together to break bread, Paul preached unto them, ready to depart on the morrow; and continued his speech until midnight."

The speaker would say that at that time most of the Christians were slaves, were forced to work, and could not have a Sunday morning service. They had Sunday night services.

It took a trip to Israel for me to understand what is there in plain English. It was not what I had always been taught.

If Paul preached until midnight on the first day of the week, it would be Saturday night. In the Jewish calendar a day starts at sundown. The dark part of the day comes first. If we are to observe the Sabbath it would be from Friday at sundown to Saturday at sundown.

Then I found Hebrews 11:1:

"NOW faith is the substance of things hoped for, the evidence of things not seen." Faith is NOW, it is a substance, and it is evidence.

Life for me became a continual growth in faith after understanding Hebrews 11:1.

How One Day at a Time Saves Money - David Newton Sneed
Homemakers, mostly women, spend many hours per year reading grocery ads and clipping and sorting cents-off coupons. They then spend time to find the best locations to use the coupons. They have to consider the various store "sales" which are announced weekly. They have to consider the "double coupons" and in some places "triple coupon" offers. With enough time and effort, they can "save" 50% or more.

With all of these "savings", someone must be losing out. Are the grocery chains going broke? Are there food processors going broke? How can the industry afford to print and process billions of coupons all to allow "discounts" on their products. How can the industry afford billions of dollars for advertising offers to "cut prices" and double or triple the coupon savings?

The answers should be of special concern to the people of God. With the Bible mentioning bread 361 times, meat 290 times, and fruit 208 times, the issue of grocery buying should be considered in a biblical context.

The first grocery ad is found in the book of Genesis. After examining the offer of fruit, Eve made the decision (Genesis 5:6) that the fruit was good, that it was well packaged, and had certain health benefits. A free sample was being offered. Eve decided that her husband would like her selection of the week. Also, even though God had said no, Eve decided that she had misunderstood. She was sure that God would be pleased with her for being so diligent at seeking out good things.

The effects of that choice have caused problems for mankind ever since. Is there a chance that Satan today still uses the grocery ad to deceive?

The whole process of grocery shopping has reached a religious fervor in the United States. Homemakers spend more time planning their strategies for grocery shopping than they spend with their families. They are too tired and mentally drained to check their children's homework or to read stories to their toddlers. Thy know more about the locations of items on the shelves of half a dozen supermarkets than they know about the locations of God's prom uses in one Bible.

Most other countries have neither supermarkets nor grocery ads and coupons. Food buying is done in open air markets where fresh items are offered strictly as commodities or in small independent stores that offer processed packaged items. The answer we are often given is that these are poor countries. From the grocery industry viewpoint that is a correct statement. From the consumer's standpoint, it is best expressed that in no other country either have or are willing to spend as much money on groceries as they do in the United States. But does that mean they are undernourished? In places like Ethiopia, yes. For the most part, no. The United States may have more food related problems tan any pithier country in the world, all because of excess, primarily because of sugar and fat. In the poorest parts of our country we find the greatest incidences of obesity from excess eating.

From a biblical perspective, the American way of buying has problems of a spiritual dimension.

The Bible teaches that we are to look on God as the provider. Jesus teaches us to ask God to "give use this day our daily bread."

In Egypt which is spiritually the world system, the Israelites had gotten used to food stockpiles. Even as slaves, they had their supermarkets, their freezers, and their pantries. All of this gave them security. Shortly after they began their walk of faith, they murmured against Moses and accused him of bringing them to the wilderness to die of hunger. Ex 16:3.

"Then said the Lord unto Moses, behold I will rain bread from heaven for you; and the people shall go out and gather a certain amount every day, that I may prove them, whether they will walk in my law, or no." Ex 16:4. God didn't tell them to keep a stockpile. He didn't say to go shopping. He didn't say to use the world system to get the best deal. He didn't say to watch for the best times to buy. What He did say was that He would provide and that there was a measurement. Ex 16:36.

God was true to His word and the food rained down. Moses told the people how much to take and how much to leave nothing over for the next day. "Notwithstanding they hearkened not unto Moses but some of them left it until morning, and it bred worms and stank and Moses was wraith with them."

"But Moses" we would say today, "If I don't clip the coupons and watch the sales I won't be a good steward." When Moses gets wroth with us, we say "But I know that they mark up the prices because they plan for the sales and the coupons, and the discounts. If I don't join the system I will pay too much." That sounds pretty good. You'll be all set when they come along and say that you have to take the mark of the beast or you can't buy or sell. Rev 13:17.

You'll have your mark, your sale papers, your coupons and your check cashing card. So you'll got out to the mall and everything will be fine until one day you go down and the store manager will be crying. Rev 18:11. The Bible says that "the fruits that thy soul lusted after are departed from thee, and all things which were dainty and goodly are departed from thee, and thou shalt find them no more at all." Rev 18:14.

God is a Living God. He has made promises and has kept them. He is not a respecter of persons. He has promised to deliver us to a land of abundance. The conditions are that we "believe that He is and that He is a rewarder of them that diligently seek Him."

The way some of God's people act, they must not believe that He is. They must not believe that He is a Living God. Otherwise they would tremble when they read Leviticus 26. Or maybe they are so busy clipping grocery coupons they do not have time to read their Bible. That might be why they miss the lesson God teaches in Deuteronomy 8.

"But I believe in God" we say today. "I read the Bible. But I'm out of work and I don't have any money." Some people say "Thank God for food stamps or I would die." Sometimes all we need is to get a little teaching. The widow of Zarephath believed in a Living God. She says so right in I Kings 17:12. But in the same breath she says that she and her son are going to eat the last of their food and die.

Elijah comes in and says "Woman you don't understand. God is going to take care of you. He is a Living God and He has promised to do so." She had gotten discouraged. The government had gone broke and had cut out her food stamps. She couldn't find a job. Her church was building a new fellowship hall to go with the new sanctuary that they had built to house the big new organ so they could praise the Lord. They had no money left to help her. She had forgotten that all she had to do was call on the name of the Lord. She had forgotten that David had "been young and now was old and had never seen a righteous man forsaken nor his seed begging bread."

But the widow was still teachable. Many people today are not. They know too much. "Times are different today," they say. "I have to cheat because everybody cheats me. I have to accumulate money because there could be hard times coming." They have all the answers. "God expects me to do this or that." The serpent is still saying "Hath God said?" The serpent still wants us to doubt God's word. He doesn't want us to know that it is "Jesus Christ, the same, yesterday and today and forever."

When Elijah told the widow what God had said she believed it. And not only did she say she believed it she went out and did what Elijah told her to do. Today we twist that around. A woman with a husband will go listen to some preacher tell her what to do and won't even listen to her husband.

The Bible talks about God's people tempting Him in their hearts because "they believed not in God and trusted not in His salvation." Ps 78:21.

Today we believe in the newspaper ad that says 10% off. We exercise our faith because we cut out the ad, get in our car, and go to the store. Sure enough, we get 10% off the price that is marked on the tag. We "saved" some money. We don't count the time we spend reading the ads and the time to go to the store. We don't count the car expenses. We don't keep records so we don't know how much of our time we devote to this exercise.

Meanwhile we don't believe God's ad when he says that we can get 100% off. Isaiah 55:1. We don't want to follow the simple plan that God has outlined in Matthew 6. We're like Naaman. He was commanded a simple thing to do and he didn't want to do it. II Ki 5:13. Naaman wanted to get rid of his disease but he wanted to stay in control. He didn't see why he had to dip in the Jordan. He liked the river in his hometown better. He was told to dip seven times. He probably thought two or three times should be enough.

Naaman probably did not like a lot of other things that God said either. If God said go to the Safeway he'd probably want to go to Kroger because he thought they had better prices.

But Naaman was teachable. He did go to the Jordan. And he did get healed.

God's people need to be taught God's word. Then they need to believe what they are taught and to do it. They need to know the voice of the serpent and the voice of God.

Good Christian women are cheating on their husbands and children by worshipping at the altar of of the supermarket. They need to throw out their coupons and their grocery ads. They need to get rid of the stockpiles of food and the security it brings and look to the security that trusting in the Lord brings.

Instead of choosing between Brand A at its regular price and Brand A at its sale price with the double coupon discount they should look at what they can create with their own hands with the children helping. They would spend less of their husband's money. He could pay off his debts and wouldn't be so tired from struggling to make the grocery stores rich.

Good Christian women should believe their husbands rather than the serpent.

Instead of clipping coupons to get discounts on a dinner of fat and sugar, she should plan mealtime as a time off fellowship for her family and a time of thanks to God.

Instead of the one or two days a week of celebrating grocery specials, she could daily buy her needs for that day or for the next day. By buying for only one day at a time she could be more aware of God's provision and by daily returning to her husband what she has saved by thoughtful planning she could strengthen her faith and her marriage. By asking for God's guidance she could provide better balance for her children's diet. By acting in faith as the widow of Zarephath did, she would find that her pantry would never run out.

CHAPTER 17. IS HEALING for TODAY?

"God's healing works with causes and not symptoms" - Anonymous

"Many will ask for prayers and for a visit from a pastor though will say that to expect healing from God is presumption." - Anonymous

Jesus Christ the same, yesterday, today and forever.
Much of the teaching we hear is that God did things in the past, will do things in the future, but at this time does nothing. Hebrews 13:8 says:

"Jesus Christ the same, yesterday, today and forever."

If you want to know what God is doing today look at what He did yesterday.

Many say that Jesus does not heal today because he has established who he is. The Bible gives a different reason in Matthew 13:58:

"And he did not many mighty works there because of their unbelief."

If you want to know what God is NOT doing today look at what He did NOT DO yesterday.

A woman with an issue of blood for 12 years spent all of her money on doctors and was not made any better. See Luke 8. Somebody, with faith, told her about this man Jesus who had healed others. The woman went and the place was crowded.

"If I can just touch His clothes" she said.

When she touched, Jesus asked,

"Who touched me?"

His disciples answered:

"Who touched you? Everyone's touching you"

He turned and saw the woman and said:

"Thy faith hath made thee whole."

That's how Jesus healed then and that's how He heals today.

If you're such a good Christian, have you told anyone that Jesus heals?

Do you believe in Hebrews 13:8: "Jesus Christ the same, yesterday, today and forever."

Was it different then because she could touch his clothes and we can't do that today? The centurion in Matthew 8 told Jesus that his servant was sick and needed a healing. Jesus said he would go to the house and heal him. The centurion said:

"I'm not worthy to have you come to my house. But speak the word only, and my servant shall be healed."

Jesus said: "as thou hast believed so be it done unto thee."

The servant was healed in the selfsame hour. As you go about as a disciple of Christ do you ask Jesus for healing of unsaved people who have no faith? Do you have the faith of the Centurion, who was not even of Israel nor a child of the kingdom?

But that healing was just for that one person you say. Well the Bible says in Matthew 4 that Jesus healed everybody that wanted to be healed. The only time that Jesus did not heal everybody was when he went back to Nazareth. The Bible says in Matthew 13:58: "And he did not many mighty works there because of their unbelief.

If you are not seeing healing is it Jesus' fault? The disciples in Matthew 17 could not cast out a demon and they asked Jesus why they could not:

"Because of your unbelief."

Jesus told them that they needed to pray and fast.

In Matthew 8, when Jesus was making some comments about how the centurion was more of a believer than the church people, Jesus said:

"But the children of the kingdom shall be cast out into outer darkness: there shall be weeping and gnashing of teeth."

Read the Bible and you'll see that he was talking about church people who don't believe in healing.

But, you say, my church does believe in healing. But we also believe that God calls people home. A few weeks ago we had Sister Jones on our prayer list. She wasn't feeling well and couldn't come to church. Then the next week we prayed that when she went for tests that they would come back negative. Then the next week we prayed that she would get through surgery ok. Then the next week we prayed for her full recovery. This week the Lord called her home and we had her funeral.

Well since your church is such a strong believer in healing why didn't it do what the Bible says? James 5:14-15 is talking to church people.

"Is any sick among you? Let him call for the elders of the church; and let them pray over him, anointing him with oil in the name of the Lord: and the prayer of faith shall save the sick, and the Lord shall raise him up; and if he have committed sins, they shall be forgiven him."

Most churches ignore this command.

If this command is followed it is usually done as a religious ritual while the believer is under the care of a doctor.

The church did not teach Sister Jones about this scripture because it really does not believe it does any good.

The church today has lost the power of the early church but it is not because Jesus changed.

There is so much carnality in the church today that like in Nazareth, Jesus can do no mighty works because of their unbelief.

For sickness it's much safer to publish a list in the church bulletin even when the sick person didn't ask for it. So what if it's not scriptural? It seems ok and we've always done it this way.

I heard one woman say:

"We used to preach it and we went to the altar and didn't get healed."

In other words she no longer believes that God heals. Maybe the churches no longer believe God saves. Maybe that's why many of them have quit giving altar calls for salvation.

I've been to healing services where people didn't get healed.

But I've been to many more evangelistic services where people didn't get saved. That does not mean that salvation is gone.

Psalm 103:3 says,

"who forgiveth all thine iniquities, who healeth all thy diseases."

If God does not heal anymore maybe he does not forgive sin anymore either.

You say you believe in Jesus in John 3:16 when Jesus says that:

"whosoever believeth in him should not perish but have eternal life."

Why do you not believe in Jesus when he says in Matthew 8:13:

"as thou hast believed so be it done unto thee."

Why do you not believe him when he says in Matthew 17:20 that you fail:

"because of your unbelief"

In Luke 17:5 the disciples said: "Lord, increase our faith."

Today we hear that God heals through doctors.

I have yet to see any scriptural basis that God now works through a system that is flawed and constantly changes.

The Bible says rough things in Revelation 22:18-19 about anyone who adds to the word or takes away from the word. It also says in Proverbs 14:12 that: "there is a way which seemeth right unto a man, but the end thereof are the ways of death."

Some say that Jesus healed then because of all the unbelievers. We've got more unbelievers today than there were then. If there was ever a time that healing was needed to show God's power it's today.

In Malachi 3:6 the Bible says: "For I am the Lord, I change not."

God has not changed. He still heals and he still saves.

What do you believe?

CHAPTER 18: DOES GOD HEAL THROUGH DOCTORS?

"Many say that assumption is presumption if God does not intend to heal; then they go to the doctor for healing and attribute it to God." -Anonymous.

The thought that God heals through doctors prevails today.
But we should be careful about this doctrine because the Bible says rough things in Revelation 22:18-19 about anyone who adds to the word or takes away from the word.

In Genesis 50:2 we read that Joseph called a physician to embalm his father.

In 2 Chronicles 16:12 we read that Asa: "was diseased in his feet, until his disease was exceeding great: yet in his disease he sought not to the Lord, but to the physicians."

In Luke 8:43, we read that: "a woman having an issue of blood 12 years, which had spent all her living upon physicians, neither could be healed of any."

The account in Mark 5 also says that there were: "many physicians" and that she "rather grew worse."

In Colossians 4:14 we read that Luke was a physician. But in Luke's account of the visit to Melita in Acts 28:8-9 it was Paul who ministered healing.

"And it came to pass, that the father of Publius lay sick of a fever and of a bloody flux: to whom Paul entered in, and prayed and laid his hands on him, and healed him. So when this was done, others also, which had diseases in the island, came, and were healed:"

Where is a there any scriptural basis that God heals through doctors? Did someone receive a special revelation that God had a new plan?

When Eve was approached in the garden she saw in Genesis 3:6:

"that the tree was good for food, and that it was pleasant to the eyes, and a tree to be desired to make one wise, she took of the fruit thereof, and did eat," The serpent convinced Eve that God must want her to eat it.

Just because something seems right does not make it right. The Bible says in Proverbs 14:12 that: "There is a way which seemeth right unto a man, but the end thereof are the ways of death."

The medical profession seems to be the right thing. Not a week goes by that we do not hear of some new drug or some new procedure. Does that mean that the medical profession is God at work? Let's see if the medical profession has the characteristics of God.

God is not a respecter of persons. See Acts 10:34. But the medical profession is a respecter of persons. If you are a white American male with private health insurance or if you are wealthy you can have the best treatments available.

God's gifts cannot be purchased. In Acts 8:20, Peter said:

"Thy money perish with thee, because thou hast thought that the gift of God may be purchased with money."

The Bible says in Revelation 22:17 that:

"Whosoever will, let him take the water of life freely."

But medical care takes money. And the more money you have the better off you are.

God's gifts are appropriated through faith. But doctors are selected by sight for their reputation. The Bible says in Ephesians 2:8-9:

"For by grace are ye saved through faith; and that not of yourselves: it is the gift of God: not of works lest any man should boast . See Ephesians 2:8-9.

A common church dinner conversation involves people bragging about the excellent coverage they have on their medical plans.

God does not take away a gift. In Romans 11:29 we read: "For the gifts and calling of God are without repentance." Then why do Christians complain when some treatment is no longer covered by their plan?

God calls his ministers through his gospel. See Ephesians 3:6-12. Medical practitioners are often unbelievers. The Bible says in John 10:27:

"My sheep hear my voice, and I know them, and they follow me:" Are these unbelievers also his sheep?

God set gifts of healings in the church. See I Corinthians 12:28. Medical profession healings are licensed by the government and often paid for by taxes collected by the government or by tax subsidies and deductions allowed by the government. If you'll watch your newspaper almost daily, medical profession deficiencies are dealt with by Congress and the Legislature and not by prayer. God does not change. But medical care keeps changing. In Malachi 3:6 we read:

"For I am the Lord, I change not."

In Hebrews 13:8 we read:

"Jesus Christ the same, yesterday, today, and forever." In Ecclesiastes 3:14 we read "I know that, whatsoever God doeth, it shall be forever: nothing can be put to it, nor anything taken away from it:"

If you believe that God heals through doctors and if you have had your life extended through medical procedures then when you give your testimony you should be sure to thank God that you are an American and not like those such and such people in some country the hav no insurance or money. You should thank God for noting how more worthy you are to be able to afford such good doctors who you believe are the ministers of God.

In Matthew 8, when Jesus was making some comments about how the Centurion was more of a believer than the church people, Jesus said:

"But the children of the kingdom shall be cast out into outer darkness: there shall be weeping and gnashing of teeth." Read the Bible and you'll see that he was talking about church people who don't believe in healing by God's ways.

The Bible says in Psalms 103:3: "who forgiveth all thine iniquities, who healeth all thy diseases."

If God now heals through heathen doctors maybe he now saves through some heathen practice. Maybe salvation is now of works.

If you run to your doctor when you're sick maybe you're closer to him than you are to Dr. Jesus. Maybe you don't really believe in eternal salvation either.

CHAPTER 19: NOT YET THE END FOR ME

"Vision is the art of seeing things invisible." - Jonathan Swift

I hope that it can be said of me what was said of Mr. Mannering in *A House in Bloomsbury, 1894,* written by, simply, Mrs Oliphant. She was a Scottish novelist and historical writer, author of many books including *The Victorian Age of English Literature,* in two volumes:

"...to the consternation of the younger men, who could not understand how anybody could believe old Mannering to be of consequence in the place; but generally his life was as obscure as he wished it to be, yet not any hard or painful drudgery; for he was still occupied with the pursuit which he had chosen, and which he had followed all his life;......."

Books.
I have realized that all the books I have collected and saved, many with multiple copies, would never again be read by me, our children nor by our grandchildren.

It had been my hope that my children and grandchildren would be seeking answers and I would be able to give them books whereby someone else's experience and insights would save them a lot of work and risk of failure.

I have weeded out my books and donated 5,631 to charity as of the end of 2018.

Of my general library, I have kept 230 books that I have yet to read.

At the end of 2019 I will donate whichever ones of those I have left of that group whether read or not.

I have a glass front case with 146 books that are really special, at least as I see it now.

I have an additional 195 books that are biographies of Christian missionaries.

I don't know what I will do with those. I have not read all of them, at least not yet. The ones I have read are of people that believed God.

Videos.
In 2018, I got rid of all of my video collection of great movies, including *The Distinguished Gentleman* starring Eddie Murphy, a movie that tells how Washington D.C. really works.

I have never had time to watch any of those movies again.

Cheri has already disposed of most of her collection.

The end of this book.
I'll end the book with three quotes that I like:

"Life is something to be spent not saved." - D H Lawrence.

"We have not lost faith; we have merely transferred it from God to the medical profession." - Bertrand Russell

"When I am dead, I hope it may be said: His sins were scarlet, but his books were read." - Hilaire Belloc

David Newton Sneed, 2019

www.ingramcontent.com/pod-product-compliance
Lightning Source LLC
Chambersburg PA
CBHW030049100426
42734CB00038B/733